LAND RECORDS OF SUSSEX COUNTY, DELAWARE 1722-1731

DEED BOOK F
NO. 6

~ *Johnita P. Malone* ~

HERITAGE BOOKS
2008

HERITAGE BOOKS
AN IMPRINT OF HERITAGE BOOKS, INC.

Books, CDs, and more—Worldwide

For our listing of thousands of titles see our website at
www.HeritageBooks.com

Published 2008 by
HERITAGE BOOKS, INC.
Publishing Division
100 Railroad Ave. #104
Westminster, Maryland 21157

Copyright © 1997 Johnita P. Malone

Other Heritage Books by the author:
Land Records of Sussex County, Delaware, 1732-1743: Deed Book G No. 7
Land Records of Sussex County, Delaware, 1742-1753: Deed Book H No. 8

All rights reserved. No part of this book may be reproduced or transmitted in any form or by any means, electronic or mechanical, including photocopying, recording or by any information storage and retrieval system without written permission from the author, except for the inclusion of brief quotations in a review.

International Standard Book Numbers
Paperbound: 978-0-7884-0775-8
Clothbound: 978-0-7884-7485-9

Dedicated To My Mother

Who First Sparked My Interest in Genealogical Research

Table of Contents

Introduction...vii

Sussex County, Delaware, Deed Book F-6..1

Index of Names...

Index of Land Names...

Sussex County, Delaware, Deed Book F-6

Introduction

In an effort to locate my own Delaware ancestors, I had occasion to read the microfilm containing the land records in Deed Book F No. 6 as held by the Delaware State Archives. During that effort, I realized that with a little more effort I could abstract all the deeds and publish them for others. This book is the end result of that effort.

These are records of land transactions, mortgages, bills of sale, bonds, and other similar transactions for the period, 1722-1731. I have included all entries in an abstract form. Included are the names of all grantees and grantors, genealogical relationships, names of individual attorneys appointed by grantors, a brief description of the land and its location, such as landmarks and rivers, and adjoining property.

In every case, the number(s) preceding each entry represents the page number of the original transaction in the deed book. The acknowledgment date, when available, is near the end of each abstract.

Included also are an every name index and a second index for names of property and land. The question marks following any of the index items indicate difficulty in reading and deciphering the exact spelling.

Johnita P. Malone
Beavercreek, Ohio
1997

Abbreviations:
Ack. = acknowledgment
dec'd = deceased
Wits. = witnesses

SUSSEX COUNTY, DELAWARE
DEED BOOK F-6
(1722-1731)

Pages 1-2. Deed. 6 Nov 17(17?). From Joseph Pyles, yeoman of Sussex Co., DE., admr & heir of William Pyles, dec'd, yeoman, of the same County, to Robert Shankland, gentleman, of the same place. For 55 pounds 268 acres. An 800-acre tract was originally granted by patent dated 8th day 5th mo 1672 from Francis Lovelace, Gov'r of New York, to Hermanus Fredrick Wiltbanck who conveyed the 800 acres to John Kirk, Sr., who had it resurveyed on 11th da 10th mo 1684 and received a patent dated 19th da 3rd mo 1686 under seal of James Claypoole and Robert Turner, commissioners for granting land under Wm Penn, Esqr. John Kirk, son and sole heir of John Kirk, Sr., by deed of sale dated 10th da 9th mo (Nov) 1688 conveyed the 800 acres to William Pyles, now dec'd. William Pyles in his will devised the 800 acres to his 4 sons, William, Isaac, Joseph and John equally. Joseph Pyles now conveys 268 acres part of the 800 acres to Robert Shankland. Tract is situated on the north side of a branch of the Broad Creek proceeding from the Cold Spring and bounded by land of William Craige. Joseph Pyles makes his mark. Wits., Daniel Hoseman and Phil. Russel, Jr. Ack. 6 Nov 1717. Recorded 20 Oct 1722.

Pages 2-4. Deed. 1 Feb 1721/2. From John Killingsworth, yeoman, of Kent Co., DE., to Cornelius Wiltbanck, gentleman, of Sussex Co., DE. For 50 pounds a house and town lot 60 by 120 feet. Lot is in Lewes Town and bounded on the SE by a lot late in the possession of John Miers, dec'd, on the NW side by a lot belonging to John Rhoads, on the front by Lewes Town Creek, and of which Richard Williams lately died possessed. John Killingsworth signed his mark. Wits., John Prettyman, Jr., and John Shiltman. Ack. 1 May 1722. Recorded 20 Oct 1722.

Pages 4-5. Deed of Release. 1 Aug 1722. From John Atkins, son of William Atkins dec'd, yeoman, of Sussex Co., DE., to his brother, William Atkins, yeoman, of Sussex Co., DE. For 5 shillings 138 acres. Land is situated in Angola Neck and is part of a larger tract that William Atkins died possessed of and is bounded by land of Woodman Stockley, Love's Creek, land of Isaac Atkins, the Mill Land and a road. John Atkins signs. Wits., Robert Burton, Sr., and Phil. Russel. Ack. 7 Aug 1722. Recorded 20 Oct 1722.

Pages 5-6. Deed of Release. 1 Aug 1722. From John Atkins, son of William Atkins, dec'd, yeoman, of Sussex Co., DE., to his brother, Isaac

Atkins, yeoman, of Sussex Co., DE. For 5 shillings 138 acres. Land is situated in Angola Neck and is part of a larger tract that William Atkins died possessed of and is bounded by Love's Branch and Richard Bundock's land. John Atkins signs. Wits., Robert Burton, Sr., and Phil. Russel. Ack. 7 Aug 1722. Recorded 21 Oct 1722.

Pages 6-7. Deed. 6 Jul 1722. From Samuel Davis, gentleman of Somersett Co., MD., to William Becket, gentleman, of the Town of Lewes. For 68 pounds a 60 by 200 foot lot in Lewes. Lot is in the second street in Lewes Town and binding on the NW side of a lot that was formerly Philip Russel's but now in the possession of William Godwin, on the SE side with the (illegible) lots and the graveyard. Samuel Davis signs. Wits., Hen: Brooke, Wm Pile, and Phil. Russel. Ack. 7 Aug 1722. Recorded 3 Dec 1722.

Page 7. Earmark. 7 Nov 1725. Jabez Fisher's ear mark is a crop and under bitt in the right ear and W in the left ear. Recorded this 7th Novr 1725. Phil. Russel, D. Rolls.

Pages 8-9. Deed of Gift. 4 May 1722. From John Fisher and Elizabeth his wife of Broadkill Hundred to their son-in-law, Enoch Cummings, weaver, and their daughter, Hannah, his wife. For the goodwill, love and amity of the parents, John & Elizabeth Fisher, for Enoch & Hannah Cummings 200 acres of land. Land is part of a larger tract of 800 acres called Mill Plantation which 200 acres was purchased by John Fisher from William Clark, dec'd, on 2 Feb 1713/4. Land is situated on the NW side of Cold Spring Branch and is bounded by Cold Spring bridge and a small branch proceeding out of Cold Spring Branch. John and Elizabeth Fisher sign with their marks. Wits., James Simson, Alexander McCullah and James White. Ack. 1 May 1722. Recorded 25 Jan 1722/3.

Pages 9-10. Deed of Mortgage. 5 Sep 1722. Thomas Murphy of Kent Co., DE., marriner, mortgages his 1/2 interest in the shallop Speedwell to William Chancellor of Philadelphia, sailmaker, for 8 pounds 7 shilling 8 pence. The Speedwell is presently in port at Philadelphia and is of the Burthen of 7 tons. Mortgage to be paid by the 17th of Oct next. Thomas Murphy signs. Wits., Edward Roberts and Jno Cadwalader. 7 Nov 1722. William Chancellor conveys mortgage to Jehu Spencer, marriner, of Sussex Co., DE. Wits., Jno Hyatt, Nicholas Grainger and John Cadwalader. 4 Dec 1722. Jehu Spencer conveys the mortgage to Nicholas Grainger. Wits., Ebenezer Robinson and Lewes Dewess. Thomas Murphy's Bond to William Chancellor for 16 pounds 15 shillings and 4 pence to be paid by 17 Oct next. Thomas Murphy signs. Wits., Edward Roberts and Jno Cadwalader. Recorded 13 Mar 1722/3.

Pages 11-12. Deed. 7 Jul 1719. From Berckley Codd, Esqr., gentleman of Sussex Co., DE., to Samuel Wattson of the same place. For 20 pounds 200 acres. The land is part of a larger tract of (acreage not given) situated in Prime Hook Neck where Samuel Wattson now lives. The land is bounded by a pond at the head of Green Branch on the south, land of John Bellamy on the north, and land of Henry Smith on the west. The larger tract was granted to Richard Perrott of Middlesex Co., VA., by Francis Lovelace, Gov'r of NY, on 21 Jun 1671 who gave the tract to his son, Richard Perrott, by deed of gift dated 4 Jun 1672, who died intestate leaving several sons the eldest of which was living on 29 Oct 1718 and whose name was Richard Perrott who sold the tract to Berckley Codd. Berckley Codd appoints Preserved Coggeshall as his attorney. Berckeley Codd signs. Wits., Joseph Peplo, Sarah Wattson and Preserved Coggeshall. Ack. 3 Nov 1719. Recorded 14 Mar 1722/3.

Pages 12-13. Deed. 5 May 1719. From James Fenwick, yeoman, of Lewes, DE., to John Shankland, blacksmith, of the same place. For 18 pounds 2 lots. The 2 lots are situated on the SW side of the meeting house lot near the town of Lewes and bounded by Hall's land and the road. James Fenwick signs. Wits., Edward Naws and Phil. Russel, Jr. Ack. 5 May 1719.

Pages 13-14. Deed. 5 May 1722. From Anthony Woodward, taylor, of Lewes, DE., to Robert Burton, Sr., yeoman, of Sussex Co., DE. For 15 pounds 3 1/9 lots. Lots are located at the south end of Lewes on the north side of the land of Nathaniel Hall, on the west side of John Shankland's lots, and on the south side of the County Road. Anthony Woodward signs. Wits., Joseph Cord and James White. Ack. 1 May 1722.

Pages 14-15. Dephearance. __ May 1722. From Robert Burton, yeoman, of Sussex Co., DE., to Anthony Woodward, taylor, of Lewes, DE. Condition is that if Anthony Woodward or his representative pays 15 pounds plus interest to Robert Burton on or before 4 May 1725, Robert Burton will reconvey 3 1/9 lots in Lewes Town to Anthony Woodward which Woodward has just sold to Burton. (See pages 13-14) Robert Burton makes his mark. Wits., Joseph Cord and James White. Ack. 1 May 1722.

Page 15. Arbitration Bond. 15 May 1716. From Richard Bracy, yeoman, of Sussex Co., DE., to Robert Burton, Sr., yeoman, of the same place. Bond for 200 pounds. Condition is that Richard Bracy, etc., will obey and observe and perform the award, arbitration, determination, and final judgment of Thomas Gordon, yeoman, Alexander Moleston, yeoman, Peter Marsh, yeoman, John Cary, yeoman, Anderson Parker, yeoman, John Prittiman, Sr., yeoman, David Gray, yeoman, Roger Train, yeoman, Simon Kollock, yeoman, Edward Crague, yeoman, Thomas Davock, yeoman, John McCullah, yeoman, concerning disputes over a tract of land in Angola Neck to be determined before 25 May 1716. Richard Bracy signs. Wits., John Hepburn and Robert Shankland.

Pages 16-17. Deed. 7 Aug 1722. From James Fenwick, yeoman, of Lewes, DE., to John Miers, shallopman, and James Miers, hatter, both of Lewes, DE. For 34 pounds 23 2/3 acres. Land is situated in Lewes Town between the land of John Chambers and a small branch that runs into Pagan Creek and is bounded by Chamber's land, the southernmost street in Lewes, a small branch, and the County Road. Sidney Fenwick, wife of James Fenwick, relinquishes her dower rights. James and Sidney Fenwick sign. Wits., Daniel Palmer, Jonathan Ozbun, and Mary Palmer. Ack. 6 Aug 1722. Recorded 18 Apr 1723.

Pages 17-18. Deed. 7 Aug 1722. From James Fenwick, yeoman, of Sussex Co., DE., to Daniel Palmer, yeoman, of the same place. For 28 pounds 20 acres. Land is situated near the town of Lewes on the southwest side of the head of a branch which runs into Pagan Creek and is bounded by the southernmost street in Lewes, the small branch, and by the 30 acres of land bought by Thomas Fenwick, dec'd, from Peter Lewis. Land is part of a tract formerly granted to John Kiphaven by patent who assigned his interest to William Clark who assigned same to Capt Nathaniel Walker who assigned same to William Dyre who assigned same to Thomas Fenwick; and also part of another tract called Middleborough granted by patent to Alexander Moleston who sold to Peter Lewes who sold 30 acres of the tract to Thomas Fenwick. Thomas Fenwick devised the 2 parcels to his son, James Fenwick. James Fenwick signs. Wits., Cornelius Wiltbank and James Miers. Ack. 8 Aug 1722.

Pages 19-20. Deed. 7 Aug 1722. From Samuel Davis, Jr., yeoman, of Sussex Co., DE., to Daniel Palmer, yeoman, of the same place. For 6 pounds 15 shillings 4 7/8 acres. Land is situated on the SW side of the head of a branch that runs into Pagan Creek near Lewes and bounded by the small branch, by the County Road, and by 30 acres bought by Thomas Fenwick from Peter Lewis, dec'd. Land is part of a larger tract called Middleborough formerly granted by patent to Alexander Moleston who sold to Peter Lewis who sold to Samuel Davis, Sr., who made over the land to Samuel Davis, Jr. Samuel Davis, Jr., signs. Wits., Henry Draper and Phil. Russel. Ack. 8 Aug 1722.

Pages 20-21. Deed. 1 May 1722. From Daniel Palmer, yeoman, of Sussex Co., DE., to William Fisher, Esqr., of the same place. For 20 pounds 100 acres. Land is situated on the NW side of the Broad Creek in Sussex Co. and bounded by a corner tree of William Fisher and Jabez Fisher, and a branch proceeding out of Prime Hooke Creek. Land is part of a larger tract of 600 acres called Howard's Choice which was granted by Edmond Andross, late Gov'r of New York, to Thomas Howard who bequeathed the land to Luke Watson, Jr., with the request that Watson should make over part of the tract to Capt John Hill and Capt Thomas Pemberton. Capt Hill afterwards purchased the rights of Luke Watson, Jr., and Capt Pemberton. Capt John Hill bequeathed the tract to his wife, Elizabeth, who sold the tract to Daniel Palmer. Daniel Palmer signs. Wits., John Thomson, Christopher Topham, and Phil. Russel. Ack. 1 May 1722.

Pages 21-22. Deed. 7 Aug 1722. From Henry Draper and Sarah his wife, of Sussex Co., DE., to Richard Hinman, of the same place. For 60 pounds 1/4 part of 800 acres. Land is situated in Rehoboth Hundred in Sussex Co., DE., and is bounded by a creek parting John King's land and John Roades' land. Sarah Draper, wife of Henry, was one of the granddaughters of John Avery, dec'd. Tract was granted by patent on 15 Jan 1675 from Edmond Andross to John Avery and called Avery's Rest. John Avery conveyed part of the tract to John Dupree (land lying in the forked neck) and afterwards John Avery died intestate owning the remainder, leaving issue of 5 children, Mary, Elizabeth, Sarah, Jemima and John who is since dec'd. John Avery's heirs were his four daughters. John Avery's daughter, Sarah, married John Kiphaven and had issue, Sarah, wife of Henry Draper. Sarah Kiphaven is now dec'd and the 1/4 part of the tract now belongs to Sarah Draper. Henry and Sarah Draper sign. Wits., Simon Kollock, Peter Marsh, and Rd Newcombe. Ack. 7 Aug 1722.

Pages 23-24. Deed. 8 Feb 1717. From Elizabeth Brown, lawful attorney of Daniel Brown, yeoman, of Kent Co., DE., and Thomas Carlile and Mary, his wife, of Sussex Co., DE., to William Fisher, gentleman, of Sussex Co., DE. For 32 pounds 300 acres. Land is situated on the west side of Delaware Bay and on the north side of a Cypress branch proceeding from the Broad Creek and is bounded by Bryant Rowles' land, Moulson's land, and laid out for 348 acres as surveyed on 18th da 11th mo 1681 by Robert Shankland and granted by the Court of Sussex on the 15th da 4th mo 1681 to Phillip Morris and David Coursey who conveyed to Barnes Garrett who had the tract confirmed by patent dated 12th da 4th mo 1684. Aneas Mahon and his wife Offiah, dau of Barnes Garrett, on 7 May 1717 conveyed the tract to Daniel Brown and Thomas Carlile. (NOTE: the discrepancy in acreage surveyed (348) and acreage sold (300) -- yet seems to be the whole tract being sold in this deed.) Elizabeth Brown signs, Thomas Carlile makes his mark, and Mary Carlile signs. Wits., Katherine Davis and Phill Russel, Jr. Ack. Feb Court 1717/8.

Pages 24-25. Deed. 8 Nov 1704. From James Marsh, Phillip Marsh, John Marsh and Peter Marsh, planters, of Sussex Co., DE., to Anderson Parker, planter, of the same place, and Matthew Spicer, planter, of Accomack Co., VA. For 90 pounds 600 acres. Land is situated in Sussex Co., DE., on the south side of Marsh's Creek and known by the name Good Hope. Tract is bounded by Marsh's Creek, the marshes of another branch, and a beaver dam. James and Philip Marsh make their marks and John and Peter Marsh sign. Wits., William Shankland, Edward Crage, and Roger Corbett. Ack. 7 May 1706.

Pages 25-26. Deed of Release. 2 Aug 1720. From John Sheltman and Tabitha, his wife, dau of Matthew Spicer dec'd, planter, of Sussex Co., DE., to Anderson Parker, Esqr., of the same place. For 35 pounds 600 acres. Land is situated in Sussex Co., DE., on the south side of Marsh's Creek and called Good Hope. The same land which Anderson Parker and Matthew Spicer purchased of James, Philip, John and Peter Marsh on 8 Nov 1704. Tract is bounded by Marsh's Creek, the marshes of another branch, and a beaver dam. Tabitha is sole heir of Matthew Spicer. John and Tabitha Sheltman make their marks. Wits., Alexander Moleston and Phil. Russel. Ack. 4 Aug 1720.

Pages 26-27. Deed. 19 Jun 17(21?). From William Orr, son and heir of William Orr, merchant, dec'd, of Sussex Co., DE., to Joseph Royall, marriner, of Lewes, DE. For 36 pounds 10 shillings one lot 60 x 200 feet. Lot is situated in the front street in Lewes, DE., and is bounded on the NW with high street, SE with lots of James Simson, NE with front street, and SW with second street. Patience Orr (alias Parker), widow of William Orr, dec'd, relinquishes her dower rights. William Orr and Patience Parker sign. Wits., Simon Kollock and Anderson Parker. Ack. 7 Aug 1721.

Pages 27-28. Patent. 2 Aug 1684. From William Penn, Proprietor and Governor of the province of Pensilvania and the Territories thereunto belonging, to William Clark. 400 acres of land. Land is situated on the SE side of the main Cypress branch proceeding from Cedar Creek and bounded by Robert Twilley's land and the Cypress branch. Land was granted at a Court in Sussex on 10 Jan 1681/2 and surveyed 30 Mar 1682 to William Page who sold on 3 Mar 1682/3 to Thomas Hassold who sold on 16 Apr 1683 to William Clark. William Clark requested that the patent be confirmed. Wm Penn signs.

Pages 28-29. Deed. 3 May 1720. From Honor Bedwell, widow & executrix of William Clark, gentleman, dec'd, of Sussex Co., DE., to Alexander Draper, yeoman, of the same place. For 22 pounds 10 shillings 300 acres. Land is part of a tract situated on the SE side of the main Cypress branch proceeding from Cedar Creek. Land was granted by patent to William Clark on 2nd da 6th mo 1684 by Wm Penn. Honor Bedwell signs. Wits., Mary Russel and Phil. Russel. Ack. 3 May 1720.

Pages 29-30. Deed. 7 Aug 1722. From James Fenwick, yeoman, and Sidney, his wife, of Sussex Co., DE., to Joseph Royall and Jacob Kollock, gentlemen, of the same place. For 73 pounds 69 1/2 acres. Land is situated on the SW side of Lewes and adjoining Pagan Creek and is bounded by 20 acres owned by Daniel Palmer, the southernmost street in Lewes, the run of Pagan Creek, and 30 acres formerly purchased of Peter Lewis by Thomas Fenwick, dec'd. Land is part of a larger tract granted by patent to John Kiphaven who sold to William Clark who sold to Capt Nathaniel Walker, and William Dyre, executor of Major William Dyre's estate (to whom Capt Walker bequeathed the land), sold the land to Thomas Fenwick, dec'd, and also part of another tract called Middleborough granted by patent to Alexander Moleston, dec'd, who sold the land to Peter Lewis who sold 30 acres to Thomas Fenwick who bequeathed the 2 parcels to his son, James Fenwick. James and Sidney Fenwick sign. Wits., Anderson Parker and James Miers. Ack. 7 Aug 1722.

Pages 30-31. Award of Arbitration. 9 Feb 1722. George Walton and John Manlove are both bound by 400 pounds to abide by the decision of Jonathan Bailey, William Fisher, and Alexander Moleston concerning the division of Walton Huling's, dec'd, lands in Sussex Co., DE. George Walton and John Manlove are claiming the lands in the right of their wives. George Walton is awarded a tract called "The Point" containing 250 acres and 2 lots in Lewes, DE. John Manlove was awarded a tract where Walton Huling died and is now in possession of John Manlove containing 400 acres together with the addition. John Manlove is to pay George Walton 10 pounds. Alexander Moleston, Wm Fisher and Jonathan Bailey sign.

Pages 31-32. Confirmation of Patent. 2 Apr 1686. From James Claypoole, Thomas Loyd, and Robert Turner, appointed commissioners by Wm Penn to grant & sign warrants & patents for land, to William Clark. 500 acres of land. Land is situated between Coole Spring and the main branch of the Mill Creek and bounded by the run of Coole Spring branch and it's bridge, by Mill Creek run, and the northwest branch of the fork of Coole Spring branch. Land granted by patent from Wm Penn on 6th da 1st mo 1684 and resurveyed on 5th da 1st mo 1686 and William Clark requested confirmation by the commissioners of this tract called "The Cold Spring". James Claypoole and Robert Turner sign.

Page 31. Assignment of Patent. 21 Nov 1717. From Honor Bedwell, gentlewoman and executrix of William Clark, to Preserved Coggeshall. Assignment of patent for land described in patent on pages 30-31 of this deed book. Honor Bedwell signs. Wits., Simon Kollock, James Simson and Elias Fisher.

Page 32. Discharge of Debt. (21 Nov 1717?.) From Thomas Bedwell, yeoman, of Sussex Co., DE., and executor in the right of his wife, Honor Bedwell, to William Clark's estate, to Thomas Harford, cordwainer. Discharges and releases Thomas Harford of all obligations due William Clark, dec'd. Thomas Bedwell signs. Wits., Richard Paynter and John Hepburn.

Pages 32-33. Deed. 12 Jul 1722. From James Finwick, yeoman, of Sussex Co., DE., to Simon Kollock, Esqr., of the same place. For 40 pounds 12 acres. Land is situated in Lewes on the SE side of the middle street (or second street) and bounded by a branch of Pagan Creek, by second street and by land of Cornelius Wiltbank. Sidney Finwick, wife of James Finwick, relinquishes her dower rights. James and Sidney Finwick sign. Wits., John Jacobs, Jno Paynter, Jr., and Rd Newcombe. Ack. 6 Aug 1722.

Pages 33-34. Deed. 4 May 1722. From James Finwick, yeoman, of Lewes, to Simon Kollock, Hannah White, Jacob Kollock, Joseph Royall and Magdelen, his wife, and Jacob Philips and Hester, his wife, of the same place. For 100 pounds one lot. Lot is situated in Lewes Town and is bounded by land that was formerly John Paynter's but is now Roger Train's, land that was formerly Thos Finwick's but is now Nathaniel Hall's and by third street. James Finwick signs. Wits., James Simson, Peter Marsh, and Rd Newcombe. Ack. 1 May 1722.

Pages 34-35. Deed of Gift. 10 Feb 1720/1. From Robert Lodge, wheelwright, of Sussex Co., DE., to Joseph Russel and Thomas Osborn. 2 acres of land. Land is situated on the east side of Cold Spring branch near to the County Road and is part of the land on which Robert Lodge lives, and on which the meeting house stands. Robert Lodge signs. Wits., Mary Russell, Naomy Davis, and Phil. Russel. Ack. 10 Feb 1720/1.

Pages 35-36. Deed. 4 May 1714. From Sarah Blundall, widow, of Sussex Co., DE., to Joseph Russell, weaver, of the same place. For 15 pounds 100 acres. Land is situated on the west side of Beaver Dam Branch proceeding out of the Cold Spring Branch and is bounded by 100 acres formerly sold by Sarah Blundall to Joseph Russell, and by Beaver Dam Branch, and was surveyed by Robert Shankland on 23 Apr 1714. Sarah Blundall signs with her mark. Wits., Mathew Osburn and Abell Pride. Ack. 4 May 1714.

Pages 36-37. Deed. 1 Aug 1718. From Joseph Carpenter, weaver, of Sussex Co., DE., to Joseph Russel, weaver, of the same place. For 4 pounds 10 shillings 31 1/2 acres. Land is situated in Sussex Co., DE., and bounded by 100 acres Joseph Russell purchased from Sarah Blundall, by Cold Spring Branch, by the mouth of the Beaver Dam, and by Harmon's land and is part of a tract of 400 acres lying on the north side of Cold Spring Branch. Joseph Carpenter signs. Wits., Sidney Finwick and Phil. Russel, Jr. Ack. 4 Nov 1718.

Page 37. Probate of Deed and Patent. 28 Jun 1723. Memorandum. Simon Kollock and James Simson, witnesses to the deed of Honor Bedwell to Preserved Coggeshall, appeared and made oath that they saw Honor Bedwell execute the deed and also the assignment of the patent and that they also saw Elias Fisher sign.

Pages 37-38. Deed. 3 Feb 1718/9. From Elizabeth Brown, attorney for Daniel Brown, yeoman, of Kent Co., DE., and Thomas Carlile and Mary, his wife, of Sussex Co., DE., heirs and administrators of Thomas Pemberton, gentleman, dec'd, to Nicholas Green, yeoman, and Margery, his wife, of Sussex Co., DE. For 25 pounds 4 shillings 70 acres of marsh. Land is situated on the north side of the Broadkill Creek and is bounded by Walton Huling's marsh, Cornelius Wiltbank's 100 acres, and Dyer's gutt. Land is conveyed to Nicholas Green and Margery, his wife, widow of Thomas Fisher, dec'd, for the use of Jabez Maud Fisher at their decease and resurveyed on 18 Feb 1717/8 by Robert Shankland. Patented to Thomas Pemberton on 14th da 3rd mo 1692 for 100 acres by the commissioners and contains only 70 acres. Elizabeth Brown and Mary Carlile sign. Wits., Thomas Wallace and Edward Naws. Ack. 3 Feb 1718/9.

Pages 39a-39b. Deed. 2 May 1721. From Thomas Marriner, yeoman, and Mary, his wife, and John Marsh, yeoman, and Elizabeth, his wife, all of Sussex Co., DE., to John Barr, yeoman, of the same place. For 20 pounds 318 acres. Land is situated on the NE side of a branch of the Broadkill called South West Branch and is bounded by Gitters Branch, one of the branches of the Broadkill. Land is the moyety of a larger tract of 650 acres granted by warrant from the Court of Sussex on __ da __ mo 1686 to John Finch who requested the tract be confirmed by patent dated in 1687. Henry

Bowman, dec'd, who obtained many patents on behalf of himself and others but after his death, William Clark, dec'd, obtained letters of administration and had several patents as part of Bowman's estate appraised. John Bowman, dec'd, son and heir of Henry Bowman, bequeathed to his 2 sisters, Mary and Elizabeth, a tract of 650 acres called Finch Hall. The sisters have now married Thomas Marriner and John Marsh and they finding the patent defective requested a resurvey dated 18 Nov 1718. Thomas Marriner and Mary Marriner make their marks, John Marsh signs and Elizabeth Marsh makes her mark. Wits., John Shankland and Richard Hinman. Ack. 1 May 1722.

Pages 39b-40. Deed. 8 Feb 1717/8. From Joseph Dod, planter, of Sussex Co., DE., to Thomas Dod, planter, of the same place. For 10 shillings 100 acres. Tract is situated in Sussex Co. on the west side of Delaware Bay, lying on the south east side of Brights Beaver Dam and adjoins Dorvalls land on the north side. The tract being conveyed is half of a larger tract of 200 acres which had been obtained by virtue of a warrant granted to Joseph Dod by Richard Hill, Isaac Morris & James Logan, the Proprietory Commissioners of Property for granting of land, bearing date 20 Sep (7th month) 1716. This tract surveyed on 1 Jan 1717 and called by the name of Dods Farm. Joseph Dod signed with his mark. Wits., David Gray and Roger Train. Ack. 8 Feb 1717/8.

Pages 40-42. Deed. 9 Nov 1721. From William Pettyjohn, yeoman, of Sussex Co., DE., to Robert Butcher, yeoman, of the same place. For 50 pounds 150 acres. Land is situated on the west side of Delaware Bay and on the south side of a branch called Long Love Branch and is called Watsons Choice. Land is bounded by land of Alexander Moleston, John Kiphaven and Samuel Gray. Land is part of a larger tract of 500 acres granted by Court at Sussex and confirmed by patent of William Penn to Luke Watson on 26th da 1st mo 1684 and surveyed 11th da 10th mo 1684. At the time of his death, Luke Watson was indebted to Anthoney Morris of Philadelphia who brought suit and had the land appraised and sold at vandue to John PettyJohn, Sr., farmer, of Sussex Co., DE., who made the land over to his sons, James and William PettyJohn. Afterwards James PettyJohn sold his moiety of the tract to his brother, William PettyJohn. William Pettyjohn signs with his mark. Wits., Jacob Kollock and Robt Perrie. Ack. Nov Court 1721.

Page 42. Deed. 7 Feb 1722/3. From Robert Shankland, lawful attorney of Daniel Brown and Elizabeth, his wife and eldest daughter of Capt Thomas Pemberton, to Robert Burton of Sussex Co., DE. For 30 pounds 150 acres of land. Land is situated on the north side of the Broad, the great Kill or

Creek, in the County of Sussex. Thomas Pemberton's daughter, Mary, wife of Thomas Carlile, has already conveyed their portion to Robert Burton by deed dated 4 Nov 1720. Tract is part of a larger tract of 400 acres called Swan Point formerly confirmed by patent bearing date in the year 1688 unto Bryan Rowles who by his deeds conveyed 200 acres to Barnes Garret, 50 acres to Henry Smith, and 150 acres by deed of sale dated thirteenth day of March 1698/9 unto Samuel Rowland. Samuel Rowland with Mary, his wife, conveyed by deed of sale dated 6 Nov 1716 the 150 acres to Capt Thomas Pemberton and then Capt Thomas Pemberton died intestate leaving two daughters. Wits., William Selthridge and Phil Russel. Ack. Feb Court 1722/3.

Page 43. Deed. 9 Aug 1722. From Archibald Smith, merchant, of Lewes Town, to Robert Smith, farmer, of Sussex Co., DE. For 100 pounds 300 acres. The land is situated on the SE side of Mill Creek and called Timber Hill. Land is bounded by land called Mulberry and by Mill Creek. Tract is part of a larger tract of 500 acres which was granted to Jno Vines by commissioners, James Claypoole and Robert Turner, on 2nd da 2nd mo 1686 and called Timber Hill. Land is bounded by land called Mulberry, the patent Bury and Abraham's Lott, Abraham Potter's land called Little Field and Mill Creek. Jno Vines sold the land to William Clark on 8th da 1st mo 1687 who sold in 1689 to Joseph Roe who sold on 15th da 4th mo 1700 to Patrick Robeson and Andrew Robeson. Andrew Robeson for 60 pounds sold the land (550 acres) to Archibald Smith. Archibald Smith signs. Wits., John Barr, Joseph Hepburn, Robt. Perrie. Ack. 9 Aug 1722.

Pages 44-45. Deed. 5 Feb 1722/3. From Francis Cornwall, yeoman, of Sussex Co., DE., to John Attkins, yeoman, of the same place. For 45 pounds 207 acres. Land is situated on the south side of the Cold Spring Branch which proceeds out of the Broadkill and is bounded by 50 acres of Humphrey Smith, the headline of Crague's land, the south side of the County Road. Land is part of a larger tract of 900 acres called Batcheller's Folley and part of one other tract of 115 acres purchased by Francis Cornwall from William White. Francis Cornwall signs with his mark. Wits., Robert Shankland and Phil. Russel. Ack. Feb Court 1722/3.

Page 45. Deed. 7 Feb 1722/3. From Daniel Palmer, yeoman, of Sussex Co., DE., to John Manlove, yeoman, of the Broadkill Hd. For 10 pounds approximately 60 acres. Land is situated on the north side of Broadkill Creek and on the SW side of Daniel Palmer's land which he purchased of his sister, Martha Huling, and is bounded by Green Branch, land laid out for Cornelius Wiltbank belonging to Palmer's tract, and John Manlove's land formerly belonging to Walton Huling. Daniel Palmer signs. Wits., George Walton and Phil. Russel. Ack. Feb Court 1722/3.

Loose Page inserted between pages 45 & 46. Deed. 30 Aug 1735. Sussex County. Whereas the within grantee John Manlove (now dec'd) Some time after the execution of the within deed made his will in writing by wch he bequeathed the within recited tract of land & premises unto his wife Sarah & to her heirs & assigns as by the sd will legally proved more at large may appear who now at this time is the lawful wife of Willm Milnor of County afsd yeom'n: Now know ye that the sd Wm (Milnor) and Sarah his wife for the consideracon of five (pounds) Curr't money of America to them in hand at & . . . the delivery hereof by James Miers of the afsd (County) yeom: well and truely pd have released & quitt claimed by these presents do absolutely release & quitt claim unto the afsd James Miers his heirs & assigns for . . . their right title & interest of in & to the within . . . agt them & their heirs & all other persons claims unto them or either of them. In witness whereof . . . Willm Milnor & wife have hereunto set their hands and seals the 30th day of Aug't in the year of our Lord (one) thousand seven hundred & thirty five. William and Sarah Milnor sign. Sarah Milnor releases her rights. Wits., Charles Dingee and Phil. Russel. Ack. 30 Aug 1735.

Page 46. Deed. 5 Feb 1722/3. From William Darter, yeoman, of Sussex Co., DE., to Joseph Cord, yeoman, of the same place. For 115 pounds 560 acres. Land is situated on Long Bridge Branch and was granted by patent from Edward Shippen, Griffeth Owen, and James Logan, commissioners of William Penn, to Honor Clark on 4 Jun 1708. Afterward Honor Clark married Thomas Bedwell who on 4 Aug 1713 sold the tract to William Darter. Margaret Darter relinquishes her dower rights. William Darter signs and Margaret Darter makes her mark. Wits., John Stewart and Phil. Russel. Ack. Feb Court 1722/3.

Page 47. Deed. 5 Feb 1722/3. From William Darter, yeoman, of Sussex Co., DE., to Joseph Cord, yeoman, of the same place. For 25 pounds 200 acres. Land is situated on the south side of Long Bridge Branch and is bounded by Darter's other land. Land was granted to Wm Darter by virtue of a warrant from the commissioners on 5 Nov 1714 and surveyed by Robert Shankland on 15 Feb 1714/5. Margaret Darter relinquishes her dower rights. William Darter signs and Margaret Darter makes her mark. Wits., John Stewart and Phil Russel. Ack. Feb Court 1722/3.

Page 48. Deed. 5 Feb 1722/3. From Timothy Dunavan, yeoman, of Sussex Co., DE., to Richard Reynolds, yeoman, of the same place. For 9 pounds 100 acres. Land is situated in Sussex Co., DE., on the NW side of the Mill

Branch proceeding out of the Broadkill and is part of a larger tract of 215 acres granted to Timothy Dunnavan by warrant from the commissioners dated 11th da 1st mo 1717 and surveyed on 26 Jan 1722 by Robert Shankland. Timothy Dunnavan makes his mark. Wits., John Hinman and Phil. Russel. Ack. Feb Court 1722/3.

Page 48. Earmark. 7 Sep 1728. Francis Wolf his mark for cattle, sheep & hogs, etc., is a swallow fork in the right ear & under bitt in the left. Recorded this 7th Day of September 1728. Test Jacob Kollock Dep Reges.

Page 49. Deed. 5 Feb 1722/3. From John Fisher, yeoman, of Sussex Co., DE., to Gideon Harrison, yeoman, of the same place. For 30 pounds 75 acres. Land is situated on a branch of the Broad Creek and bounded by the Kings Road at the Round pole branch. Land is part of a larger tract of 1000 acres called Millford and purchased by John Fisher from Thomas and Honor Bedwell, executors of William Clark, dec'd of Lewes Town, on 7 May 1713. Elizabeth Fisher relinquishes her dower rights. John and Elizabeth Fisher make their marks. Wits., William Seltheridge and Phil. Russel. Ack. Feb Court 1722/3.

Page 50. Deed. 2 May 1721. From Samuel Rowland, Esqr., of Sussex Co., DE., to Thomas and William Rowland of the same place. For 200 pounds 250 acres. Land is situated on the west side of Lewes Town between Lewes and Pagan Creek. Samuel Rowland signs. Wits., William Shankland, Simon Kollock, and Phil. Russel. Ack. May Court 1721.

Page 51. Deed of Gift. 5 May 1722. From James Simson, yeoman, and Margaret his wife, of Lewes, Sussex Co., DE., to Robert Heaton, weaver, and Mary his wife, of the same place. For natural love and affection and 5 shillings a 60 by 40 foot lot. Lot is situated in Lewes and bounded by second street, land of Simson and by land of John Jacobs. James Simson signs. Wits., Robert Smith, Thomas Gear, and Richard Newcombe. Ack. 1 May 1722. Recorded 9 Aug 1723.

Pages 51-52. Deed. 9 May 1723. From Henry Moleston, gentleman, of Kent Co., DE., son and heir of Hendrick Molleston, Esqr., of Kent Co., DE., to Andrew McGill, gentleman, of Sussex Co., DE. For 25 pounds 43 acres. Land is situated in Sussex Co., DE., in Cedar Creek Hd on the NW side of Cedar Creek and is bounded by land of Thomas Fleman. Hendrick Moleston, dec'd, sold the land to John Harmonson, dec'd, for 7 pounds 13 shilling & 9 pence and Hendrick Molleston, dec'd, did also bind himself to make over the land to John Harmonson's, dec'd, children, Hendrick and John Harmonson. Hendrick and John Harmonson sold the land to Andrew

McGill for 25 pounds. Henry Molleston, son of Hendrick Molleston, dec'd, now conveys to Andrew McGill. Henry Molleston signs. Wits., Thomas Stapleford, James White, and Samuel Wattson. Ack. May Court 1723.

Pages 53-54. Lease. 22 Jun 1721. From Henry Loyd, gentleman, of the mannor of Queen's Village in Queen's County on the Island Nassaw, NY., to Isaiah Harrison, blacksmith, of Smith Town in the County Suffolk on the Island, NY. For 100 pounds 907 acres. Land is situated 8 miles from the Town of Lewes in Sussex Co., PA. (DE.), and called by the name Maiden Plantation and is bounded by land of James Fisher and Bright's Beaver Dam. Land was formerly laid out for William Darval of Kent Co., PA. (DE.), by warrant from the Sussex Court for 1000 acres who sold the land to John Nelson, merchant, of Preston in New England, on 2 Feb 1687 who by deed of gift made over the land to his son-in-law, Henry Loyd, on 16 Nov 1713. The land was resurveyed on 1 Jan 1717/8 in pursuance of a warrant from the commissioners by Jacob Taylor, surveyor, for 907 acres. Henry Loyd signs. Wits., Thomas Everet and Samuel Pecton. Ack. Suffolk 23 Jun 1721. John Wickes. Ack. Sussex County 6 Aug 1722.

Pages 54-55. Letter of Attorney. 9 Jun 1722. From Henry Loyd of the mannor of Queen's Village in Queen's County on the Island Nassaw, NY., gentleman, to Capt Jonathan Bailey of Port Lewes, County of Sussex, PA. (DE.). Attorney to appear in Sussex Court instead of Henry Loyd and acknowledge a lease and release of a tract called Maiden Plantation dated 22 Jun 1721 to Isaiah Harrison of Smith Town, NY. H. Loyd signs. Wits., Thomas Brush and Robert Mackbeth.

Pages 55-56. Deed. 8 Aug 1723. From William Godwin, of Sussex Co., DE., to Ryves Holt, gentleman, of Lewes, DE. For 110 pounds a 60 by 200 foot lot. Lot is situated in Lewes Town and is bounded by land formerly belonging to Samuel Davis but now is Rev. Mr. William Becket, a new street lately laid out, Snitting Street, and second street. Elizabeth Godwin relinquishes her dower rights. William and Elizabeth Godwin sign. Wits., John Pritteman, Jr., and Thomas Gordon. Ack. 10 Aug 1723.

Page 57. Deed. 8 Aug 1722. From Nathaniel Hall, merchant, of Lewes, DE., to William Thomson, yeoman, of Sussex Co., DE. For 30 pounds 200 acres. Land is situated at the head of Cedar Creek and is bounded by land formerly belonging to Luke Watson, dec'd. Land was granted by warrant to Thomas Wilson on 19th da 12th mo 1714 and by him sold to Nathaniel Hall on 1 May 1716. Nathaniel Hall signs. Wits., Alexander Draper and James White. Ack. 6 Aug 1722.

Page 58. Bill of Sale. 30 May 1720. Sussex Supr. Delaware. Be it remembered that I the within named Wm Till, Gent: doe hereby acquit, & renounce all my right, title & interest to ye within negroe woman & children during the full time & term of the naturall life of my grandmother Mary Codd Gent: And I doe hereby give, grant, make & sett over ye use of the sd Negroes to my sd Grand Mother only dureing the term afsd. As witness my hand the 30th of May 1720. Wm Till signs. Wits., Hen: Brooke and Preserved Coggeshall. The above was endorsed on ye back of a certain Bill of Sale for ye above Negroes made by Berkley Codd Esqr to ye above Wm Till wch sd Bill of Sale was recorded heretofore in Record Book E No 4 page (383) per me. Phil Russel D Roll.

Page 58. Deed. 1 May 1681. From John Crew, planter, of Deal County, to Robert Hignot, planter, of the same place. For one cow and calf John Crew's interest in 900 acres. Land is situated by a Creek that comes out of Rehobah Bay and by a branch. Land was granted to Robert Hignot and John Crew by St Edmond Andross on 20 Aug 1679. John Crew makes his mark. Wits., William Clark, Alexander Draper and Andrew Depree.

Pages 58-59. Deed of Gift. 30 Nov 1689. From Cornelius Wiltbank, planter, of Sussex Co., PA. (DE.), to brother-in-law, John Williams, and Rebeckah, his wife, and their only daughter, Rebeckah Williams, Jr. For natural love and affection 40 acres. Land is situated on the SW side of the first branch lying SW from Lewes Creek to Pagan's Creek, and binding on the SE side of the Town Land and is part of the land on which Cornelius Wiltbank lives situated on Lewes Creek. Land given to John and Rebeckah Williams during their lives and after their decease to their daughter Rebeckah. Cornelius Wiltbank signs. Wits., Henry Stretcher and William Rodeney. Ack. Feb Court 1689/90.

Pages 59-60. Deed. 8 Feb 1721/2. From John Hinman, of Sussex Co., DE., to Woodman Stockley, of the same place. For 164 pounds a tract called Love's Choice. Land is situated in Angola Neck on the westernmost creek called Love's Creek and is known by the name Love's Choice and contains that quantity of land lying between Love's Creek and a certain branch proceeding therefrom to the southward of the land to the head of the branch. Land is near land of Woodman Stockley and is all the land that Richard Hinman sold his brother, John Hinman. John Hinman signs. Wits., James Simson and James White. Ack. 10 Feb 1720/1.

Pages 60-61. Deed. 10 Feb 1720/1. From Joseph Atkins and Elizabeth, his wife, of Sumersett Co., MD., to Woodman Stockley, yeoman, of Sussex Co., DE. For 25 pounds 175 acres. Land is situated on the westernmost side of Love's Creek and is part of a larger tract called Love's Choice by Thomas Pemberton and Joseph Atkins and is bounded by Love's Creek. Joseph Atkins signs and Elizabeth Atkins makes her mark. Wits., Alexander Moleston and James White. Ack. 10 Feb 1720/1.

Pages 61-62. Deed. 1 Nov 1723. From Berkley Codd, gentleman, to Caleb Kirwithen, yeoman, both of Sussex Co., DE. For 5 pounds 300 acres. Land is situated on the north side of Prime Hook. Land is part of a larger tract of 600 acres originally granted by patent of Francis Lovelace to John and Samuel Wattson on 17th da 3rd mo (May) 1688 on the north side of Prime Hooke who conveyed to Capt William Pyles, dec'd, in Jun 1688. Capt Pyles conveyed 300 acres of the tract to Luke Wattson, Jr., yeoman, dec'd, it being that part which adjoins William Bellamy. William Pyles conveyed the other 300 acres to Caleb Kirwithen, dec'd, on 10 Aug 1698 which was part of a larger tract granted to Richard Perrott of Middlesex Co., VA., dec'd, by patent of Francis Lovelace, Governor of NY., on 1 Jun 1671, who gave it to his son, Richard Perrott on 2 Jun 1672 who died intestate leaving several sons the eldest of whom was living on 29 Oct 1718 named also Richard Perrott who conveyed to Berkley Codd, gentleman, who now conveys to Caleb Kirwithen, son of the first mentioned Caleb Kirwithen, dec'd, 300 acres of the 600 acres. Berkley Codd appoints Preserved Coggeshall his attorney. Berkley Codd signs. Wits., Jane Wallace and James White. Ack. Feb Court 1723/4. Recorded in Liber F of Entrys near the end.

Pages 63-64. Deed. 10 Jul 1717. From Edward Morris, and Sarah, his wife, sole heir of Thomas Branscomb, of Sussex Co., DE., marriner, dec'd, to Joseph Godwin, house carpenter, of Sussex Co., DE. For 26 pounds 12 shillings 6 pence 200 acres. Land is situated at head of Lewes Creek and bounded by the SE point of Kickout Neck, John Kipshaven's land, Jeremiah Scott's land, a branch of Roades' Creek, Roades's Creek, and a pond. Land is part of a larger tract of 500 acres formerly surveyed by Cornelius Verhoofe, dec'd, for Stephen Whiteman and likewise part of another tract granted by patent from Governor Andross of NY to John Lemon who sold to Stephen Whitman who sold on 5th da 4th mo 1688 the afsd 200 acres to Thomas Branscomb. Edward and Sarah Morris sign. Wits., Hen: Brooke and William Godwin. Ack. 4 Aug 1719. Edward and Sarah Morris appoint Robert Clifton as their attorney.

Page 64. Deed of Gift. 7 Feb 1723. From Samuel Davis, gentleman, of Sumerset Co., MD., to Philip Russel and Mary, his wife. One negro girl named Abigail with future issue. Samuel Davis signs.

Pages 64-65. Deed. 3 Aug 1719. From Robert Lodge, house carpenter, of Sussex Co., DE., to John Roades, yeoman, of the same place. For 36 pounds 300 acres. Land is situated on the north side of Long Love Branch and called Gray's Inn. Tract was granted by Court of Sussex on 8th da 10th mo 1681 and surveyed 8th da 10th mo following for 632 acres and confirmed by patent of Wm Penn on 26th da 1st mo 1684 to Samuel Gray, gentleman, dec'd. David Gray, son and heir of Samuel Gray, sold 300 acres of the 632 acres to John Roades. John Roades sold the 300 acres on 4 Aug 1718 to Robert Lodge. Robert Lodge signs. Wits., Cornelius Wiltbank and W. White. Ack 3 Nov 1719.

Pages 65-66. Deed. 7 May 1723. From John Parsons, executor of Thomas Bate, yeoman, of Sussex Co., DE., to Archibald Smith, merchant, of Lewes. For 17 pounds 10 shillings 232 acres. Land is situated on the south side of Bracy's Branch and is bounded by Joseph Russel's land which formerly belonged to Thomas Besant and by John Fox's land. Land was originally granted to Thomas Bate on 20th da 3rd mo 1717 by the Commissioners and upon his decease, John Parsons was appointed administrator as the principal creditor. Since Bate's personal estate was insufficient to satisfy all of his debts, this land was sold. John Parsons signs. Wits., Thos. Gear, Daniel Palmer, Robt Shankland. Ack. May Court 1723.

Pages 66-67. Deed. 26 Feb 1722. From Thomas Gear, cordwayner, of Sussex Co., DE., to Archibald Smith, merchant, of Lewes. For 24 pounds 242 acres. Land is situated on the west side of Herring Creek proceeding out of Rehobah Bay and is bounded by land sold to William Hanzor by Thomas Gear, Aminadab Hanzor's land, Jacob Burton's land and by Herring Creek, and is part of a larger tract of 342 acres called Bottle and Cake which was granted to Thomas Gear by warrant from the Commissioners on the 5th da 10th mo 1714 and surveyed 8 Jan 1714 by Robert Shankland. Mary Gear relinquishes her dower rights. Thomas and Mary Gear appoint John Jacobs and/or Preserved Coggeshall as their attorneys. Thomas Gear signs and Mary Gear makes her mak. Wits., Nathaniel Hall, James Simson, Phil. Russel. Ack. May Court 1723.

Pages 67-68. Deed. 4 Feb 1723. From Archibald Smith, merchant, of Lewes, to John Parsons, yeoman, of Sussex Co., DE. For 40 pounds 242 acres. Land is situated on the west side of Herring Creek proceeding out of Rehobah Bay and is bounded by land of William Hanzor which was sold to him by Thomas Gear, Aminadab Hanzor's land, Jacob Burton's land, and by Herring Creek. Land is part of a larger tract of 342 acres called Bottle and Cake granted to Thomas Gear by warrant from the Commissioners and 242 acres was sold to Archibald Smith by Thomas Gear. Archibald Smith signs. Wits., Alexander Moleston, Phil. Russel. Ack. Feb Court 1723.

Pages 68-69. Deed of Release. 11 Feb 1720. From Joseph Atkins, eldest son of William Atkins, yeoman, deceased of Sussex Co., DE., to John Atkins, yeoman, of the same place. Quit claim for 203 acres. Land is situated on the southwest side of Long Love Branch near the head of a neck of land called Angola Neck and is bounded by land formerly laid out for Richard Bundock and land formerly laid out for Robert Bracy, Sr. Land formerly belonged to William Atkins, deceased. Joseph Atkins signs and Elizabeth Atkins makes her mark. Wits., Alexander Moleston, James White. Ack. Feb Court 1720.

Page 69. Deed of Gift. 4 Dec 1723. From Margret Paynter to her children, Luke Shield, John Paynter, and Doogood Paynter. 100 pounds to her 3 sons -- 50 pounds to Luke Shield and the remaining 50 pounds to be divided between John and Doogood Paynter when they reach age 21 -- to be paid out of her estate after her decease. Margaret Paynter signs. Wits., Simon Kollock Anderson Parker and Wm Becket.

Pages 70-71. Deed. 26 Feb 1717. From John Warren, waterman, of Philadelphia and son of William Warren, dec'd, of Sussex Co., DE., to William Godwin, yeoman, of Sussex. For 60 pounds and one merchantable cow and calf 300 acres. Land is situated on Potthook Creek and on the east side of Whorekill Town. Land was granted on 29 Sep 1677 by Edmond Andross to William Warren abovesaid and was called Warren's Choice. Martha Johnson, widow of Adam Johnson, by virtue of a purchase from Edward Bendbrick, son and heir of Edward Bendbrick, dec'd, claimed the land. Martha Johnson sold the land to John Warren by her deed of release dated 13 Feb 1717. John Warren signs with his mark. Wits., Simon Kollock and W. White. John Warren appoints Archibald Smith as his attorney. Ack. 5 Aug 1718.

Pages 71-72. Deed. 5 Nov 1719. From Patience Bowman, widow and executrix of John Bowman, dec'd, late of Kent Co., DE., to Stephen Henry, yeoman, of Sussex Co., DE. For 7 pounds 10 shillings 100 acres. Land is situated in Slaughter Neck and is bounded by land of James Carpenter and was surveyed 23 Mar 1718 by Robert Shankland. Patience Bowman makes her mark. Wits., Samuel Wattson and James White. Ack. 3 Nov 1719.

Pages 72-73. Deed. 7 May 1723. John Cary, yeoman, to Thomas Gray, yeoman, both of Sussex Co., DE. For 160 pounds 259 acres of land. Tract is situated in Angola Neck, binding on James Walker's land, Ayleff's line,

Webley's land, David Hazzard's land, and is part of a larger tract granted by patent to Robert Bracey in 1674 and by Robert Bracey sold to William Clark and by William Clark's executor conveyed to John Cary. John and Bridget Cary sign. Wits., Catherine Holt and Phil Russel. Ack. 6 Aug 1723.

Pages 73-74. Deed. 7 Nov 1723. From Joseph Carpenter, weaver, of Sussex Co., DE., to Thomas Cade, carpenter, of the same place. For 47 pounds 169 acres. Land is situated on the northwest side of Cold Spring Branch in Sussex Co. and bounded by Cold Spring Branch, by Henry Harmon's land, and by a small branch and contains 400 acres in the whole and known by the name Rotterdam. Land was granted by patent of William Penn on the 1st da 1st mo 1682 to Cornelius Johnson and whose successive heirs have been in possession since his decease. Joseph Carpenter, as the present possessor, sells 169 acres of the 400 acre tract to Thomas Cade. The 169 acres are bounded by land called Abraham's Lott and (illegible) Russell's land. Joseph Carpenter makes his mark. Wits., Samuel Hand and James Finwick. Ack. Feb Court 1723.

Pages 74-75. Deed. 23 Jul 1721. From James Walker, gentleman, of Sussex Co., DE., to John Parsons, house carpenter, of the same place. For 25 pounds 100 acres. Land is situated in Sussex Co., DE., and known by the name of Webley. Land is bounded by Bracey's Branch and a little branch called Green Branch. Land is part of a larger tract of 800 acres called Webley which was granted by patent of William Penn to Robert Bracey, Sr. Robert Bracey, Sr., gave the land to his son, Robert Bracey, Jr., except for 100 acres and a little neck which he gave his two daughters, Mary and Elizabeth. The 800 acres is bounded by a beaverdam branch called Bracey's Branch and is on the west side of another branch and the head of the said branch. Robert Bracey, Jr., sold the land to William Clark who for 135 pounds sold 400 acres to James Walker. The 400 acres were bounded by Bracey's Branch and on the west side of another small branch and the little neck, and by the head of the small branch. James Walker signs. Wits., Benjamin Stockley, John Prise, and Cord Hazzard. Ack. Aug Court 1721.

Pages 75-76. Deed. 5 May 1721. From Elizabeth Stutchbury/Touchberry, widow of Henry Touchberry, yeoman, of Sussex Co., DE., deceased, to John Price, yeoman, of the same place. For 40 shillings 1/2 of 239 acres or 100 acres more or less. Land is situated on Indian River Hundred on the south side of Bracey's Branch and bounded by Robert Richard's land, Jacob Kollock's land, and on the north side of Fishing Branch one of the branches of Middle Creek. Land is part of a larger tract of 239 acres which was granted by warrant of Jacob Taylor, Commissioner, to Henry Touchberry on 16th da 12th mo 1714 and surveyed by Robert Shankland on 23 Apr 1717.

Elizabeth Touchberry sells to John Price 1/2 of the tract of 239 acres which is on the south side of the tract where John Price now lives and it contains 100 acres more or less. Elizabeth Touchberry makes her mark. Wits., Thomas Gear and Robt Perrie. Ack. May Court 1721. Endorsement on back of deed acknowledges receipt of forty shillings the full consideration for the land. Elizabeth Touchberry makes her mark.

Page 77. Deed. 1 Feb 1718. From James Finwick, yeoman, of Lewes, to Anthony Woodward, taylor, of the same place. For 13 pounds 10 shillings 3 1/9 lots. The lots are situated at the south end of Lewes and bounded on the north by land of Nathaniel Hall, Jr., on the west side of John Shankland's lots and on the south side of the County Road. James Finwick signs. Wits., Samuel Rowland and Phil. Russel. Ack. 7 Aug 1722.

Pages 77-78. Deed. 12 Feb 1723/2. Thomas Carlile & Mary, his wife, of Sussex Co., yeoman, to Christopher Topham, merchant, of Philadelphia. For 15 pounds 217 acres. Whereas by virtue of a warrant by Jacob Taylor, surveyor, gentleman, bearing date at Philadelphia on the thirteenth day of the eleventh month requiring him to take up 200 acres of land vacant in the forest of Sussex County for Thomas Carlisle. Land is situated at the head of the northwest branch of the Broadkill in the place called Pemberton's Savannah. Robert Perrie is the attorney of Thomas Carlile. Thomas and Mary Carlile make their marks. Wits., Edward Stretcher, Alexander Moleston, Archibald Smith, Joseph Hepburn. Ack. May Court 1723.

Pages 78-79. Power of Attorney. 8 Feb 1722. From Thomas Carlile to Robert Perrie to acknowledge the above deed in Court and sale of land to Christopher Topham. Thomas Carlile makes his mark. Wits., Edward Stretcher and Alexander Moleston.

Pages 79-80. Deed. 3 Aug 1724. From Christopher Topham, merchant, of Lewes, to William Cornwallis, gentleman, of Philadelphia. For 50 pounds 217 acres. Land is situated at the head of the northwest branch of the Broad Kill in the place called Pemberton's Savannah and bounded on the northwest side by a Savannah. Land was assigned to Christopher Topham on 12 Feb 1722 by Thomas Carlile and Mary, his wife. Christopher Topham signs. Wits., William Moliston and Joseph Hepburn. Receipt for consideration money. Christopher Topham signs. Wits., Wm Moliston and Joseph Hepburn. Ack. 4 Aug 1724.

Pages 80-81. Deed. 7 May 1723. From William Darter, yeoman, of Sussex Co., DE., to Christopher Topham, merchant, of Lewes. For 30 pounds 442 acres. Land is situated at the head of Long Bridge Branch and is bounded by

Thomas Davock's land called Green Meadows and William Darter's land and contains 232 acres. Also another tract of land adjoining to the first tract which is bounded by Thomas Davock's land called Green Meadows and on the southeast side of Barnes' Savannah containing 210 acres. The first tract was originally granted by warrant dated 14th da 8th mo 1715 to John Hinman and by him assigned on 5 Oct 1721 to William Darter. The second tract was granted by warrant dated 10th da 5th mo 1718 to William Darter. Wm Darter signs. Wits., Roger Train and Phil. Russel. Ack. May Court 1723.

Pages 81-82. Deed. 1 May 1722. From Daniel Palmer, yeoman, of Broad Kill, to Cornelius Wiltbanck, gentleman, of Sussex Co., DE. For 50 pounds 193 acres. Land is situated on the north side of Broad Creek and bounded by William Fisher's land and the head of a branch which proceeds out of the Broad Kill. Tract contains 193 acres called Howard's Choice and was granted by Edmond Andross, Governor of New York, to Thomas Howard whose heir being deceased bequeathed the tract to Luke Watson, Jr., with the request that he make over the tract to Capt John Hill and Capt Thomas Pemberton. Capt John Hill afterwards purchased the rights of Luke Watson, Jr., and Capt Thomas Pemberton. Capt Hill bequeathed the tract to his wife, Elizabeth Hill, who conveyed the tract to Walton Huling. Martha Huling as executrix of Walton Huling conveyed the tract to Daniel Palmer. Daniel Palmer signs. Wits., Christopher Topham and John Hinman, Jr. Ack. May Court 1723.

Page 82. Deed. 5 Dec 1723. From John Kiphaven Johnson, yeoman, of Sussex Co., DE., to Archibald Smith, merchant, of Lewes. For 35 pounds 560 acres. Land is situated on Long Bridge Branch. Tract was originally granted by patent dated 11 Oct 1714 to Honor Clark, executrix of William Clark, deceased, who in his lifetime was indebted to Patrick Williams. Martha Johnson, administrator of Patrick Williams, for the recovery of the debt commmenced an action against Honor Clark and obtained judgement on 29 Apr 1714 and execution was issued on 10 Jul following on this tract of land. Tract was therefore sold by John Hepburn, sheriff, to Martha Johnson on 25 Oct 1715. Martha Johnson by several deeds of gift dated 6 May 1720 gave the land to her two sons, John Kiphaven and Isaac Johnson. Isaac Johnson bequeathed by his will dated 9 Feb 1721 his part to John Kiphaven Johnson. John Kiphaven Johnson appoints Martha Johnson and/or John Jacobs his attorneys. John Kiphaven Johnson signs. Wits., Joseph Hepburn and Phil. Russel. Ack. Feb Court 1723. Recorded in Liber F of Entrys near the end.

Page 83. Deed. 4 Feb 1723. From John Parsons, yeoman, of Sussex Co., DE., to Archibald Smith, merchant, of Lewes. For 20 pounds 100 acres. Land is situated in Angola Neck and is bounded by Bracey's Branch and Green Branch. Tract is part of a larger tract of 800 acres called Webley which was granted by patent from William Penn to Robert Bracey who gave the tract to his son, Robert Bracey, who conveyed the tract to William Clark who sold 400 acres to James Walker who sold 100 acres of the 400 acres to John Parsons. John Parsons signs. Wits., Alexander Moleston and Phil. Russel. Ack. Feb Court 1723.

Pages 83-84. Deed. 11 May 1724. From Nathan Whitehead and Mary, his wife, of Kent Co., DE., to Archibald Smith, merchant, of Lewes. For 40 pounds 2 lots. The lots are situated on Second Street in the Town of Lewes and is bounded by the lot of Richard Hinman, the lot where Archibald Smith now dwells, and a street lately laid out. The lots were formerly granted to William Orion. Nathan and Mary Whitehead appoint Ryves Holt to be their attorney. Nathan Whitehead signs and Mary Whitehead makes her mark. Wits., Lydia Sipple and Robert Hodgson. Ack. 16 Jun 1724.

Pages 84-85. Deed. 11 Dec 1723. From John Jacobs, Esqr., Sheriff of Sussex Co., DE., to Richard Hinman, Esqr, of the same place. For 24 pounds 10 shillings 1 lot of land. The lot is situated in Lewes Town and bounded by Second Street, by land of James Simson, and by land of John Jacobs. Lot was sold by James Simson and Margaret, his wife, to Robert Heaton and Mary, his wife, by deed dated 5 May 1722. John Jacobs, Sheriff, took the lot in execution, finding no other effects, on 6 Nov 1723 and the lot was sold at public vendue on 28 Nov 1723 to Richard Hinman. John Jacobs signs. Wits., Robert Smith and Preserved Coggeshall. Ack. Feb Court 1723.

Pages 85-86. Deed. 8 Mar 1722. From Robert Lodge, house carpenter, of Sussex Co., DE., to Francis Cornwall, cordwayner, of the same place. For 36 pounds 98 acres. Land is situated on the west side of Delaware Bay and on the north side of Long Love Branch and is bounded by land occupied by Francis Cornwall and contains 100 acres except for 2 acres granted by deed of gift to the people called Quakers. Land is part of a larger tract of 632 acres called Gray's Inn which was granted by order of the Court of Sussex Co. on 8th da 10th mo 1681 and surveyed on the 8th da 10th mo following and confirmed by patent of William Penn on the 26th da 1st mo 1684 to Samuel Gray. David Gray, son and heir of Samuel Gray, sold 300 acres of the tract to John Roades who by his deed of sale dated 5 Aug 1719 conveyed 100 acres of the 300 acres to Robert Lodge. Robert Lodge signs. Wits., Thomas Cade and Enoch Cummings. Ack. May Court 1723.

Pages 86-87. Deed. 1 May 1716. From John Coe, Esqr, of Kent Co., DE., to Thomas Cale, Jr., yeoman, of Sussex Co., DE. For 37 pounds 10 shillings for 90 acres. Land is situated in Rehoboth and is on the west side of small gutt and is bounded by a tract called South Hampton, on the south side of a small branch, and the head of a valley. Land is part of a larger tract of 350 acres called South Hampton formerly granted and confirmed to John Roades, dec'd, by patent of Edmond Andross, Governor of New York, dated 25 Mar 1676. John Roades, son and heir of John Roades, dec'd, by deed of release dated 4 May 1706, conveyed the 350 acres to John Coe. John Coe signs. Wits., John McCullach and Phil. Russel, Jr. Ack. 1 May 1716.

Pages 87-88. Deed. 2 Aug 1721. From Sarah Lucas, executrix of Peter Lucas, yeoman, deceased, of Sussex Co., DE., to William Stewart, yeoman, of the same place. For 20 pounds 210 acres. Land is situated in the fork of Pemberton's Branch, one of the branches which proceeds out of the Broad Creek, and is bounded by the southernmost fork of the branch, the mouth of the fork, and the other fork of the branch. Tract was originally granted by the Commissioners on 13th da 11th mo 1717 to Peter Lucas who bequeathed the land to Sarah Lucas. Sarah Lucas signs. Wits., Abrm Potter, John Stewart, Sam'l Stewart. Ack. Aug Court 1721.

Page 88. Deed. 7 Feb 1720. From Anderson Parker, Esqr., of Sussex Co., DE., to John and William Stewart, yeomen, of the same place. For 15 pounds 166 acres. Land is situated on the south side of Long Bridge Branch which proceeds out of the Broad Creek and called by the name of Walton's Choice and is bounded by land of Thomas Davock and a small swamp. Tract was granted by Commissioners warrant dated 5th da 7th mo 1718 to Anderson Parker. Anderson Parker signs. Wits., Daniel McSeachram, Wm Micky, and Dan'l Micky. Acknowledged but no Court date.

Page 89-90. Deed. 7 May 1723. From Thomas Stapleford, joyner, of Philadelphia, to Alexander Draper, of Sussex Co., DE. For 15 pounds 5 shillings 231 acres. Land is situated on the northwest side of Cedar Creek and bounded by land which does now belong to Alexander Draper, by the County Road, by Cedar Creek Branch, by land of John Walton, which was resurveyed by Robert Shankland on 3 Apr 1723. Land is part of a greater tract of 700 acres which on 21 Jan 1681 was surveyed and laid out for Robert Hart, Sr., who on 9 Dec 1684 conveyed to William Darvall, dec'd, of Kent Co., DE., merchant. William Darvall absented himself from the Government not taking care to pay his debts; therefore, the tract was taken in execution at the suit of William Emmot, dec'd, executor of the estate of John Vines, dec'd, who in his lifetime obtained a judgment against William

Darvall. John Hill, high sheriff, took the land in execution and it was conveyed to William Clark who conveyed to John Richards, butcher, of Philadelphia, and John Richards by William Clark, his attorney, conveyed 400 acres of the tract to William Stapleford on 3 Jul 1704, and William Clark, lawful attorney of John Richards, made over the other 300 acres to Thomas Stapleford, planter, of Sussex Co., DE., on 20 Jul 1704. Thomas Stapleford conveyed 100 acres of the 300 acres to John Walton of Sussex Co., DE., yeoman. Now Thomas Stapleford, son of the elder Thomas Stapleford, conveys the remaining portion of the 300 acres to Alexander Draper. Thomas Stapleford signs. Wits., Ryves Holt, Preserved Coggeshall, and James White. Ack. May Court 1723.

Pages 90-91. Deed. 4 Feb 1723. From Cornelius Wiltbanck, yeoman, of Sussex Co., DE., to Abraham Wiltbanck, yeoman, of Lewes. For 100 pounds 150 acres. Land is situated on the northwest of Lewes Town and is bounded by Abraham Wiltbanck's house, by the dividing line between this land and the land of Cornelius Wiltbanck, a minor son of Isaac Wiltbanck, dec'd, by Lewes Creek, by William Clark's land, and by Pagan Creek. Cornelius Wiltbanck signs. Wits., William Shankland and Phil. Russel. Ack. Feb Court 1723. Recorded in Liber F of Entrys near the end.

Page 91. Deed. 7 Nov 1723. From William Crammer, yeoman, of Kent Co., DE., son and heir of Thomas Crammer, house carpenter, deceased, of Sussex Co., DE., to Abraham Wiltbanck, yeoman, of Sussex Co., DE. For 4 pounds a 4-acre lot. Lot is situated on the west of Lewes town and adjoyning the land of Abraham Wiltbanck. The lot was granted and confirmed by the Court of Sussex to Thomas Crammer. William Crammer appointed Philip Russel to be his attorney. William Crammer signs. Wits., Margt Bodall and Wm Shankland. Ack. Feb Court 1723. Recorded in Liber F of Entrys near the end.

Page 92. Division of Lands. Between Abraham Wiltbanck and Cornelius Wiltbanck. Cornelius Wiltbanck's, son and heir of Isaac Wiltbanck, bounds. Land joins to and is on the northwest side of Lewes town and is part of a great tract of land that did belong to Halmanius Wiltbanck, dec'd, by patent and is on the west side of Lewes Creek that runs into Delaware Bay and is bounded by the corner stone of the street of the town of Lewes at the bank of Lewes Creek, by Lewes Creek, by Abraham Wiltbanck's old dwelling house, by the Ship & Carpenter yard and street, and by one of the branches of Pagan Creek commonly called Finwick's branch. Land was divided by William Becket, guardian of Cornelius Wiltbanck, and Abraham Wiltbanck. Surveyed by Robert Shankland on 10 Jan 1723. Robert Shankland signs. Abraham Wiltbanck's bounds. Land is bounded by William Clark's land, by

Lewes Creek, by Pagan Creek, and a little to the south east of Clark's great house. Surveyed 15 Jan 1723. Robert Shankland, deputy surveyor, signs.

Pages 92-93. Deed of Release. 7 Feb 1720. From William Field, youngest son of Nehemiah Field of Sussex Co., DE., dec'd, gentleman, to Elias Fisher, weaver, of Sussex Co., DE. For 12 pounds (most of this deed is illegible) William Field signs. Wits., Alexander Moleston and Phil Russel. Ack. Feb Court 1722.

Pages 93-94. Deed. 7 May 1724. Thomas Dod, yeoman, of Sussex Co., DE., to John Pettyjohn, Sr., yeoman, of the same place. For 10 pounds 100 acres of land. Tract is situated on the south east side of Bright Beaver Dam bounded by Darval's land and is part of a larger tract granted to Joseph Dod by warrant dated 20th day 7th month 1716 and Joseph Dod sold this 100 acres to Thomas Dod on 8th day of Feb 1717. Thomas Dod signs with his mark. Wits., John Pettyjohn, Jr., and Phil Russel. Ack. May Court 1724.

Pages 94-95. Deed. 7 May 1724. William Spencer, yeoman, of Sussex Co., DE., and his wife, Sarah, to William Pettyjohn of the same place. For 75 pounds 500 acres. Land is situated in Sussex Co., DE., and bounded by a corner of Alexander Moleston and John Kiphaven. Tract was originally patented to Roger Gum and by him sold to John Fisher whose sons, Thomas and John Fisher, by deed of gift, conveyed on 4(?) May 170(3?) to Sarah Spencer. William and Sarah Spencer sign. Wits., Francis Conwell(?) and Phil Russel. Ack. May Court 1724.

Page 95. Deed of Release. 5 Aug 1718. James Pettyjohn, yeoman, of Sussex Co., DE., to William Pettyjohn, yeoman, of the same place. For 40 pounds 400 acres. Land is situated at the head of Long Love Branch alias Bundock's Branch. Land was formerly purchased by James and William Pettyjohn from Thomas Fisher, gentleman, and is part of a greater tract of 500 acres taken up by Luke Watson and called Watson's Choice. James Pettyjohn signs. Wits., Richard Bracey(?) and James White. Ack. 5 Aug 1718.

Page 96. Deed of Gift. 7 May 1724. John Pettyjohn, Sr., to his granddaughter, Isabelle Pettyjohn, daughter of Thomas and Elizabeth Pettyjohn. The 100-acre tract is situated near the head of Long Bridge Branch and part of a 200-acre tract granted to William Arey who assigned his interest to John Pettyjohn. If Isabell should die before reaching 21 years or without lawful issue then the tract reverts to her mother, Elizabeth. John Pettyjohn signs with his mark. Wits., Thomas Dod and Phil Russel. Ack. May Court 1724.

Pages 96-97. Deed of Gift. 7 May 1724. John Pettyjohn, Sr., to his son, Richard Pettyjohn. The 100-acre tract is situated near the head of Long Bridge Branch, near the County Road, and is part of a larger tract of 200 acres granted to William Arey who assigned his interest to John Pettyjohn, Sr. John Pettyjohn signs with his mark. Wits., Thomas Dod and Phil: Russel. Ack. May Court 1724.

Pages 97-98. Deed. 2 Aug 1715. From Joseph & John Pyles, yeoman, of Sussex Co., DE., to John Fisher, yeoman, of the same place. For 16 pounds 50 acres of marsh land. Land is situated on the west side of Delaware Bay and on the south side of Broad Creek and is bounded on the south side by Broad Creek, on the northeast side by the plantation where John Fisher lives, and the mouth of a gutt proceeding out of the Broad Creek. Marsh land was granted to William Pyles, father of Joseph and John, by warrant from the Commissioners and surveyed by Thomas Pemberton on 3 Mar 1709. Joseph Pyles makes his mark and John Piles signs. Wits., Philip Russell, and Phil Russel, Jr. Ack. 4 Aug 1715.

Pages 98-99. Deed. 8 Aug 1723. From Philip Russel, Esqr., of Sussex Co., DE., to William Godwin, yeoman, of the same place. For 25 pounds one town lot 60 by 200 feet. Lot is situated in the town of Lewes and bounded on the southeast with the lot of Mr. William Becket, on the southwest by a street lately laid out, on the northwest Snitting Street or Mulberry Street, and on the northeast by Second Street. Mary Russel, wife of Philip, relinquishes her dower rights. Phil Russel and Mary Russel both sign. Wits., Robt Shankland and Ryves Holt. Ack. Aug Court 1723.

Pages 99-100. Deed of Release. 16 Jun 1724. From Elias Fisher, weaver, of Sussex Co., DE., to John Shankland, blacksmith, of Lewes, DE. Quit claim for 32 acres. Land is situated on the north side of the flatt land in Sussex Co. and is bounded by a pond in the line of Otto Woolgast's land. Elias Fisher signs. Wits., Arch: Smith and Phil. Russel. Ack. 16 Jun 1724.

Pages 100-101. Deed. 1 Feb 1724. From David Smith, Esqr, and Sarah, his wife, of Sussex Co., DE., to Robert Turk, Turn:, of the same place. For 14 pounds 195 acres. Land is situated in the fork of Cedar Creek which proceeds out of Delaware Bay and is bounded on the north side by the southernmost branch or fork of Cedar Creek, on the west side of the County Road above the bridge, by Cedar Creek, and near the Church. Land was surveyed on 1 Aug 1716 for David Smith by virtue of a warrant of the Commissioners dated 29th da 6th mo 1715 by Robert Shankland. David Smith signs and Sarah Smith makes her mark. Wits., John McDowell and

John Hunter. Ack. Feb Court 1723. Recorded in Liber F of Entrys near the end.

Pages 101-102. Deed. 4 Feb 1723. From Stephen Henry, yeoman, of Sussex Co., DE., to Robert Miller, weaver, of the same place. For 20 pounds 100 acres. Land is situated in Slaughter Neck and is bounded by James Carpenter's land, and by some land unknown. Land was surveyed 23 Mar 1718 by Robert Shankland. Stephen Henry makes his mark. Wits., Mary Russel and Phil Russel. Ack. Feb Court 1723.

Pages 102-103. Deed. 7 May 1724. From William Becket and Jacob Kollock, gentlemen, of Sussex Co., DE., and executors of Cornelius Wiltbanck, yeoman, deceased, last of Sussex Co., DE., to Abraham Parsley, yeoman, of the same place. For 34 pounds 275 acres. Land is situated on the south side of Broad Kill and is part of a larger tract called Luck by Chance and bounded by Dawson's Branch and by a little swamp. Cornelius Wiltbanck died legally possessed of the land which by his will dated 10 Mar 1723 authorized his executors to make over to Abraham Parsley. Wm Becket and Jacob Kollock sign. Wits., Wm Till and A. D. Peyster(?). Ack. May Court 1724.

Pages 103-104. Deed. 6 May 1724. From William Walton, yeoman, and Patience , his wife, late of Sussex Co., DE., now of Kent Co., DE., to George Walton, yeoman, of the said County. For 80 pounds 91 acres. Land is situated on the north side of Cedar Creek and bounded by George Walton's land, by Art Vankirk's land, by Nicholas Grainger's land, by a small gutt or branch, and resurveyed on 24 Mar 1724. Land is part of a greater tract of 933 acres of land and marsh granted to Henry Bowman, dec'd, by patent of the Commissioners dated 9 Aug 1690. Henry Bowman sold 100 acres of the 933 acres to John Walton but died before making the deed. William Clark, dec'd, as administrator of Henry Bowman, conveyed 97 acres to John Walton by deed dated 1 Jun 1700. John Walton bequeathed the 97 acres to his son, William Walton. William and Patience Walton sign. Wits., Wm Spencer and Robt Shankland. Ack. May Court 1724.

Pages 104-105. Deed. 8 Feb 1722/3. From Archibald Smith, merchant, of Lewes, to Arthur Johnson, farmer, of Sussex Co., DE. For 11 pounds 210 acres. Land is situated at the head of Laws' ponds which proceeds out of Bracy's Branch and joining on the west side with Laws' lands and is bounded by Laws' lands and known by the name The Glades. Land was originally granted by virtue of a Commissioners warrant dated 13th da 1st mo 1717 to Robert Davis and was surveyed by Robert Shankland on 12 Apr 1717.

Archibald Smith, the principal creditor of Robert Davis, yeoman, deceased, who dying intestate, obtained administration of Robert Davis' estate on 13 Jun 1719. Archibald Smith employed two sworn appraisers/surveyors, Robert Clifton and Anderson Parker; thereafter, Archibald Smith employed John Hepburn, sheriff, to have the lands sold at vendue and the land was sold to Arthur Johnson. Arch: Smith signs. Wits., Robt Perrie and Rob: Smith. Ack. Feb Court 1722.

Pages 105-106. Deed. 7 May 1723. From John and Albertus Jacobs, sons of Albertus Jacobs, deceased, gentleman, of Sussex Co., DE., to Thomas Stockley, yeoman of the same place. For 55 pounds 100 acres. Land is situated in Warrens Neck and is bounded by Potthooks Creek, land of Jonathan Henry, and a small branch proceeding out of Potthooks Creek. Land is part of a larger tract formerly taken up by Otto Woolgast, yeoman, deceased. John Jacobs, Hannah Jacobs, Albertus Jacobs, and Abigail Jacobs all sign. Wits., Phil Russel and John Shankland. Ack. 10 Sep 1723.

Pages 106-107. Deed. 9 Aug 1722. From James Finwick, yeoman, of Sussex Co., DE., to Joseph Eldridge, carpenter, of the same place. For 20 pounds 5 1/2 lots. The lots are situated in Lewes town and are bounded by a lot of John Bywater purchased of the Conveyor, by the County Road, by a corner of a parcel of ground left by a street by James Finwick, by the southernmost street in Lewes, and by lots of Philip Russel purchased from the Conveyor. Sidney Finwick relinquishes her dower rights. James and Sidney Finwick sign. Wits., John Hines and Jean Little. Ack. 9 Aug 1722.

Pages 107-108. Deed. 2 Aug 1720. From Richard Dobson, cooper, of Sussex Co., DE., to Capt Jonathan Baily, Esqr., of the same place. For 10 pounds a lot 60 by 200 feet. Lot is situated in the second street of the town of Lewes and is bounded by Thomas Marshall's lot and Thomas Jenkins' lot. Richard Dobson signs. Wits., Arch: Smith and Philip Russel. Ack. Aug Court 1720.

Pages 108-109. Deed. 9 May 1723. From William Dyer, of Sussex Co., DE., to John Allen, of the same place. For 6 pounds 205 acres. Land is situated in the forest on the head of a glade of Ivy Branch which proceeds out of Middle Branch that comes of Rehoboth Bay and is bounded by John Prettyman's land. Land was surveyed and laid out for 205 acres on 20 Nov 1718 by Robert Shankland by virtue of a warrant from the Commissioner, Jacob Taylor, dated 30th da 1st mo 1717 to William Dyer and known by the name Dyer's Choice. William Dyer makes his mark. Wits., Joseph Shankland, James Baily, and Jas White. Ack. May Court 1723.

Pages 109-110. Deed of Gift. 4 Aug 1724. From Francis Cornwall, yeoman, of Sussex Co., DE., to his sister, Mary Woolfe alias Moore, widow, of the same place. For 5 shillings 15 acres. Land is situated in a neck called White Oak Neck and is bounded by the mouth of a gutt which proceeds out of Marshes Creek and by a large pond which heads the gutt. Francis Cornwall makes his mark. Wits., Mary Russel and Phil. Russel. Ack. Aug Court 1724.

Page 110. Deed of Gift. 6 Aug 1724. From Mary Moore, to her son, Francis Woolfe, son of Rice Woolfe, deceased, of Sussex Co., DE. For natural love and affection 15 acres. Land is situated in White Oak Neck and is bounded by the mouth of a gutt which proceeds from Marshes Creek and by a large pond which heads the gutt. Mary Moore makes her mark. Wits., Mary Russel and Phil Russel. Ack. Aug Court 1724.

Pages 110-111. Deed. 6 May 1724. From Robert Burton, yeoman, of Sussex Co., DE., to Anthony Woodward, taylor, of Lewes. For 17 pounds 8 shillings 5 pence 3 1/9 lots. Lots are situated on the south end of the town of Lewes and is bounded by land of Nathaniel Hall, by lots of John Shankland, and by the County Road. The lots were purchased by Robert Burton from Anthony Woodward on 5 May 1722. Robert Burton appoints John Shankland, blacksmith, of Lewes, to be his attorney. Robert Burton makes his mark. Wits., Mary Russel and Phil. Russel. Ack. 26 May 1724.

Pages 111-112. Deed. 4 Feb 1723. From Joseph Cord, yeoman, of Sussex Co., DE., to Nathaniel Racklief, yeoman, of Sumerset Co., MD. For 90 pounds 121 acres. Land is situated on the west side of Delaware Bay on the south west side of Love's Creek which proceeds out of Rehoboth Bay and is bounded by Woolfe's Pitt Branch, by John McCullah's land, and surveyed by Robert Shankland. Joseph Cord signs and Anne Cord makes her mark. Wits., William Shankland and Phil. Russel. Anne Cord assented to the sale of the land. Ack. May Court 1724.

Pages 112-113. Deed. 5 May 1724. From Robert Hart, planter, of Sussex Co., DE., to George Walton, yeoman, of the same place. For 10 pounds 56 acres. Land is situated in Cedar Creek Neck on the south side of Mispillion Creek adjoining the west side of land on which John May, Esqr., and Art Johnson Vankirk live on and is bounded by a small branch, by Clandening's land, and by the Neck road and surveyed by Robert Shankland on 24 Mar 1723. Land is part of a larger tract of 900 acres as by certificate dated 3rd da 4th mo 1685 under the hand of Joshua Barsted, surveyor, which was resurveyed by virtue of a warrant granted by order of the Court to William Clark, Chief Surveyor, for Robert Hart and named Hart's Range. The 900 acres was formerly in two tracts. One tract of 400 acres, Robert Hart obtained from James Louton; and the other tract of 500 acres, Robert Hart obtained patent from New York dated the 29th da 10th mo 1677. Robert Hart makes his mark. Wits., William Spencer and Robert Shankland. Ack. May Court 1724.

Pages 113-114. Deed. 7 May 1724. From John Watson, of Sussex Co., DE., to John Smith, yeoman, of the same place. For 20 pounds 100 acres of marsh land. Land is situated in Prime Hook Neck and known by the name Watson's Marsh and is bounded by Samuel Watson's land on the beach, by the beach, and by Prime Hook Creek. The land was formerly purchased by Luke Watson, dec'd, brother to John Watson, from his father, Luke Watson, dec'd, by deed dated 6 Feb 1704. Luke Watson, the younger, on 4 Feb 1706 by deed of gift gave the land to John Watson. Sarah Watson relinquishes her dower rights. John and Sarah Watson appoint James White to be their attorney. John and Sarah Watson make their marks. Wits., Richard Shockley, William Haverloe, and James Jones. Ack. May Court 1724.

Pages 114-115. Deed. 4 Feb 1719. From Isaac Watson, yeoman, of Sussex Co., DE., to Samuel Watson, yeoman, of the same place. For (not given) pounds 200 acres. Land is situated in Prime Hook and is bounded by the marshes of Prime Hook Creek. Isaac Watson obtained the land from his father, Luke Watson, gentleman, deceased, by deed of gift dated 6 Dec 1697 and acknowledged in open Court on 9 Jun 1698. Land is part of a larger tract of 600 acres called Fairfield. Isaac Wattson signs. Wits., Robert Shankland and James White. Ack. 4 Feb 1719.

Pages 115-116. Deed of Release. 4 Feb 1719. From William Walton, yeoman, of Sussex Co., DE., to John Walton, yeoman, of the same place. Quit claim for 50 acres. Land is situated on the north the cypress or swamp of Cedar Creek. Land is part of a larger tract of 700 acres which was bequeathed to William Walton by his father, John Walton, deceased, to include the water mill. William Walton signs. Wits., Alexander Draper and Tho: Wallace. Ack. 4 Feb 1719.

Pages 116-117. Deed of Release. 8 Feb 1723. From James Miers, to his brother, John Miers, marriner, of Lewes. Quit claim for 5 pounds for 10 acres. Land is situated on the south side of Alexander Moleston's plantation and is part of a tract which formerly belonged to Samuel Dickason which their father, John Miers, deceased of Lewes, purchased of Samuel Dickason and bequeathed to James Miers. James Miers signs. Wits., Sarah Smith and Joseph Eldridge. Ack. Feb Court 1723.

Page 117. Deed of Gift. 9 Mar 1723. From George Claypoole, Joseph Claypoole, and Mary Cooke, of Philadelphia, to cousin, Jeremiah Claypoole, yeoman, of Broadkill. For natural love and affection 500 acres. Land is situated in Indian River Hundred and the 500 acres is part of a larger tract of 1200 acres which formerly belonged to Richard Bundock who sold the 500 acres to Norton Claypoole who died possessed of it. Afterwards, Nehemiah Field and Rachel, his wife, widow of Norton Claypoole, sold the 500 acres to Francis Cooke, administrator of the estate of their father, James Claypoole, deceased, merchant, of Philadelphia. George Claypoole, Joseph Claypoole, and Mary Cooke sign. Wits., Christopher Topham and Jno Kiphaven Johnson. Ack. Aug Court 1723 by Jacob Kollock, their attorney, and proved by Christopher Topham and John Kiphaven Johnson.

Page 118. Deed. 1 May 1722. From Anne May, widow and executrix of Thomas May, Jr., deceased, yeoman, of Sussex Co., DE., to William Selthridge, gentleman, of Philadelphia, and Lucilla, his wife. For 20 pounds 100 acres of land. Land is situated on the south side of Mispillion Creek and is bounded by the mouth of Holly Branch and up the branch, by the mill road, and was surveyed by Robert Shankland on 1 May 1722. Land is part of a larger tract of 400 acres called Pennington which 400 acres formerly belonged to Henry Pennington who conveyed the land to Thomas May who sold the land to his son, Thomas May, Jr. Thomas May, Jr., by his last will and testament, authorized Anne May to convey the 100 acres to Lucilla. Anne May makes her mark. Wits., John Roades, Roger Train, and James White. Ack. 1 May 1722

Page 118. Acknowledgement. 11 May 1724. I acknowledge to have rec'd of Wm Selthridge full satisfaction for all debts dues bonds bills or other accts whatsoever from the beginning of the world to this date as witness my hand & seal this eleventh day of May Anno 1724. Willm Huston signs. Test. John May. The above discharge in full was prov'd by the oath of John May to be given under ye hand & seal of the above Huston before me this 23d of April 1725. Test. David Smith signs.

Page 119. Deed. 6 Aug 1720. From William Townsend, planter, of Sussex Co., DE., to George Bushop, yeoman, of the same place. For (consideration not given) 200 acres. Land is situated on the north side of the northernmost branch of Cedar Creek and is bounded by the dividing line of the tract, by the other part of the tract which now belongs to Denis Bryan, by the said branch, by the mouth of Polecatt Branch which comes out of the main branch and binding with the said branch. Land is part of a larger tract of 450 acres. William Townsend signs. Wits., William Shankland, John Pettyjohn, Sr., and Arch. Smith. Ack. Feb Court 1720.

Page 119. Earmark. 30 Dec 1731. Daniel Harrison his ear mark for cattle sheap & hoggs is as follows (vis) swallow fork & underbitt the left ear and over bit the right ear recorded the 30th day of Decem'r 1731. Jacob Kollock Dep Regr.

Page 120. Deed. 23 Jun 1721. From Patrick Delany, of Lewes, DE., to Robert Pirrie, school master, of the same place. For 13 pounds one town lot. Lot is situated in Mulberry Street in the town of Lewes. Lot was originally granted by the Court at Lewes in Sep 1696 to Samuel Crowell, gentleman, of Cape May in West Jersy which lot adjoins the lot of Nehemiah Field and in the proportion and size and Field's lot and being on Mulberry Street. Yelwerton Crowell, son and heir of Samuel Crowell, sold the lot to Patrick Delany on 27 Aug 1718. Patrick Delany makes his mark. Wits., Simon Kollock, Joseph Hepburn, and Rd Newcomb. Ack. Aug Court 1721.

Page 121. Deed. 1 May 1721. From Samuel Rowland, Esqr., of Sussex Co., DE., to John Hall, Esqr, executor of the last will and testament of Thomas Bedwell, gentleman, deceased, of Sussex Co., DE. For 57 pounds 15 shillings 71 1/2 acres. Land is situated on the west side of Lewes Town Creek and is bounded by William Clark's land, by Lewes Town Creek, and by Pagan Creek. Samuel Rowland had sold the land to Thomas Bedwell during his lifetime; however, actual conveyance is now occuring. Samuel Rowland signs. Wits., Charl. Harrison, John Jacobs, and Phil. Russel. Ack. May Court 1721.

Pages 122-123. Deed. 1 Jan 1721. From John Hall, gentleman, of Kent Co., DE., executor of Thomas Bedwell, deceased, to William Rodeney, gentleman, of Sussex Co., DE. For 26 pounds 5 shillings 71 1/2 acres. John Hall, as executor of Thomas Bedwell, had filed his administration account at an Orphans Court on 6 Sep 1720 and it showed that Thomas Bedwell's personal estate would not satisfy his debts; John Hall then on 4 Aug 1721 petitioned the Court to take this tract of land in execution which was then sold at vendue on 27 Sep 1721 to William Rodeney. John Hall signs. Wits., Thos. Ward and James Pepper. John Hall appoints Philip Russel his attorney. Ack. Feb Court 1721.

Pages 123-124. Deed. 6 Feb 1721. From William Rodeney, yeoman, of Sussex Co., DE., to Philip Russel, yeoman, of the same place. For 25 pounds 34 acres. Land is situated near the town of Lewes and is bounded by Lewes Creek and by William Clark's land. Land is part of a larger tract granted by Francis Lovelace, Governor of New York, to Harmanus Fredrick Wiltbanck on 1 Jul 1672 which land was bounded by the land of William

Classen, by land of the heirs of Jan Jardyne, a frenchman, containing in breadth 114 rods, each rod being 11 feet , and into the woods to Pagan Creek which tract of land was called West India Fort. Harmanus Wiltbanck conveyed the tract to Norton Claypoole who sold the tract to James Claypoole, of Philadelphia, merchant. James Claypoole bequeathed the tract to his youngest son, Joseph Claypoole, who conveyed the tract on the 12th da 9th mo 1703 to Samuel Rowland. Samuel Rowland conveyed 71 1/2 acres of this tract to John Hall, executor of Thomas Bedwell, who, in order to satisfy the just debts of Thomas Bedwell, sold the land at vandue to William Rodeney on 1 Jan 1721. William Rodeney signs. Wits., James Simson and Elias Fisher. Ack. Feb Court 1721.

Pages 124-125. Deed. 6 Feb 1721. From William Rodeney, yeoman, of Sussex Co., DE., to Nathaniel Hall, merchant, of the same place. For 35 pounds 37 acres. Land is situated near the town of Lewes and bounded by the land of William Clark, by Lewes Town Creek, by Philip Russel's land, by a small swamp, and by Pagan Creek. Land is part of a larger tract granted by Francis Lovelace, Governor of New York, to Harmanus Fredrick Wiltbanck on 1 Jul 1672 which land was bounded by the land of William Classen, by land of the heirs of Jan Jardyne, a frenchman, and into the woods to Pagan Creek which tract of land was called West India Fort. Harmanus Wiltbanck conveyed the tract to Norton Claypoole who sold the tract to James Claypoole of Philadelphia, merchant. James Claypoole bequeathed the tract to his youngest son, Joseph Claypoole, who conveyed the tract on the 12th da 9th mo 1703 to Samuel Rowland. Samuel Rowland conveyed 71 1/2 acres of this tract to John Hall, executor of Thomas Bedwell, who in order to satisfy the just debts of Thomas Bedwell, sold the land at vendue to William Rodeney on 1 Jan 1721. Wm Rodeney signs. Wits., Phil. Russel and Arch. Smith. Ack. Feb Court 1721.

Page 126. Deed of Release. 1 Aug 1710. From Francis Bagwell, son of of Thomas Bagwell, yeoman, deceased, of Accomack Co., VA., to his brother, William Bagwell. Quit claim for 250 acres. Land is situated in a neck called Long Neck in Indian River Hundred and is bounded by Rehoboth Bay and land where William Bagwell is now seated and surveyed by Jonas Greenwood, surveyor, on 2 May 1710. The 250 acres is one-half of a larger tract of land which Thomas Bagwell purchased of William Burton, yeoman, deceased, of Accomack Co., VA. Francis Bagwell signs. Wits., Philip Russel, Cornelius Wiltbanck, and Thomas Fisher. Ack. 3 Aug 1710.

Page 126. Earmark. 12 Dec 1725. Jabez Fisher his ear mark for cattle sheep & hoggs is a crop & under bitt in the right ear and a W in the left. Recorded this 12th Decemb'r 1725. Phil. Russel D. Regr.

Page 127. Deed. 4 Aug 1724. From John Jacobs, yeoman, of Sussex Co., DE., to John Shankland, blacksmith, of the same place. For 8 pounds 5 shillings 11 acres. Land is situated near the town of Lewes and is bounded by land of Adam Johnson, dec'd, and by land of John Shankland. John Jacobs signs. Wits., Robert Shankland and Phil. Russel. Ack. Aug Court 1724.

Pages 127-129. Deed. 6 Nov 1724. From Martha Johnson, widow, John Kiphaven Johnson, yeoman, and Elizabeth Johnson, spinster, all of Sussex Co., DE., to John Shankland, blacksmith, of the same place. For 8 pounds 15 acres. Land is situated on the southeast side of Lewes and is bounded by land of Albertus Jacobs, by the other half part of the 30 acres now belonging to Archibald Smith and was surveyed and divided on 1 Nov 1724. Land is part of a larger tract of 611 acres originally granted by patent from Edmond Andross, Governor of New York, on 25 Mar 1677 to Alexander Moleston who for diverse good causes on 8 Jan 1703 gave and bequeathed the land to his son, Alexander Moleston, Jr., and is all that land on the southeast side of Lewes Town. The remainder part of the 611 acres not yet disposed of, which is in the tenor and possession of Alexander Moleston, Jr., Alexander Moleston, Jr., conveyed to John Stutchbury (30 acres). John Stutchbury on 20 Apr 1709 conveyed the 30 acres to Adam Johnson. The 30 acres were bounded by Alexander Moleston's land and by Samuel Davis's land and surveyed by Jonas Greenwood, surveyor. Adam Johnson by his last will and testament bequeathed 1/3 part of his property both real and personal to his wife, Martha Johnson, and the remaining two thirds part, he bequeathed to be divided amongst his three children, Isaac, John Kiphaven, and Elizabeth. The survivors now sell the 1/2 of the 30 acres to John Shankland. Marthew Johnson makes her mark, Jno Kipshaven Johnson and Elizabeth Johnson sign. Wits., John Jacobs, Robert Shankland and James Sangster. Ack. Nov Court 1724.

Pages 129-130. Deed. 6 Nov 1724. From Martha Johnson, widow, John Kipshaven Johnson, yeoman, and Elizabeth Johnson, spinster, all of Sussex Co., DE., to Archibald Smith, merchant, of Lewes. For 8 pounds 15 acres. Land is situated on the southeast side of Lewes and is bounded by John Shankland's land and surveyed by Robert Shankland on 3 Nov 1724. Land is part of a larger tract of 611 acres granted by patent from Edmond Andross, gentleman, Governor of New York, on 25 Mar 1676 to Alexander Moleston, yeoman, of Sussex Co., DE., who for diverse good causes by deed of gift dated 8 Jan 1703 gave and bequeathed the land to his son, Alexander Moleston, Jr. Alexander Moleston, Jr., conveyed 30 acres of the 611 acres to John Stutchbury who conveyed the 30 acres to Adam Johnson on 20 Apr 1709. The 30 acres were bounded by Alexander Moleston, Jr's, land and by Samuel Davis's, gentleman, land and was surveyed by Jonas Greenwood. Adam Johnson, by his last will and testament dated 16 Dec 1713, bequeathed 1/3 of his property in America both personal and real to his wife, Martha Johnson, and the remaining two thirds to be divided between his three children, Isaac, John Kipshaven, and Elizabeth. The survivors now sell 1/2 of the 30 acres to Archibald Smith. Martha Johnson signs with her mark, Jno Kipshaven Johnson and Elizabeth Johnson sign. Wits., John Jacobs, Robert Shankland, and James Sangster. Ack. Nov Court 1724.

Pages 130-131. Deed. 7 Nov 1724. From James Simson and Margret, his wife, of Sussex Co., DE., to Richard Hinman, gentleman, of the same place. For 52 pounds one lot 60 X 200 feet. Lot is situated in the Front Street of Lewes and is bounded by land of John Price and by land of Richard Hinman and with land of Alexander Moleston and with Second Street. Margret Simson relinquishes her dower rights. James and Margt Simson sign. Wits., David Smith, Jabez Fisher, and Phil. Russel. Ack. Nov Court 1724.

Pages 131-132. Deed. 3 Nov 1719. From Jacob Kollock, merchant, of Lewes, to Harmon Harmonson, cooper, of Sussex Co., DE. For 45 pounds 300 acres. Land is situated on the east side of Loves Creek which proceeds from Rehobah Bay. Land was purchased by John Deprey, Sr., dec'd, from Robert Hignot, dec'd, and John Deprey sold it to his son, Andrew Deprey, dec'd, and after the death of Andrew Deprey, the land was sold to John Deprey, Jr., a second son of John Deprey, Sr., and brother of Andrew Deprey. Mary Deprey, widow of John Deprey, Jr., pursuant to John Deprey's will for a consideration paid to John Deprey, Jr., during his lifetime, conveyed the land to Jacob Kollock on 6 Feb 1710. The land now to be sold is to be the northernmost part of the tract purchased of Robert Hignot by John Deprey, Sr., as per the deed of sale between John Deprey, Sr., and Andrew Deprey. Jacob Kollock signs with his mark. Wits., Robert Pirrie and Cornelius Kollock. Ack. 3 Nov 1719.

Pages 132-133. Deed. 7 Nov 1724. From James Simson and Margret, his wife, of Sussex Co., DE., to John Price, mariner, of Lewes. For 60 pounds one lot 60 X 160 feet. Lot is situated in Front Street of Lewes and bounded by the lots of Jno Jacobs and by the lots of Richard Hinman. Margaret Simson relinquishes her dower rights. James and Margret Simson sign. Wits., David Smith, Jabez Fisher, and Phil. Russel. Ack. Nov Court 1724.

Pages 133-134. Deed. 3 Nov 1724. From Joseph Royall, mariner, of Lewes, and Alexander Moleston, yeoman, of Sussex Co., DE. For 80 pounds one town lot 60 X 200 feet. Lot is situated in Front Street of Lewes and bounded by High Street, by lots of James Simson, by Front Street, and by Second Street. Joseph Royall signs. Wits., Ryves Holt, Richard Hinman, and Phil. Russel. Ack. Nov Court 1724.

Pages 134-135. Deed. 13 Jan 1724. From Mary Kollock, widow of Jacob Kollock, merchant, of Lewes, deceased, Simon Kollock, Esqr., Hannah Wiltbanck, widow, Jacob Kollock, gentleman, Jacob Phillips, gentleman, and Hesther, his wife, and Jane Hirons, heirs of Jacob Kollock, deceased, to Woodman Stockley, yeoman, of Sussex Co., DE. For 60 pounds 550 acres. Land is situated in Sussex Co., DE., and is bounded by some of Darvall's lands, by Law's Branch, by Bracy's Branch, and near some ponds called Law's ponds. The land was granted by the Court of Sussex in 1681 to Richard Law and was resurveyed to Richard Law by virtue of the Commissioners warrant on 25 Nov 1708 and sometime after Richard Law conveyed the land to Jacob Kollock, deceased, who by his last will and testament, bequeathed the land to his seven children: Simon, Hannah, Jacob, Jane, Magdalen, Hesther and Cornelius. Jane Hirons signs, Jacob and Hesther Phillips sign, Mary Kollock signs, Simon Kollock signs, Hanah Wiltbanck signs, and Jacob Kollock signs. Wits., Oliver Stockley and Phil. Russel. Ack. Feb Court 1724.

Pages 135-136. Deed of Release. 11 Nov 1724. From Joseph Royall, marriner of Lewes, to Jacob Philips, merchant of the same place. For 45 pounds 69 1/2 acres. Land which was purchased jointly by Joseph Royall and Jacob Phillips is situated on the south side of Lewes and on the north side of Pagan Creek and is bounded by Daniel Palmer's land, the southern most street of Lewes, the run of Pagan Creek Branch, and 31 acres which formerly belonged to Peter Lewes and containing 69 1/2 acres. J Royall signs. Wits., Arch. Smith and John Roades. Ack. Nov Court 1724.

Pages 136-137. Deed. 3 Nov 1724. From Elizabeth Brown, lawfull attorney of Daniel Brown, yeoman, of Kent Co., DE., to Christopher Phillipson, yeoman, of Sussex Co., DE. For 20 pounds 5 shillings 210 acres. Land is situated on the north side of Sow Bridge Branch, one of the branches of Prime Hooke Creek, and is bounded by Sow Bridge Branch below the County Road and bridge and by Prime Hooke Branch. Land was granted virtue of a warrant from the Commissioners dated the 13th da 11th mo 1717 and surveyed for Daniel Brown. Elizabeth Brown, attorney, signs. Wits., Roger Train and Phil. Russel. Ack. Nov Court 1724.

Pages 137-138. Deed. 4 Aug 1724. From John Williams, planter, of Sussex Co., DE., to Margret Pope, widow of Francis Pope, deceased, of the same place. For 16 pounds 105 acres. Land is situated in Mark's Neck on the west side of Swan Creek branch which runs into Indian River and surveyed 3 Aug 1724. Land is part of a larger tract of 210 acres which was granted by virtue of a warrant from the Commissioners dated the 26th da 6th mo 1717 and surveyed on 11 Jan 1717 to John Williams. John Williams makes his mark. Wits., Willm Crige, Robert Shankland, and Robert Pirrie. Ack. Aug Court 1724.

Pages 138-139. Deed. 10 Aug 1724. From John Sanderson, planter, of North Hampton Co., VA., to Wrixham Lewis, yeoman, of Sussex Co., DE. For 35 pounds 200 acres. Land is situated on the south side of Herring Creek which proceeds out of Rehobah Bay and adjoining land of Francis Williams and is bounded by Herring Creek. John Sanderson makes his mark. Wits., Jonathan Henry and Phil. Russel. Ack. Nov Court 1724.

Page 139. Deed. 1 Aug 1713. From Edward Parker, Esqr., Sheriff of Sussex Co., DE., to John Cary, yeoman, of the same place. For 15 pounds 15 shillings 394 acres. Land is situated on the north side of Indian River and bounded by a cypress branch. Land was taken in execution from Thomas Bedwell and Honor, his wife, executors of the estate of William Clark, gentleman, deceased, at an Orphans Court on 3 May 1713 at the suit of John Cary for 37 pounds and costs. Land was granted by warrant of the Commissioners dated the 9th da 6th mo 1693 to William Clark and surveyed on the 19th da 7th mo 1695. The land was valued at 15 pounds 10 shillings by a jury and sold at public vendue and John Cary as the highest bidder bought the land. Edward Parker signs. Wits., Phillip Russel and Phil. Russel Jr. Ack. May Court 1715.

Page 140. Deed. 5 Aug 1712. From John Fisher and Nathaniel Starr, both yeoman of Sussex Co., DE., administrators of the estate of John Haggester, deceased, to Babtist Newcomb, yeoman, of the same place. For (consideration not given) 200 acres. Land is situated in Kimball's Neck and is part of two tracts of land. One of the tracts was land of William Pyles and bequeathed by William Pyles to James Carpenter who sold the land to John Haggester and is bounded by William Pyles' (deceased) other land and contains one (or 100 acres?) acre. The other is part of Babtist Newcomb's land and bequeathed by him to John Haggester and bounded by lands of John Haggester and Daniel Newcomb and contains 100 acres. John Fisher and Nathaniel Starr are transferring land which Babtist Newcomb purchased from John Haggester during his lifetime but deed and confirmation were not yet completed. John Fisher makes his mark and Nath'l Starr signs. Wits., Edward Crage and Thomas Fisher. Ack. Aug Court 1712.

Pages 140-141. Deed. 2 Aug 1715. From Francis Dunavan and Elizabeth, his wife, of Sussex Co., DE., to Babtist Newcomb, yeoman, of the same place. For 39 pounds 189 acres. Land is situated on the west side of Delaware Bay and on the south side of the great Creek or Broad Creek and bounded by the bridge on Point(?) Gutt or Branch, by land of Daniel Newcomb, and by land of Jno Haggester and known by the name of Trotters Point. Land is part of a larger tract of 500 acres granted by patent by the Commissioners in 1689 to Babtist Newcomb, deceased, who bequeathed 189 acres to his son, William Newcomb. William Newcomb, by his last will and testament, bequeathed the 189 acres to his wife, Elizabeth, except for a part he had before sold to William Light. Francis Dunnavan and Elizabeth, his wife, widow of William Newcomb, now sell the 189 acres to Babtist Newcomb. Francis and Elizabeth Dunnavan make their marks. Wits., Anderson Parker, Phil Russel, Jr. Ack. Nov Court 1715.

Pages 141-142. Deed. 4 May 1722. From William Smith, yeoman, of Sussex Co., DE., and Rebecca, his wife, to John Hill, taylor, of the same place. For (consideration not given) 61 acres. Land is situated on the head of a branch which proceeds out of Bracy's Branch and is bounded by land which was formerly taken up by Francis Meads and John Crawley and known by the name of Soulsters Inheritance. The 61 acres is 1/4 part of a larger tract of 244 acres which was originally granted by virtue of a Commissioner's warrant dated 1 Apr 1681 to Richard Solster of Sussex for 244 acres who sold the 244 acres to Richard Cantwell/Kentwell of Sussex who sold the 244 acres to Thomas Smith. Thomas Smith, by his last will and testament dated 25 Apr (no year), bequeathed the land to his daughter, Rebecca, who married William Smith. John Hill is to have the use of the land until the youngest heir shall come of age to possess her part of the 244 acres. William Smith makes his mark and Rebecca Smith signs. Wits., Sam. Davis and Thomas Gordon. Ack. 1 May 1722.

Page 142. Receipt. 22 Apr 1724. Rec'd of my mother Martha Johnson, wid'w some time since administratrix of the estate of my dec'd father, Albertus Jacobs, the sum of eight pounds four shillings & ten pence, it being in full of my part or share of my sd father's personall estate. Rec'd the 22th April 1724 (or 1722?) and also rec'd more the sum of eleven pounds ten shillings being due to me for sundry cattle sold of mine by Adam Johnson dec'd. I say both sd sums rec'd date above per me. John Jacobs signs. Wits., Nathaniel Baily and Jno Kipshaven Johnson.

Page 142. Receipt. 22 Apr 1724. Rec'd of my mother Martha Johnson wid'w some time since admin'x of the estate of my dec'd father Albertus Jacobs the sum of four pounds two shillings & five pence, it being in full of my part or share of my sd father's personall estate, rec'd the 22th April 1724 per me. Albertus Jacobs signs. Wits., Nathaniel Baily and Jno Kipshaven Johnson.

Pages 142-143. Deed of Gift. 28 May 1716. From John Bennett, Sr., of Sussex Co., DE., to his son, John Bennett, Jr. For love, good will & affection 150 acres. Land is situated on Cedar Creek. Land is part of a larger tract of 300 acres which was formerly William Emmat's and bought by John Bennett, Sr., from William Fisher. John Bennet signs. Wits., Tho. Toole and Thomas Davis. Ack. 7 Aug 1716.

Pages 143-144. Division of Lands of William Bagwell. 12 May 1725. By virtue of an Order of Orphan's Court dated -- Mar 1724 upon petition of John Adams and Agnes, his wife, daughter of William Bagwell, dec'd, for the division of the lands of William Bagwell, dec'd, which he died possessed of in Indian River Hundred. Ryves Holt, James Walker, Samuel Davis, Philip Askie, and John Russel were appointed to set off Agnes Adams' part of the lands. The appointees are to divide the lands allowing the heir-at-law, William Bagwell, 2 parts and if there being occasion they are to first run a dividing line between these lands and the land of Woolsey Burton, Esqr., and make report at the Orphans Court in next Sep. The appointees report that they have made division of the lands between where Woolsey Burton lives adjoining to Indian River and the lands of William Bagwell lying on Rehobah Bay. The land is bounded by the 640 acres of land formerly laid out for Woolsey Burton and Francis Bagwell, dec'd, between the River and the Bay, by the neck road, by fishing or Indian Cabin Creek that runs into Indian River, by the head of Roberson's Branch that runs into Rehobah Bay and divided for 991 acres on each side (north and south) of the dividing line with land of Woolsey Burton on the south side adjoining the River and land of the Bagwell's on the north side adjoining the Bay. Agnes' part of the 991 acres was the lowermost part down the neck and bounded by Rehobah Bay, by the 640 acres of Burton and Bagwell, by the neck road, by a gut at the head of Ragged Hammock Creek and down to the mouth of the Creek where it joins Rehobah Bay and laid out for 390 acres. William Bagwell's part contained 610 acres of the 1/2 part of Long Neck. John Russell signs, James Walker signs, Philip Askie signs and Robert Shankland, D. Surveyor signs.

Pages 144-145. Deed. 8 Aug 1722. From James Finwick, yeoman, of Lewes, to John Chambers, joyner, of Sussex Co., DE. For 54 pounds 16 1/2 acres. Land is situated on the Whorekill in Delaware Bay near the town of Lewes and between the County Road and the southernmost street in Lewes and is bounded by the southernmost street, by the County Road, by Alexander Moleston's land, and by the lane that goes into Mr. Davis's plantation and was surveyed on 2 Aug 1722 by Robert Shankland. Land is part of a larger tract of 69 acres granted by patent from New York dated 15 Jan 1675 to John Kiphaven and bounded by the Whorekill in Delaware Bay, by Alexander Moleston's land and by Pagan Creek, and surveyed by Edmond Cantwell. John Kiphaven conveyed the land to William Clark who on 12 Apr 1681 conveyed to Capt Nathaniel Walker who, by his last will and testament, bequeathed the land to Major William Dyre, dec'd. The land, by warrant of resurvey, belonging to William Carter was found to be surplusage 27 acres and on 27 Sep 1686 William Carter conveyed the land to William Clark who conveyed to Major William Dyre on the 3rd da 4th mo 1687 so that the whole tract is deemed to be 96 acres. William Dyre, oldest son and executor with Mary, his mother, dec'd, and wife to their father, Major William Dyre, dec'd, conveyed the land to Thomas Finwick. Additionally, Alexander Moleston, Sr., conveyed 440 acres situated near the town of Lewes to Peter Lewes called Middleborough who conveyed the 440 acres to Jacob Kollock, Sr., except 6 acres previously sold to Thomas Finwick of Lewes. James Finwick, being the proper heir of Thomas Finwick, conveys part of the 2 tracts to John Chambers. James Finwick signs. Wits., Arch. Smith, Roger Traine, and Jos. Hepburn. Ack. 6 Aug 1722.

Page 146. Letter of Attorney. 12 Jun 1703. From George Thomson, marriner, of Lewes, to Roger Corbett, of the same place. Authority to acknowledge deed of gift to Peter Lewis. Georg Thomson signs. Wits., John Miers and John Coe.

Page 146. Deed of Gift. 12 Jun 1703. From George Thomson, marriner, of Lewes, to Peter Lewis, cordwayner, of Sussex Co., DE. For love and affection one town lot 60 X 200 feet. Lot is situated in Lewes on Front Street and bounded by the lots of John Miers, the lots in ye (illegible) of Baltus(?) Finwick. Lot to Peter and Grace Lewis during their natural lives and after their decease to their son, Wrixham Lewis. George and Anne Thomson sign. Wits., John Miers, John Coe and Roger Corbett. Ack. 1 Aug 1704.

Page 147. Deed. 8 Feb 1722. From Joseph Russel, weaver, of Sussex Co., DE., to Thomas Marshall, cordwayner, of the same place. For 12 pounds one lot. Lot is situated in Lewes and taken up by Richard Paynter, Sr., and is on Second Street and is bounded by the lot of Capt Jonathan Baily, and by lots once belonging to Richard Dobson. Joseph Russel signs. Wits., Robert Pirrie and Joseph Godwin. Ack. Feb Court 1722.

Pages 147-148. Deed 4 Feb 1717. From John PettyJohn, Sr., yeoman, of Sussex Co., DE., to John Thomson, gentleman, of the same place. For 47 pounds 200 acres. Land is situated on the south or southwest side of Love Long Branch and bounded by land of John PettyJohn. The land is part of a larger tract of 1200 acres formerly belonging to Richard Bundock who sold 540 acres to Thomas Jones and John Jones, dec'd, and Thomas Jones released his right and title to John Jones. Jane Jones, widow and administratrix of John Jones, and Henry and Ruth Dixon, daughter of John Jones, conveyed the 540 acres to John PettyJohn on 3 Aug 1715. John Pettyjon makes his mark. Wits., William Shankland and Benjamin Stockley. John PettyJohn appoints Jacob Kollock, Sr., his attorney to acknowledge the deed in Court. John Pettyjon makes his mark. Wits., Thomas Gordon and Jacob Kollock, Jr. Ack. 4 Feb 1717.

Page 149. Deed of Gift. 1 May 1705. From William Fisher, cordwayner, of Sussex Co., DE., to Yeates Conwill, planter, of Lewes, and Rebecca, his wife, daughter of William Fisher. For the love and affection William Fisher has for his son-in-law, Yeates Conwill and Rebecca, his only daughter, 100 acres and after their decease to the children of Yeates and Rebecca. Land is situated in a neck of land between the Broad Creek and Prime Hooke and is bounded by Beaverdam Branch, by land of Anthony Haverly, by land of John Hill, gentleman, by a neck of land of William Fisher, and by a gutt which runs into Prime Hooke Creek. Land is part of a larger tract that William Fisher bought from William Dyre. William Fisher signs. Wits., William Clark, Thomas Fisher and Jonas Greenwood. Ack. 1 May 1705.

Page 150. Receipt. 6 Apr 1724. Sussex County. Rec'd the 6th day of April 1724 of Mary Codd of the County aforesaid Executrix Joyntly with Mr. St Ledger Codd of the province of Mary Land to the Last Will & Testament of Berckley Codd Esqr dec'd my full part or porportion of all the goods & chattells rights & credits which of right belonged to me by the afsd Last Will & Testament & in full of all demands witness my hand. Tho. Pattison signs. Wit., Wm Till. Memorandum: there is some corn, wheat & hogs yet unaccounted for.

Page 150. Receipt. 22 May 1725. Rec'd of Mary Codd widdow & executrix of Berckley Codd Esqr dec'd the sum of ten pounds being a legacy due to me by vertue of his Last Will & Testament. I say rec'd by me. Wm Becket signs.

Pages 150-151. Deed. 29 Apr 1725. From Thomas Willson, yeoman, of Sussex Co., DE., to Joseph Hickman, yeoman, of the same place. For 42 pounds 200 acres. Land is situated in Slaughter Neck and is bounded by land formerly belonging to Luke Watson, Jr., dec'd. Land is known by the name of Scidmore's Choice, part of a tract known as Bowman's Farms, which Henry Scidmore, dec'd, bought of Henry Bowman, dec'd, and left to his son, Henry Scidmore, who conveyed the tract to Thomas Willson on 7 May 1719. Thomas Willson signs. Wits., Mercy Willson, Rebecca Willson and James White. Ack. 5 May 1725.

Pages 151-152. Deed. 29 Apr 1725. From Thomas Willson, yeoman, of Sussex Co., DE., to Joseph Hickman, yeoman, of the same place. For 4 pounds 2 1/2 acres. Land is situated upon the inlet point of Nutter's Neck in Slaughter Neck and is bounded by a pond called Inlet Pond. Land is part of a larger tract of 10 acres that Thomas Willson bought of Christopher Nutter, yeoman, on 7 Aug 1716. The 2 1/2 acres, being 1/3 of the 10 acres, was measured out by Thomas Willson and Joseph Hickman. Thomas Willson signs. Wits., Mercy Willson, Rebecca Willson and James White. Ack. 5 May 1725.

Pages 152-153. Patent. 29 Sep 1677. John Prettyman's Patent. Land is situated in Delaware Bay on Love's Creek and is bounded by the mouth of a little creek and by the mouth of Love's Creek. Land was certified at a Court at the Whorekill for John Johnson and called Johnson's Purchase and warranted by E. Andross, Governor of New York, for 400 acres. E. Andross signs and Matthias Nicholls examines. Endorsement on the back of the patent shows that John Johnson sold the patent to William Futcher by the order and consent of John Barker on the 8th da 7th mo 1685 in Lewes.

Pages 153-154. Deed. 1 Feb 1725. From James Walker, gentleman, of Sussex Co., DE., to John Prettyman, gentleman, of the same place. For 37 pounds 200 acres. Land is situated on the west side of Love's Creek in Angola Neck and is bounded by the mouth of a small creek which proceeds out of Love's Creek. Land is part of a larger tract of 400 acres granted by patent to John Johnson who assigned the patent to William Futcher who died intestate leaving diverse sons and daughters by which means the 200 acres were allotted to daughter, Sarah Futcher, who married James Askew. Sarah, thereafter, died intestate and the land descended to her son, James Askew who bequeathed the land to James Walker. James Walker signs. Wits., John Welbore and Phil. Russel. Ack. Feb Court 1725.

Pages 154-155. Deed 1 Feb 1725. From Ruth Russel, of Kent Co., DE., formerly widow and administratrix of John Wheeler of Sussex Co., DE., dec'd, to Jehosaphat Hallands, carpenter, of Sussex Co., DE. For 24 pounds 125 acres. Land is situated on the south side of Mispellion Creek. Ruth Russel, as administratrix of John Wheeler, appeared in Sussex Orphans

Court on the 2nd Tuesday in Mar 1723 and made appear by a former record that she had overpaid the inventory of her deceased husband's personal estate and petitioned to sell real property. The Court appointed Joseph Booth, John May, Esqr., George Walton, Samuel Spencer, and Art Vankirk to value and lay out unimproved lands of John Wheeler sufficient to satisfy debt and make return at next Sep Orphans Court. At Orphans Court in Sep 1724, John May Esqr., was replaced by John Walton and return to be made Mar next. Return made 28 Nov 1724 for 125 acres. Ruth Russel makes her mark. Wits., John Russel and Henry Moleston. Ack. Feb Court 1725.

Pages 155-156. Deed. 5 May 1725. From Enoch Cummings, weaver, of Lewes, and Hannah, his wife, to Robert Smith, yeoman, of the Broadkill. For 80 pounds 200 acres. Land is situated on the northwest side of Cold Spring Branch and is bounded by the bridge of Cold Spring Branch, by Cold Spring Branch, and by a small branch proceeding out of Cold Spring Branch. Land is part of a larger tract of 800 acres bounded by Cold Spring Branch, by a tract called Abraham's Lott, by land called Little Field, by Mill Creek, and Cold Spring bridge and called Mill Plantation. The 800 acres were granted by patent to William Clark, of Lewes, dec'd, by two commissioners, viz. James Claypoole and Robert Turner. William Clark conveyed 200 of the 800 acres to Mathew Osborn who conveyed the 200 acres to Thomas Bedwell and Honor, his wife, who on 4 Aug 1713 conveyed the 200 acres to William Clark, son of the previous William Clark. William Clark, the younger, conveyed the 200 acres to John Fisher who by deed of gift conveyed to Enoch Cummings and Hannah, his wife on 4 May 1722. Enoch Cummings signs and Hannah Cummings makes her mark. Wits., Robt Shankland, Thos. Gordon, and Alex'r Richey. Ack. May Court 1725.

Page 156. Earmark. 21 May 1731. Charles Farganson his ear mark for cattle, sheap & hoggs &ct is as follows (viz) a crop and hole in each ear. Recorded this 21st of May 1731. per Jacob Kollock Dp Rols.

Page 156. Earmark. 21 May 1731. David Mackklain his ear mark for cattle, sheap & hoggs &ct is as follows the right ear under halfed and the left ear hole. Recorded this 21st of May 1731. per Jacob Kollock Dp Rols.

Pages 157-158. Deed. 5 Nov 1724. From Abraham Potter, yeoman, of Sussex Co., DE., to John Stewart, miller, of the same place. For 165 pounds 150 acres and a mill. Land in two tracts. The first tract is situated on the northwest side of Mill Creek which proceeds out from Broad Kill Creek and is bounded by Mill Creek, a small distance from the mill dam, by land belonging to the heirs of Nathaniel Starr, dec'd, and by land belonging to the heirs of Cornelius Wiltbanck. Also a second parcel of land adjoining the first which Abraham Potter bought from Nathaniel Starr. Abrm Potter signs. Wits., Chris. Topham, Robt Lodge, and Enoch Cummings. Ack. Nov Court 1724.

Page 158. Deed of Gift. 20 Apr 1726. From William Cornwallis, gentleman, of Kent Co., DE., to William, John, Elias and Hannah Conwill. For love and affection, 4 negroes. Abigail to William; Andrew to John; Venus to Elias; and Margaret to Hannah. William Cornwallis signs. Wits., Philip Russel and Wm Becket.

Pages 158-159. Bond. 1 Jun 1726. From Elias Fisher, Esqr., of Broadkill Hundred, to Henry Fisher, Dr. in physick, of Sussex Co., DE. For 400 pounds 98 acres. Elias Fisher mortgaged his land to William Till, treasurer and trustee of the Loan Office, in 1724. Land is near the town of Lewes. Henry Fisher is paying the mortgage and Elias Fisher is obligated to Henry Fisher. Elias Fisher signs. Wits., Jeremiah Claypoole, John Jackson, and William Cornwallis.

Pages 159-160. Deed. 6 May 1726. From Robert Lodge, house carpenter, of Sussex Co., DE., to Robert Maccarrel, planter, of the same place. For 30 pounds 200 acres. Land is situated northwest side of Cold Spring Branch and is bounded by land of the heirs of Robert Cade, dec'd, by Cold Spring Branch, by land of Robert Smith, and by land of Richard Dobson. Robert Lodge signs. Wits., Baptis Newcomb, Christopher Topham, and Jno Long. Ack. May Court 1726.

Pages 160-161. Deed. 4 Aug 1720. From Thomas Marriner, yeoman, of Sussex Co., DE., to William Stockley, yeoman, of the same place. For 10 pounds 100 acres. Land is situated on the south side of Ivy Branch and is bounded by Ivy Branch and the land of Gilbert Marriner. Land is part of a larger tract which Thomas Marriner bought of Aminadab Hanzer. Thomas Marriner makes his mark. Wits., Richard Hinman and James White. Ack. Aug Court 1720. Second Ack. 17 Aug 1723 and witnessed by Wm Till, Phil Russel and Samuel Rowland.

Pages 161-163. Deed. 3 Nov 1725. From Joseph Pevey and Jean, his wife, (daughter of John Dyall, yeoman, dec'd, of Sussex Co., DE., and co-heiress with sisters, Eleanor, Mary, and Elizabeth), to John Atkins, yeoman, late of Sussex Co., DE. For 16 pounds 50 acres. Land is situated in Sussex Co., DE., and is bounded by a savannah and by land of William White and was surveyed by Thomas Pemberton. Land is 2/3 part of the tract of land which was conveyed by William White, yeoman, late of Sussex Co., DE., to Eleanor, Jean, Mary, and Elizabeth Dyall, daughters of John Dyall, deceased, by deed dated 4 Aug 1713. Joseph Pevey signs and Jane Pevey makes her mark. Wits., James Mackelwan and John Welbore. Ack. Nov Court 1725.

Pages 163-164. Deed. ___ ___ 1721. From Owen Hill, yeoman, of Sussex Co., DE., to Elener Coulter, widow, and William Coulter, her son, both of Sussex Co., DE. For 19 pounds 210 pounds. Land is situated in the forest adjoining land of William Darter and bounded by Gravilly Hill Swamp, by a savannah, and surveyed on 6 Jan 1717 by Robert Shankland. Tract was originally granted by commissioners warrant to Owen Hill, planter, for 200 acres and when surveyed the tract contained 210 acres. Owen Hill makes his mark. Wits., John Coulter and Robt Pirrie. Ack. May Court 1721.

Pages 164-165. Deed. 3 Aug 1726. From Jeremiah Claypoole, Esqr., of Sussex Co., DE., to John Allen, yeoman, of the same place. For 70 pounds 500 acres. Land is situated on the south side of Love Long Branch. Tract was given to Jeremiah Claypoole by a deed of gift dated 9 Mar 1722 from George and Joseph Claypoole and Mary Cook. Jeremiah Claypoole signs. Wits., Jonathan Baily and Phil Russel. Ack. Aug Court 1726.

Pages 165-166. Deed. 1 Feb 1725. From William Cornwallis, Esqr., of Philadelphia, to James Holland, yeoman, of Sussex Co., DE. For 15 pounds 270 acres. Land is situated in Pemberton's Savannah. Land previously belonged to Christopher Topham. William Cornwallis appoints Philip Russell, Esqr., Symon Collet, Esqr., or Christopher Topham, merchant, to be his attorney to acknowledge the deed in court. Willliam Cornwallis signs. Wits., Hester Holland and William Holland. Ack. Nov Court 1726.

Page 166. Earmark. 4 May 1732. Peris Chipman his ear mark for cattle, sheep & hoggs &ct is as followeth (viz) two holes in the right ear & crop in the left ear this 4th of May 1732. Jacob Kollock signs.

Pages 167-168. Deed. 3 Nov 1719. From William Arey, yeoman, of Sussex Co., DE., to John Coulter, yeoman, of the same place. For 15 pounds 98 acres. Land is situated on the north side of Bright's Beaverdam and is bounded by 50 acres of land which was formerly Charles Bright's, by land of John Morris, and on the west side of a kill. Land is part of a larger tract of 300 acres granted by a warrant from Sussex County Court on 1st da 11th mo 1682 to William Trippit who on 2 Feb 1682/3 conveyed the warrant to John Hill, dec'd, whose heir, John Hill, assigned his right and title on 11 Jan 1689/90 to Charles Bright who on 10 Apr 1697 by virtue of the warrant had the land surveyed by Mr. Thomas Pemberton. The tract was on the west side of Delaware Bay, and on the east and west of a Beverdam Branch and bounded by land of William Darvall. Charles Bright conveyed 50 acres of the land to Robert Inkins, labourer, dec'd. John Sheltman, executor of the last will and testament of Robert Inkins, dec'd, conveyed the 50 acres William Arey on 4 Feb 1717 in addition to part of a tract (48 acres) granted to Robert Inkins by a warrant from the Commissioners dated 20th da of 7 mo 1716. William Arey appoints Robert Pirrie of Lewes to be his attorney to confirm the deed in Court. Robt Pirrie signs. Wits., John Hall and John Stevenson. Ack. 3 Nov 1719.

Pages 168-169. Power of Attorney. 13 Oct 1719. From William Arey, yeoman, of Sussex Co., DE., to Robert Pirrie, yeoman, of the same place. Authority to convey, acknowledge and confirm a tract of land to John Coulter, yeoman, of Sussex Co., DE. Land is in the forrest near the land of John Hall, shoemaker, and contains 90 acres more or less. William Arey makes his mark. Wits., John Hall and John Stevenson. Ack. 3 Nov 1719.

Pages 169-170. Deed. 5 May 1726. From Samuel Rowland, Esqr., of Lewes, to Enoch Cummings, weaver, of Sussex Co., DE. For 51 pounds 396 acres. Land is situated in Kimball's Neck and is bounded by a fork of a branch which bounds the land of Baptist Newcomb, by land called Millborrow, and known by the name Harlem or Orphans Choice. Land was granted by warrant from the Court of Sussex on 27 Mar 1678 to Mathew Everston, dec'd, whose heirs conveyed the tract to Samuel Rowland, Esqr. Samuel Rowland signs. Wits., Phil. Russel and Robert Shankland. Ack. Aug Court 1726.

Pages 170-171. Deed of Gift. 31 Oct 1726. From Katherine Davis, wife of Thomas Davis, Jr., of Sussex Co., DE., to her husband, Thomas Davis. For love and affection 100 acres. Land is situated Slaughter Neck and is bounded by a savannah, by land of Alexander Draper, by Bowman's Farm, by land of Thomas Tillton, and surveyed on 12 Apr (16)93. Land is known by the name Susan's Pallas and is part of a tract of Henry Bowman's land called Bowman's Farms. Katherine Davis appoints Luke Wattson and Andrew Haverloe of Sussex Co., DE., to be her lawful attornies. Katherine Davis makes her mark. Wits., Richard Davis, Luke Wattson, and Jas White. Ack. Nov Court 1726.

Pages 171-172. Deed. 9 Feb 1726. From James Walker, gentleman, of Sussex Co., DE., to James Shirley, merchant, of the same place. For 100 pounds 300 acres. Land is situated on Bracy's Branch in Angola Neck and is bounded by a beaverdam of Bracy's Branch, on the west side of the little neck, at the head of a small branch. Land is part of a larger tract of 400 acres which James Walker bought from Jacob Kollock, dec'd. James Walker sold 100 acres of the 400 acres to John Parsons. James Walker signs. Wits., Anderson Parker and Phil. Russel. Ack. Feb Court 1726.

Pages 172-173. Deed. 10 Feb 1726. From Charles Cade, yeoman, of Sussex Co., DE., to Arthur Johnson, cordwainer, of the same place. For 27 pounds 100 acres. Land is situated on the northwest side of the Cold Spring Branch. The land is part of a larger tract of 300 acres known as Abraham's Lott which was granted by warrant of the Commissioners, James Claypoole and Robert Turner, to Abraham Potter by patent dated 2nd da 2nd mo 1686. Abraham Potter conveyed the tract to Jacob Warren who by deed of sale conveyed the land to John Haynes who conveyed on 2 Dec 1695 to Robert Cade, cordwainer, whose son and heir was Robert Cade. Robert Cade, the younger, by deed of sale dated 5 May 1724 conveyed to Charles Cade. The 100 acres is on the northeast side of the 300-acre tract. Charles Cade signs. Wits., Thomas Hide and John Wilbore. Ack. Feb Court 1726.

Page 174. Certificate of Marriage. 31 Oct 1717. Sussex Supr Delaware. After due publication made according to the Laws of this Government & by vertue of an Act of Assembly in that case made and provided on the thirty first day of October and the yeare of our Lord One thousand seven hundred hundred and seventeen was solemnly maried according to God's holy ordinance, George Walton of the above County Batchalor and Hester Hulling daughter of Walton Hulling late of this county Gent Decesed by Jonathan Bailly, Esqr., one of his Majties Justices for this County & before the following Evidences: Jonathan Baily, Sarah Fisher, Mary Attkinson, Martha Hulling, Jonathan Manlove, Ann Draper, Alee Walker, Mary Walton, Nathanel Hall, John Nutter, Will Fisher, Nicholas Green, Mary Walton, Cornelius Wiltbanck, Elias Fisher, John Hepburn. George and Esther Walton sign.

Pages 174-175. Deed. 21 Sep 1722. From William Hanzer, yeoman, of Sussex Co., DE., and Elizabeth, his wife, to Nathan Frame, yeoman, of the same place. For (consideration not given) 100 acres. Land is situated at the head of Long Neck of Fishing Branch and is bounded by land of Aminadab Hanzer, on the east side of Fishing Branch, by land of Jacob Burton, and surveyed by Robert Shankland. Land is part of a larger tract of 300 acres called Bottle and Cake which was granted by the commissioners to Thomas Greer and which William Hanzer bought of Thomas Greer, cordwainer, in 1715. William Hanzor signs. Elizabeth Hanzer makes her mark. Wits., Tho. Gear and Steven Keney. Ack. 6 Nov 1722.

Page 175. Power of Attorney. 8 Sep 1722. From William Hanzor, planter, of Sussex Co., DE., to Woolsey Burton, Esqr., yeoman, of the same place.

Authority to make over and acknowledge in open Court all right and title that William Hanzor has in a certain tract of land near the head of Long Neck known by the name Bottle and Cake. William Hanzor signs. Wits., Thomas Foster and Frances Hardy. Proved in Nov Court 1722 by Thos. Foster.

Pages 176-177. Deed. 9 Feb 1726. From Richard Hinman, Esqr., of Sussex Co., DE., to John Marsh, yeoman, of the same place. For 55 pounds 200 acres. Land is situated on the west side of the mouth of Delaware Bay adjoining to the seashore and is bounded by Roades pond, by a branch of the pond, by land that John Roades lives on, by the other part of the tract purchased by Peter Marsh, and surveyed by Robert Shankland on 15 Jan 1713. Land is part of a larger tract of 427 acres which formerly belonged to John Roades. Richard Hinman signs. Wits., William Burton and Robert Lacey. Ack. Feb Court 1726.

Pages 177-179. Deed. 9 Feb 1726. From Robert Lacey, yeoman, of Sussex Co., DE., and son of John Lacey, dec'd, to William Burton, of the same place. For 20 pounds 150 acres. Land is situated on the north side of Indian River and on the east side of Swan Creek and Branch and is bounded by Swan Creek. Land is part of a larger tract of 400 acres which Richard Ward, carpenter, of Sussex Co., purchased from William Clark. Richard Ward conveyed the 400 acres to John Gibb of Lewes on the 1st da 12th mo 1702 with the provision that if Richard Ward should pay John Gibb 12 pounds and 11 shillings before 1 Feb 1703 with lawful interest that John Gibb should reconvey the tract to Richard Ward. Richard Ward did pay the amount specified and the tract was reconveyed on 29th da 11th mo 1703. Richard Ward afterwards conveyed 200 acres to John Lacey on 3 Feb 1703. Robert Lacey now conveys 150 acres of the 200 acres to William Burton. Robert Lacey signs. Wits., Richard Hinman and John Welbore. Ack. Feb Court 1726.

Pages 179-180. Deed of Gift. 6 Nov 1722. From John Mullinux, yeoman, of Sussex Co., DE., to his sister, Mary Mullinux, spinster, of the same place. For 5 shillings 100 acres. Land is situated between the Misspillion and Ceder Creeks and is bounded by land of Richard Manlove. Land was conveyed to John Mullinux by Art Johnson Vankirk. John Mullinux makes his mark. Wits., Mary Russel and Phil Russel. Ack. 6 Nov 1722.

Pages 180-181. Deed. 3 Nov 1719. From Samuel Rowland, Esqr., of Sussex Co., DE., to Joseph Hepburn, yeoman, of the same place. For 25 pounds 250 acres. Land is situated on the south side of Broadkill Creek. Land is part of a greater tract of 1000 acres called Millford of which Samuel Rowland purchased 500 acres from William Clark, Esqr., dec'd. The 250 acres is to be laid out from the lower or easternmost end of the 500 acres. Samuel Rowland signs. Wits., James Walker and Phil Russel, Jr. Ack. 3 Nov 1719.

Pages 181-183. Deed. 4 Nov 1713. From Lazarus Kening and Martha, his wife, and Stephen Kening, all of Sussex Co., DE., to Phillip Askie, of the same place. For 20 pounds 100 acres. Land is situated the north side of Indian River and is bounded by the Indian River, by land where William Kening did live now in the possession of Phillip Askie, and by the mouth of the beaverdam. Land is part of a larger tract of 300 acres bounded by land where William Kening did live and by Indian River. The 300 acres was laid out for William Kening on the 13th da 1st mo 1685 who sold the 100 acres to John How, dec'd. John How conveyed the 100 acres to Peter Waples who absented himself out of the Government with paying his debts; therefore, John Barren, tanner, caused the 100 acres to be attached at his suit for a debt owed to him by Peter Waples and obtained judgment. William Dyre, high sheriff, took the land in execution. The land was appraised by a jury of twelve men and sold at public sale and William Clark bought the land. William Dyre conveyed the land to William Clark on 1 Feb 1698. William Clark sold the 100 acres to William Kening, father of Lazarus Kening, and Martha, his wife, and Stephen Kening. All rights, titles, appurtenances, etc., are conveyed except Royall mines. Lazarus, Martha and Stephen Kening make their marks. Wits., Francis Bagwell, Joseph Burton, and Thos. Toole. Ack. Nov Court 1718.

Pages 183-184. Deed. 4 Feb 1722. From John Cary, planter, of Sussex Co., DE., to Job Barker, planter, of the same place. For 12 pounds 187 acres. Land is situated on the east side of Cow Bridge Branch, one of the branches which proceeds out of the Indian River, and adjoining land of Thomas Walker and is bounded by Cow Bridge Branch and by land of Thomas Walker. Land is known by the name Strife and was surveyed on 20 Apr 1717 for John Cary by virtue of a commissioners warrant from Jacob Taylor, Surveyor General, dated 26 Nov 1716. John Cary makes his mark. Wits., Robert Cornwell and Catherine Holt. Ack. Aug Court 1723.

Pages 184-185. Deed. 4 Feb 1723. From James Sangster, yeoman, of Lewes, to John Townsend, marriner, of the same place. For 12 pounds one lot 60 X 200 feet. Lot is situated on Mulbery Street in Lewes and is bounded by on the northeast side with the lot of Robert Pirry and on the southwest side with the lot of William Godwin. James Sangster signs. Wits., William Shankland and Phil Russel. Ack. Feb Court 1723.

Pages 185-186. Deed. 3 Nov 1724. From Richard Bracy, planter, of Sussex Co., DE., to Joseph Aylif, planter, of the same place. For 20 pounds 150 acres. Land is situated on Middle Creek or Fishing Creek coming out of Rehoboth Bay and is bounded by land of William Simmons, by land of Robert Bracy, Jr., and by the head of a beaverdam. Land is part of a larger tract of 300 acres granted by patent from Edmond Andross, Governor of New York, dated 29 Sep 1677 granted to Richard Bracy. Richard Bracy makes his mark. Wits., James Sangster and Danet Pennoyre. Ack. Nov Court 1724.

Pages 186-188. Deed. 4 Aug 1720. From Jacob Kollock, merchant, of Lewes, to John Russell, yeoman, of Sussex Co., DE. For 85 pounds 200 acres. Land is situated on the west side of Delaware Bay and the south side of Middle Creek proceeding out the westernmost side of Rehoboth Bay and is bounded by Middle Creek and by land of Abraham Moleston, dec'd. Land is part of a greater tract of 400 acres called Tanner's Hall and granted by patent dated 1 Mar 1684 from William Penn, Esqr., to William Emmott. William Emmott conveyed the land to Francis Williams who conveyed 1/2 (200 acres) to John Barker who conveyed to Jacob Kollock who conveyed to Daniel Fling, yeoman. Daniel Fling conveyed the 200 acres to Jacob Kollock. Jacob Kollock makes his mark. Wits., Jacob Kollock, Jr., and James White. Ack. Aug Court 1720.

Pages 188-189. Deed. 5 Nov 1722. From Gilbert Marriner, yeoman, of Sussex Co., DE., to Joseph Piles, of the same place. For 30 pounds 100 acres. Land is situated on the south side of Ivy Branch proceeding out of Rehoboth Bay and is bounded by Ivy Branch. Land is part of a larger tract of land formerly under the tenure of Aminadab Hanzer who conveyed to Thomas Mariner who conveyed to Gilbert Mariner. Gilbert Mariner makes his mark. Wits., Jno Russell and Thos. Gear. Ack. May 1723.

Pages 189-190. Deed. 10 Aug 1722. From John Russell, yeoman, of Sussex Co., DE., to Benjamin Stockley, yeoman, of the same place. For (consideration not given) 200 acres. Land is situated on the north side of Stuchbury's Neck and on the south side of Bracies Branch and is bounded by the mouth of Bracy's Branch and across Stuchbury's Neck. Land formerly belonged to Robert Richard. Jno and Elizabeth Russell make their marks. Wits., Abraham Parsly and Anderson Parker. Ack. 10 Aug 1722.

Pages 190-191. Deed. 1 Jul 1717. From William Milliner, yeoman, of Sussex Co., DE., and John Bowman, yeoman, of the same place, to Joshua Hickman, yeoman, of the same place. For 4 pounds 10 shillings 20 acres. Land is situated in Slaughter Neck on the east side of the plantation of

Joshua Hickman and joining the land of Mr. Berckley Codd and is bounded by Joshua Hickman's land and surveyed 2 Aug 1716 by Robert Shankland. William Milner signs and Patience Bowman makes her mark. Wits., Samuell Wattson and James White. Ack. 3 Nov 1719.

Pages 191-192. Deed. 4 Nov 1724. From John Laughland, planter(?), of Sussex Co., DE., to William Milliner, yeoman, of the same place. For 8 pounds 50 acres. Land is situated on the south side of Ceder Creek and is bounded by land of Elias Fisher and the mouth of a small branch which proceeds out of Ceder Creek. Land is part of a larger tract which John Laughland formerly bought of Josuah Cowdry. John Loughland signs. Wits., John May and David Smith. Ack. Nov Court 1724.

Pages 192-193. Deed. 9 Nov 1721. From Robert Cade, cordwainer, of Sussex Co., DE., to George Manlove, yeoman, of Kent Co., DE. For 90 pounds 200 acres. Land is situated on Muspillin Creek and is bounded by land called Hill's Content, by a branch called Little Creek, and by the mouth of a gutt. Land which Robert Cade purchased on 18 Oct 1703 from Josuah Bawler and Mary, his wife, then of Philadelphia. Robert Cade signs. Wits., Roger Train and John May. Ack. Nov Court 1721.

Pages 193-194. Deed. 1 Apr 1709. From Art Vankirk Johnson (or Arthur Johnson Vankirk) to Penellope Mullinux, widow of John Mullinux, dec'd. For 8 pounds 100 acres. Land is situated on the west side of Delaware Bay and between the Mispellin Creek and the Ceder Creek in Sussex and is bounded by land of Richard Manlove. Land is part of a greater tract of of 500 acres granted by warrant dated 1 Apr 1686 to Richard Bundick who assigned his right to his son-in-law, Arthur Johnson Vankirk, on the 15th da 1st mo 1687. Arthur Johnson Vankirk had the land laid out to him and surveyed for 400 acres. Arthur Johnson Vankirk sold 100 acres of the 400 acres to John Mullinux before his decease and now conveys the land to his widow with the reservation that the land descend to his son, John Mullinux. Arthur Johnson Vankirk makes his mark. Wits., Thos. Fisher and Philip Russell. No acknowledgement.

Pages 194-195. Deed. 6 Dec 1712. From Jeffrey Summerford and Anne, his wife, of Sussex Co., DE., to Samuel Dowling, of the same place. For 6 pounds 200 acres. Land is situated on the north side of Broad Creek near the Sipras Swamp and is bounded by the sipras branch of the Broad Creek, by Broad Creek, and by the tracts of land of Bryant Rolles. Land is part of a larger tract owned by Bryant Rolles who sold 200 acres to Barnes Garrett, father of Anne Summerford. Barnes Garrett died intestate possessed of this 200-acre tract and died upon the same and one other tract of 300 acres adjoining the first. Barnes Garrett left as descendants 2 daughters and when the lots were cast for his land, Jeffrey Summerford and Anne, his wife, received the 200-acre tract. Jefray and Anne Sumerford make their marks. Wits., Thomas Marshall and John Colleman. Proved by the oath of Tho. Marshall Feb Court 1712.

Pages 195-196. Deed. 3 Aug 1721. From William Spencer, son of Henry Spencer, dec'd of Sussex Co., DE., to John Smith, sergint, of the same place. For 27 pounds 88 acres. Land is situated on the west side of Delaware Bay and on the south side of Muspillin Creek and is bounded by land of Robert Hart and by a branch. Land is part of a larger tract of 1000 acres granted by patent dated 29 Sep 1667 from Edmund Andross, Governor of New York & Albiny, to Richard Hill who sold on 11 Jul 1678 the 1000 acres to Benjamin Cowdry who on 26 Aug 1683 gave and assigned 500 acres of the 1000 acres to his daughter, Frances Spencer, wife of Major William Spencer. Joseph Booth after marrying Frances Spencer sold 100 acres of the 500 acres to Mark Manlove who sold the 100 acres to Henry Spencer. Henry Spencer gave his bond to John Smith, Sergant, to sell him the 100 acres except 12 acres which Henry Spencer sold to Mark Gendron and John Smith paid part of the bond to Henry Spencer and the remainder to William Spencer. The 12 acres adjoins 47 acres which Henry Spencer also sold to Mark Gendron. William Spencer signs. Wits., Thomas Goldsmith and John May. Ack. Aug Court 1721.

Pages 196-197. Deed. 5 Aug 1718. From John Morris, yeoman, of Sussex Co., DE., to William McGraughan, planter, of the same place. For 7 pounds 10 shillings 98 acres. Land is situated on the north side of Bright's Beaver Dam and is bounded by land of William Arey and by the headline of a tract of 300 acres. Land is part of a two tracts of land. One tract which was granted to Robert Jenkins as per commissioners warrant dated 20th da 7th mo 1716 and another tract of 50 acres which formerly belonged to Charles Bright and was by John Sheltman, executor of Robert Jenkins, sold to John Morris by deed of sale dated 4 Feb 1717. John Morris makes his mark. Wit., Robert Craige. Ack. 5 Aug 1718.

Pages 197-198. Deed. 5 Aug 1718. From John PettyJohn, Jr., yeoman, of Sussex Co., PA., to George Dodd, yeoman, of the same place. For 2 cows and calves 100 acres. Land is situated on the west side of Delaware Bay and on the south side joining Long Loved Branch which proceeds into Rehoboth Bay and is the southern part of 340 acres. Land is part of a larger tract of 1200 acres which formerly belonged to Richard Bundick who sold 500 acres to Thomas and John Jones. Thomas Jones conveyed his part of the 500 acres to John Jones and Jane Jones, widow of John Jones, and Henry Dixon and Ruth, his wife, alias Ruth Jones, daughter of John and Jane Jones, sold 340 acres of the 500 acres to John PettyJohn, Jr. The 100 acres was surveyed on 4 Jan 1717. John Pettijohn makes his mark. Wits., John Allen and Robert Shankland. Ack. 5 Aug 1718.

Page 199. Power of Attorney. 31 Oct 1710. From Joshua Cowdry, of Northampton Co., VA, on the Eastern Shore, to his Uncle Joseph Booth, of Kent Co. Joshua Cowdry appoints his Uncle Joseph Booth to be his lawful attorney to make over a tract of land situated on the south side of Cedar Creek in Sussex Co. which contains 200 acres of land to John Laughland. Joshua Cowdry signs. Wits., Robert Glandon and Anne Glandon. Ack. by her Majesties Justices of the Peace for the County of Northampton on 31 Oct 1710. Hillary Stringer signs and John West signs.

Pages 199-200. Deed. 16 Jul 1714. From Joshua Cowdry, of Northampton County in Accomack on the Eastern Shore of Virginia, to John Laughland, weaver, of the County of Sussex in the terrytories of the province of Pensilvaniah and on the west side of Delaware Bay. For 4500 pounds of tabaccoe and cask 200 acres of land and marsh. Land is situated on the south side of Cedar Creek and is bounded by William Fisher's pasture, by the head of a small branch, by Cedar Creek, being so divided as appears in the deed of Jonathan Wynne to Joshua Cowdry and called Callis. Land is part of a larger tract granted to Henry Pennington as may be shown by the deed of Jonathan Wynne to Joshua Cowdry dated 8 Dec 1698 and recorded by Nehemiah Field, Clerk of Sussex County Court. Joshua Cowdry appoints his uncle-in-law Joseph Booth of Kent Co. as his attorney to acknowledge the deed in open Court. Joshua Cowdry signs. Wits., Thomas Williams and Samuel Davis. Proven in Northampton Co., on 16 Jul 1714 before two of her Majesties Justices by Thomas Williams and Samuel Davis. Hillary Stringer and John Savage sign. Ack. 6 Aug 1714.

Pages 200-201. Deed. 5 Aug 1717. From Joshua Cowdry, son and heir of William Cowthery, dec'd, to Art Johnson Vankirk, yeoman, of Sussex Co., DE. For 50 pounds 300 acres. Land is situated on Cedar Creek and is bounded by on the south side of Thomas May's gut or branch in his pasture, by the head of the said gut or branch, on the south side of a swamp, by the head of Nicholas' branch, across one of the forks of sd branch, and by Walton's land. Joshua Cowthery's father, William Cowthery, prior to his decease, sold the land to Art Johnson Vankirk but did not make it over by deed. Joseph Booth, gentleman, of Kent Co., DE., as lawful attorney, by power attorney dated 4 Aug 1709, of Joshua Cowthery now makes over the land by deed to Art Johnson Vankirk. Jos. Booth, attorney, signs. Wits., John Hinman and Phil. Russel, Jr. Ack. 5 Aug 1717.

Page 201. Receipt. 10 Dec 1700. From Isack Ong to John Stewart. Received of John Stewart the sum fifteen pounds fore shillins it being the last pament of A bond that was due to me that He past for Twenty eight pounds odd money I say received by me this Tenth of December In the yeare 1700(?). Isack Ong makes his mark. Received at the request of Jno Stewart the 4th day of January 1728.

Page 202. Deed. 1 Jun 1723. From James Finwick, gentleman, of Sussex Co., DE., son and heir of Thomas Finwick, to Philip Russel, of Lewes. For 8 pounds two 4-acre lots. One lot is situated in the town of Lewes on the southwest side of the easternmost branch of Pagan Creek and between the southernmost street and the middle street of Lewes. The other lot is situated on the southwest side of and adjoining to the first lot. The first lot was granted by warrant from the Court of Sussex County on 6 Feb 1689 to Thomas Hollyman who conveyed the lot by deed of gift dated 2 Mar 1689 to his son-in-law, William Rodeney. The second lot was granted by warrant by the same Court on 6 Feb 1689 to Henry Stretcher who conveyed on 2 Mar 1689 to William Rodeney. William Rodeney on 7 Feb 1693 assigned his interest in the 2 lots to Charles Haynes who on 3 Sep 1695 conveyed to Thomas Finwick. Thomas Finwick, by his last will and testament dated 2 Mar 1707/8, gave the lots to his son, James Finwick. James Finwick signs. Wits., John Shankland and Mary Shankland. Ack. Aug Court 1723. On 1 Jun 1723, James Finwick acknowledges receipt of payment of 8 pounds from Philip Russel. James Finwick signs and John Shankland witnesses.

Pages 203-204. Deed. 1 Feb 1725. From George Manlove, yeoman, of Kent Co., DE., to Abraham Parsley, yeoman, of Sussex Co., DE. For 100 pounds 200 acres. Land is situated on the south side of Muspelion Creek and is bounded by land called Hill's Content and by a branch of the Muspelion called Little Creek. Land formerly belonged to Joseph Booth who conveyed to Peter Goyt who, by his last will and testament, bequeathed it to a son and daughter of one Ruth Williams at Marvelhead in New England named Peter and Mary. Peter died in his minority and Mary married Joshua Bawler of the City of Philadelphia who together conveyed the land to Robert Cade, cordwainer, of Sussex Co., DE., dec'd. Robert Cade, son of Robert Cade, conveyed the land to George Manlove. George Manlove appoints Ryves Holt to be his lawful attorney. George Manlove signs. Wits., John May, Elizabeth May, Jr. Ack. Feb Court 1725.

Pages 204-206. Deed. 4 May 1725. From Abraham Pasley and Frances, his wife, of Sussex Co., DE., to George Walton, yeoman, of the same place. For 200 pounds 250 acres. Land is situated in Cedar Creek neck and is bounded by the head of a branch, by George Walton's land, by Art Vankirk's land, by the head of a gut, by Mispelion Creek, and by the edge of a small gut and known by the name of Granger's Field. Abraham and Frances Parsley sign. Wits., John Russell and John Jackson. Ack. May Court 1725.

Pages 206-207. Deed. 7 May 1725. From George Walton, yeoman, of Sussex Co., DE., to Abraham Pasley, yeoman, of the same place. For 200 pounds 250 acres. Land is situated in Cedar Creek Neck and known by the name of Granger's Field and is bounded by the head of a branch, by George Walton's land, by Art Vankirk's land, by the head of a gut, by Mispelion Creek, and by the edge of a small gut. (An apparent error in the deed which says: "And the sd George Walton for himself his heirs Exers adminrs & assigns the sd two hundred & fifty acres of Land Marsh & premises with the appurtenance unto the sd Abraham Parsly his heirs Execrs adminrs & assigns against him the sd George Manlove his heirs & assigns and against all person or persons whatsover claiming . . ..") George Walton signs. Wits., John Russell and John Jackson. Ack. May Court 1725.

Pages 207-208. Deed. 18 Aug 1725. From James Dyre, gentleman, of Newcastle Co., DE., to Thomas Groves, yeoman, of Sussex Co., DE. For 20 pounds 300 acres of land and 100 acres of marsh. Land is situated on the south side of Prime Hook Creek and is bounded by the Beaver Dam with the 100 acres of marsh adjoining the 300 acres of land. Land was bequeathed to James Dyre by his father, Major William Dyre. James Dyre signs. Wits., John Wells and William Robinson. Ack. Feb Court 1725.

Pages 208-209. Deed. 2 Nov 1725. From Jabez Maud Fisher, brother to Elizabeth Seatown; Margery Miers, sister to Elizabeth Seatown, and her husband, James Miers, to Samuel Spencer, Jr., planter, of Sussex Co., DE. For 5 pounds 200 acres. Land is situated on the south side of Herring Branch that runs into Muspillion Creek, and is bounded by Piney's Branch, and known by the name of Richland. Land was granted virtue of a warrant dated 20 Aug 1715 from the Commissioners to James Seatown and surveyed by Robert Shankland. James Seatown, by his last will and testament, bequeathed the 200 acres to his wife, Elizabeth, who bequeathed the 200 acres to her brother and sister. Jabez Maud Fisher, Margery Miers and James Miers sign. Wits., Robert Lodge, Joshua Fisher, and Jehu Spencer. Ack. May Court 1726.

Pages 209-210. Deed of Gift. 6 Aug 1725. From Samuel Rowland, Esqr., and Jane, his wife, of Sussex Co., DE., to their son, Joshua Stockley, cordwayner, of the same place. For natural love and affection 200 acres. Land is situated in Angola Neck. The 200 acres were bequeathed to Jane

Rowland by William Simmonds, yeoman, deceased, of Sussex Co., DE. If Joshua Stockley should die without lawful issue, the land is to descend to Benjamin Stockley and Oliver Stockley, brothers of Joshua. Land given without money for consideration except two hhds of cyder to be paid yearly & every year at Lewes to Samuel and Jane Rowland. Samuel and Jane Rowland sign. Wits., Mary Eldridge and Phil. Russel. Ack. Aug Court 1725.

Page 210. Deed. 2 Aug 1725. From Robert Burton, yeoman, and Comfort, his wife, of Sussex Co., DE., to James Walker, gentleman, of the same place. For 21 pounds 2 shillings 180 acres. Land is situated on Love's Creek in Angola Neck. Land was purchased by Robert Burton from James Walker as by deed dated 1 Aug 1722 and is known by the name of Johnson's Purchase. Comfort Burton relinquishes her dower rights. Robert and Comfort Burton make their marks. Wits., Oliver Stockley and Thomas Leatherbury. Ack. Aug Court 1725.

Page 211. Deed of Deference. 8 Aug 1725. From Alexander Draper, merchant, of Sussex Co., DE. to Richard Davis, yeoman, of the same place. Richard Davis has made over to Alexander Draper the plantation on which he lives which contains 100 acres by separate deed dated the same date of even with these presents contingent upon paying and discharging a bond conditioned for the payment of 30 pounds plus interest to Alexander Draper before 1 Aug 1732. Alexander Draper signs. Wits., Thomas Willson, Costin Townsend and Jas White. Ack. Aug Court 1725.

Pages 212-213. Deed. 5 May 1725. From Henry Skidmore, yeoman, of Sussex Co., DE., to Thomas Willson, yeoman, of the same place. For 35 pounds 55 acres of land and marsh in 3 parcels. Land is situated on the south side of Indian Branch in Slaughter Neck and the 46 acres are bounded by Indian Branch, by Isaac Watson's thirds, and by the cornfield fence; the 4 acres are bounded by Indian Branch and by a little house; and the 5 acres is 1/2 of a tract of marsh which Christopher Nutter sold to Thomas Willson (as the deed says, but believe that this should be Henry Skidmore) and is the northernmost half. Henry Skidmore makes his mark. Wits., Joseph Dodd, Thomas Gray and Jas White. Ack. May Court 1725.

Pages 213-214. Deed. 1 Nov 1725. From Isaac Watson, yeoman, of Sussex Co., DE., to Thomas Willson, of the same place. For 12 pounds 88 acres. Land is situated on the west side of Delaware Bay and on the north side of Slaughter Creek and known by the name of Schoolfield and is bounded by land formerly surveyed for Thomas Price, dec'd, by the line of a dividend of land of John Nutter, dec'd, called Nutter's Farm, and by a branch dividing Nutter's land from Thomas Davis's land. Land is part of a larger tract formerly surveyed for Henry Bowman, dec'd. Isaac Wattson signs. Wits., Thomas Davis, Elizabeth Davis, and Jas White. Ack. Nov Court 1725.

Pages 215-216. Deed. 29 Jan 1725. From John Ponder, yeoman, of Sussex Co., DE., to Thomas Groves, yeoman, of the same place. For 10 pounds 151 acres. Land is situated in the Broad Kill Neck and is bounded by Ponder's land, by Barnwill's land, by the County Road, by Hill's Bridge Branch which proceeds out of Prime Hook Creek, and by Darval's land. John Ponder makes his mark. Wits., Luke Wattson and Mary Woodward. Ack. Feb Court 1725.

Page 216. Deed. 4 May 1725. From Richard Dobson, cupper, of Sussex Co., PA.,to John Roades, planter, of the same place. For 20 pounds a house and lot 60 X 200 feet. Lot is situated in the town of Lewes on second street, is now in the possession of Thomas Ginkins, and is bounded by the lot of Jonathan Baily and by a lot of James Simson. Richard Dobson signs. Wits., John Allen, Jno Russell and John Long. Ack. May Court 1725.

Pages 217-218. Deed. 3 May 1726. From John Adams, cordwayner, of Lewes, and Agnes, his wife, to Woolsey Burton, Esqr., of Sussex Co., DE. For 23 pounds 8 shillings 9 pence 75 acres of land and marsh. Land is situated between the Indian River and Rehoboth Bay in Long Neck and is bounded by the division line of the neck, a gut of Ragged Hammock Creek, and by another gut. Land of part of a larger tract of 390 acres of which this 75 acres was divided out of the west end and was allotted to Agnes as her part of her father's, William Bagwell, land of which he died possessed. John J. Adams and Agnes Addams sign. Wits., Arch Smith and Phil Russel. Ack. May Court 1726.

Pages 218-219. Deed. 3 Aug 1725. From Elias Fisher, yeoman, of Sussex Co., DE., to Joshua Hickman, yeoman, of the same place. For 8 pounds 10 shillings 55 acres. Land is 1/2 of an island called Persimon Island which contains 85 acres of land and 25 acres of marsh and is in Slaughter Neck. The island is bounded by the seashore, a pond that runs into the Bay, and the 25 acres added adjoin the island. Land was granted by commissioners warrant dated the 1st da 1st mo 1714 from Jacob Taylor to William Fisher and surveyed by Robert Shankland on 14 Jan 1715. Elias Fisher signs. Wits., Humphry Marshall, John Draper, and Jas White. Ack. Aug Court 1725.

Pages 219-220. Deed. 4 Aug 1726. From Robert Lodge, wheelwright, of Sussex Co., DE., to Francis Dunavan, yeoman, of the same place. For 28 pounds 100 acres. Land is situated on the northwest side of Mill Creek proceeding out of the Broadkill and bounded by Mill Creek. Land is part of a larger tract of 215 acres granted by warrant from the commissioners on the 11th da 1st mo 1716 and surveyed by Robert Shankland on 26 Jan 1722. Robert Lodge signs. Wits., James Miers and John Welbore. Ack. Aug Court 1726.

Pages 220-222. Deed. 8 Dec 1725. From Rose Hanzer, widow and administratrix of Aminadab Hanzer, dec'd, to Job Barker, planter or yeoman, of the same place. For 33 pounds 10 shillings 150 acres. Land is situated on the south side of Herring Creek which proceeds out of the Middle Creek from Rehoboth Bay and is bounded by Edward Carey's land now possessed by Aminadab Okey and by Herring Creek by a spring. Land is part of a larger tract of 400 acres known by the name of Ebenezer and was granted by patent dated 26 da 1st mo 1684 from William Penn to William Emmott of Sussex who conveyed the tract to Richard Painter, Sr., dec'd, on 8 Dec 1687. Sarah Painter, deceased, widow of Richard Painter, in fulfillment of a contract made by her husband, conveyed the 400 acres to Edward Carey and Aminadab Hanzer, dec'd, on 3 Sep 1695. The 400 acres were bounded by Herring Creek, by a branch proceeding from a Creek, and by land of Capt John Avery. Rose Hanzer conveys the land to Job Barker in order to satisfy a bond past by Aminadab Hanzer during his lifetime to Jacob Kollock. Rose Hanzer makes her mark. Wits., John Hill, William Robinson, and John Welbore. Ack. in Dec being the Nov adjourned Court 1725.

Pages 222-223. Deed. 3 Aug 1725. From Richard Davis, yeoman, of Sussex Co., DE., to Alexander Draper, merchant, of the same place. For 30 pounds 100 acres. Land is situated in Slaughter Neck and is the plantation that Richard Davis now lives on and is bounded by Henry Draper's land on the the north side of the Log House Branch, by the head of the branch, by the land of Thomas Davis and by the land of Alexander Draper and on his branch. Richard Davis signs. Wits., Thomas Willson, Costin Townsend and Jas White. Ack. Aug Court 1725.

Pages 223-224. Deed. 8 Dec 1725. From Samuel Rowland, Esqr., of Sussex Co., DE., to Enoch Cummings, of the same place. For 46 pounds 350 acres. Land is situated in Kembles Neck on the south side of Broadkill Creek and is bounded by land of Joshua Fisher, by a small gut that runs into the Broadkill, by land of Baptist Newcomb, by the head of the gut or branch, and known by the name of Virgin's Choice. Samuel Rowland signs. Wits., Edward Naws, Baptist Newcomb, and John Long. Ack. Dec Court 1725.

Sussex County, Delaware, Deed Book F-6   59

Pages 224-225. Deed. 1 Feb 1725. From Nathaniel Hall, merchant, of Sussex Co., DE., to James and Charles Coulter, yeomen, of the same place. For 24 pounds 325 acres. Land is situated on the north side of a branch of the Broadkill called the Southwest Branch and is bounded by a small branch and by the main branch and is on the north side of a 650 acre tract. Land is part of a larger tract of 650 acres and formerly belonged to Henry Bowman, dec'd, and was by John Bowman conveyed to his two sisters, Mary Marriner and Elizabeth Marsh. The tract was resurveyed to the two sisters by virtue of a warrant from the Surveyor General dated 28 Nov 1718 and the former errors were corrected by the survey return. Mary Marriner and Elizabeth Marsh with their husbands, Thomas Marriner and John Marsh, by their deed dated 2 May 1722, conveyed 325 acres to Nathaniel Hall. Nathaniel Hall signs. Wits., William Coulter and Phil. Russel. Ack. Feb Court 1725.

Pages 225-226. Deed 1 Feb 1725. From John Parsons, house carpenter, of Sussex Co., DE., to William Prittyman, yeoman, of the same place. For 40 pounds 242 acres. Land is situated on the west side of Herring Creek proceeding out of Rehoboth Bay and is bounded by land lately sold by Thomas Gear to William Hanzer in the line of Aminadab Hanzer's land, and by land of Jacob Burton. Land is part of a larger tract of 342 acres called Bottle & Cake granted to Thomas Gear by virtue of a warrant from the Commissioners who conveyed 242 acres to Archibald Smith who conveyed the 242 acres to John Parsons. John Parsons signs. Wits., William Field and Phil. Russel. Ack. Feb Court 1725.

Pages 226-227. Deed. 4 May 1725. From Abraham Parsley and Frances, his wife, of Sussex Co., DE.,to James Finwick, of the same place. For 50 pounds 275 acres. Land is situated on the south side of the Broadkill and is bounded by by a small branch that runs into the marsh and by Dawson's Branch. Land is part of a larger tract called Luck by Chance. Abraham and Frances Parsley sign. Wits., Rob. Smith and Phil Russel. Ack. May Court 1725.

Page 228. Deed. 3 Feb 1725. From Job Barker, yeoman, of Sussex Co., DE., to Thomas Walker, yeoman, of the same place. For 20 pounds 187 acres. Land is situated on the east side of Cow Bridge Branch one of the branches which proceeds out of the Indian River and adjoining the land of now in possession of Thomas Walker and is bounded by Cow Bridge Branch. Land is known by the name of Strife and formerly granted by warrant to Jno Cary, dec'd, who conveyed the land to Job Barker. Job Barker makes his mark. Wits., Oliver Stockly and Joseph Hazard. Ack. Feb Court 1725.

Pages 229-230. Deed. 31 Jul 1725. From Elias Fisher, weaver, of Sussex Co., DE., to Gabriel Henry, yeoman, of the same place. For 9 pounds 55 acres. Land is situated on an island in Slaughter Neck on the west side of Delaware Bay and known by the name of Persimon Island. The 55 acres is 1/2 of 85 acres of land and 25 acres of marsh which was resurveyed on 14 Jan 1715 by Robert Shankland to William Fisher, yeoman, by virtue of a commissioners warrant dated 1st da 1st mo 1714 from Jacob Taylor. The island (55 acres) is bounded by the sea shore, by a pond that runs into the Bay, and the 25 acres of marsh are bounded by the island, by a gut, and by the mouth of an inlet by the Bay shore. Elias Fisher signs. Wits., Humphry Marshall, John Draper, and Jas White. Ack. Aug Court 1725.

Pages 230-231. Deed. __ Dec 1725. From John Marsh, yeoman, of Sussex Co., DE., to Mary Gray, widow of George Gray, dec'd, of the same place. For 25 pounds 75 acres. Land is situated on the north side of Ivy Branch and bounded by Ivy Branch. Land is part of a larger tract of land formerly pertaining to Thomas Pemberton, dec'd, who conveyed the land to Thomas Marriner who conveyed 75 acres to John Marsh. John Marsh makes his mark. Wits., John Roades and Arch. Smith. Ack. Feb Court 1725.

Page 232. Deed. 2 May 1727. From Philip Dirnie, marriner, of Sussex Co., DE., to William Burton, yeoman, of Somersett Co., MD. For 10 pounds 50 acres. Land is situated on the north side of the Broad Kill and is bounded by land of Bryan Rowles. Philip Dirnie signs. Wits., Margret Addams and Phil. Russel. Ack. May Court 1727. Recorded 8 Jun 1727.

Page 233. Deed. 2 May 1727. From Elias Fisher, yeoman, of Sussex Co., DE., to Elizabeth Marshall, widow, of the same place. For 43 pounds 135 acres. Land is situated in Slaughter Neck adjoining land of Joshua Hickman now in the possession or occupation of Elizabeth Marshall and is bounded by John Bennet's land and on the north side of a branch. Elias Fisher signs. Wits., John May and Phil. Russel. Ack. May Court 1727.

Page 234. Deed. 3 May 1727. From James Pettejohn, yeoman, late of the County of Sussex, to John Chapman, yeoman, of Sussex Co., DE. For 25 pounds 150 acres of land. Land is situated on the east side of Peterkins Branch one of the branches that runs into the Indian River in Rosemary Neck and surveyed on 14 Apr 1719 by Robert Shankland. James Pettyjhon makes his mark. Wits., Jacob Kollock, Sam'l Halbert and John Welbore. Ack. May Court 1727.

Page 235. Deed. 7 Feb 1726. From William Stewart, yeoman, and Mary, his wife, of Sussex Co., DE., to John Hall, yeoman, of the same place. For 36 pounds 210 acres. Land is situated in a fork of Pemberton's Branch one of the branches which proceeds out of Broad Creek and is bounded by the southernmost fork of the branch. Land was originally granted by warrant from the commissioners on 13th da 11th mo 1717 to Peter Lucas who bequeathed the land to his sister, Sarah Lucas, who conveyed the land on 2 Aug 1721 to William Stewart. Wm Stewart signs. Wits., Sam'l Stewart and Thomas Cade. Ack. May Court 1727.

Pages 236-237. Deed. 3 May 1727. From John Marsh, yeoman, of Sussex Co., DE., to Philip Marsh, of the same place. For 39 pounds 5 shillings 140 acres. Land is situated on the west side of Delaware Bay adjoining the seashore on the side of Roades pond that runs into the sea and is bounded by land of Roades, by the branch of the pond, by 200 acres belonging to the heirs of Peter Marsh, dec'd, and surveyed by Robert Shankland in 1727. Land is part of a larger tract of 227 acres conveyed by Richard Hinman to John Marsh in Feb Court 1727 which 227 acres is also part of a larger tract of 427 acres granted by patent to John Roades, dec'd, and known by the name of Hatter's Land. John Marsh makes his mark. Wits., Wm Godwin, Jos. Godwin, and John Welbore. Ack. May Court 1727.

Page 237. Lease. 14 Feb 1726. From Jacob Kollock, and William Becket, gentlemen, of Lewes, to Edward Naws, yeoman, of Sussex Co., DE. For 5 pounds 10 shillings for 10 years (acreage not specified). Land is situated on the north side of the Broadkiln and belonged to the estate of Cornelius Wiltbanck, dec'd, of Sussex Co., DE. Jacob Kollock and William Becket are executors of Cornelius Wiltbanck. Edward Naws is to keep the buildings in tenantable repair, may use the timber on the land for the plantation but may not sell it as also he may not sell the land, and he is to try to raise an orchard of 100 apple trees. Jacob Kollock and Wm Becket sign. Wits., Jacob Philips and John Welbore. No acknowledgement.

Pages 238-239. Deed. 3 May 1727. From Enoch Cummings, gentleman, of Sussex Co., DE., to Hugh King, yeoman, of the same place. For 32 pounds 200 acres. Land is situated in Kembills Neck on the side of the Broad Kiln Creek and bounded by land of Middle Burrey and surveyed 3 Apr 1727 by Robert Shankland. Land is part of a larger tract of 396 acres formerly surveyed by Cornelius Verhoofe on 27 Mar 1678 by virtue of a warrant granted by the Court of Sussex and again surveyed by virtue of a warrant from William Clark, Chief Surveyor of the Countys of Kent and Sussex, for Gartharight Everson by whom it was seated and originally called

New Heveloe or the Orphans Choice. Enoch Cummings signs. Wits., Anderson Parker, Robert Cade, and John Welbore. Ack. May Court 1727.

Pages 239-240. Deed. 4 Nov 1720. From Thomas Carlile, yeoman, and Mary, his wife, of Sussex Co., DE., to Robert Burton, yeoman, of the same place. For 30 pounds 9 shillings 10 pence 150 acres. Land is situated on the west side of Delaware Bay and on the north side of a Creek called Broad alias Great Creek. Land is part of a larger tract of 400 acres called Swan Point which Bryand Rowles had laid out for him by patent dated 1688. Rowles sold 200 acres to Barnes Garret; 50 acres more was sold by Rowles to Henry Smith on 14 Mar 1698; and on 17 Sep 1698 Rowles sold the residue, 150 acres, to Samuel Rowland. Samuel Rowland and Mary, his wife, on 6 Nov 1716 sold the 150 acres to Thomas Pemberton, gentleman, of Sussex Co., DE. Thomas Carlile makes his mark and Mary Carlile signs. Wits., Joseph Godwin and Jas White. Ack. Nov Court 1720. Recorded 21 Aug 1727.

Pages 240-241. Appointment of Supreme Court Justices. 8 Sep 1727. From Patrick Gordon to David Evans and Richard Grafton, Esqrs, of Newcastle Co., DE., Robert Gordon and Benjamin Shurmer, Esqrs., of Kent Co., DE., and Henry Brooks and Jonathan Baly, Esqrs., of Sussex Co., DE.

Pages 241-243. Deed. 11 Dec 1727. From Evan Morgan and Elizabeth, his wife, of Kent Co., DE., to William Manlove, carpenter, of the same place. For 30 pounds 308 acres. Land is situated in Cedar Creek Neck and on the south side of the Mispelion Creek and is bounded by Mispelion Creek, by James Brown's land, and by John Richard's land. Land is part of a larger tract which was formerly surveyed and laid out to William Clark who conveyed the land to James Brown who conveyed 308 acres of the tract to Richard Manlove, dec'd, father of Elizabeth Morgan. Evan Bradbury Morgan signs and Elizabeth Morgan makes her mark. Wits., Jehosaphat Hallands and William Donley. Evan and Elizabeth Morgan appoint John May as their attorney to acknowledge the deed in Court. Jehosaphat Hallands proves the deed in Court on 12 Feb 1727. Ack. 12 Feb 1727.

Pages 243-244. Deed. 14 Dec 1727. From Robert Cade, yeoman, of Sussex Co., DE., to Thomas Cade, yeoman, of the same place. For 37 pounds 130 acres. Land is situated on the northwest side of the Cold Spring Branch on the northeast side of a larger tract and is bounded by land of Arthur Johnson. The 100 acres is part of a larger tract of 300 acres called Abraham's Lott which was granted by patent dated 2nd da 2nd mo 1686 from the commissioners appointed by Wm Penn, James Claypoole, and Robert Turner, to Abraham Potter who conveyed the 300 acres to Jacob

Warrin who conveyed to John Haynes. John Haynes on 2 Dec 1695 conveyed the land to Robert Cade, cordwainer, deceased, of Sussex Co., DE., whose son, Robert Cade, on 5 May 1724 conveyed 100 acres on the northeast side of the tract to Charles Cade who on 10 Feb 1726 conveyed the 100 acres to Arthur Johnson. Robert Cade signs. Wits., James Camel, Jos. Hepburn and Edward Naws.

Page 245. Deed of Gift. 4 Aug 1727. From Alexander Moleston to his children, William, Elizabeth, Hannah, Alexander, Ann, Naomi, and Jhon Moleston. For love and affection the northeast one half of a lot 60 X 200 feet. Lot is situated in Lewes on Front Street and is bounded northwest with High Street, southeast with lots formerly called James Simson's and now in the possession of Richard Hinman, Esqr, northeast with Front Street and southwest with Second Street. Alexander Moleston reserves the right for himself and his wife, Elizabeth, to possess the lot for the rest of their natural lives. Alexander Molston signs. Wits., James Simson, Phil. Russel and John Welbore. Ack. 2 Aug 1727.

Pages 246-247. Deed. 3 Nov (1702-1714). Thomas Bedwell and Honor, his wife, executors of William Clark, gentleman, deceased, of Sussex Co., DE., to William Clark, merchant, of Lewes. For 45 pounds 50 acres. Land is situated on the west side of Delaware Bay near the town of Lewes and called New Hall and is bounded by Whorekill Creek and by Pagan Creek. The land was granted by patent dated 15 Jan 1675 of Edmond Andross, Esqr., formerly Governor of New York, to Simon Pawling who by his assignment on the back of the patent dated 9 Sep 1679 conveyed the patent to Capt Nathaniel Walker who reassigned the patent on 11 Jun 1681 to William Clark. The 45 pounds is in part of a judgment obtained by Anthony Hueston against the estate of William Clark, dec'd. Thomas and Honor Bedwell sign. Wits., Edw. Parker, John Prettiman, and Gabriel Thomas. No acknowledgement.

Pages 247-248. Deed. 20 Nov 1727. From William Cornwallis and Rebecca, his wife, daughter and heir of William Fisher, Esqr., deceased, of Sussex Co., DE., to John Conwill, of the same place. For 1000 pounds 1764 acres. Land is situated in Broadkill Neck and is bounded by land of Anthony Haverloe, Land is made up of several tracts of land formerly owned by William Fisher. One parcel of 200 acres situated in Broadkill Neck is part of a tract of Daniel Palmer which he sold to William Fisher. Another parcel was granted by warrant from the commissioners on 13 Feb 1693 to William Dier for 200 acres of land and marsh in Broadkill Neck and also by another warrant granted on 2 Jun 1693 for 89 acres to William Dier which were both surveyed on 21 Jul 1693 and were situated on the northwest side of Broad Creek and are bounded by Broad Creek and Prime Hook Creek, and by indorsement on the back of the patents on 23 Sep 1693 and as acknowledged in Court on 2 May 1704, the 289 acres were conveyed by William Dier to William Fisher. Another patent which was granted by warrant of survey from William Penn on 12th da 5th mo 1701 and surveyed to William Dyer for 1100 acres in Broadkill Neck and bounded by land of Anthony Haverloe. A final warrant also dated 12th da 5th mo 1701 was granted to William Dyer for 175 acres in Broadkill Neck and bounded by land called Knight Howard's Land. William Dyer by his assignment dated 23 Jul 1703 conveyed the 1275 acres to William Fisher. William and Rebecca Cornwallis appoint John May, Esqr., Alexander Moleston, Benjamen Orem, and/or Anderson Parker to be their attornies to acknowledge the conveyance in Court. Wm and Rebekah Cornwallis sign. Wits., John Fisher, Wm Fisher, Robert Gillespe and Jos. Ewing. Ack. 12 Dec 1727.

Pages 249-250. Deed. 28 Nov 1727. From John Conwill, of Sussex Co., DE., to William Cornwallis, gentleman, of the same place. For 1100 pounds 1764 acres. Land is situated in Broadkill Neck and are all of the lands of William Fisher, dec'd, which John Conwill purchased in the deed on pages 247-248. John Conwill signs. Wits., Robert Gillesp, Wm Fisher, John Fisher, and Jos. Ewing. Ack. 12 Dec 1727.

Pages 250-251. Deed. 7 Nov 1727. From Alexander Moleston, yeoman, of Lewes, to Robert Shankland, Esqr., of the same place. For 20 pounds one half of a lot 60 X 200 feet. The lot is situated in Lewes and bounded by Front Street and Market Street. The lot was formerly granted to Jacob Kollock who on 13 Dec 1692 conveyed the lot to Adam Birch who by his attorney John Hill conveyed the lot to William Orr on 28 Aug 1696. William Orr, by his deed of mortgage on 1 Jul 1697, conveyed the lot to Capt John Hill. After John Hill's death, Elizabeth Hill, being the sole heir & legatee, on 6 May 1712 conveyed the lot to John and William Orr. Afterwards, John Orr died under age and without issue and the lot descended to William Orr. William Orr conveyed the lot on 19 Jun 1721 to Joseph Royall who on 3 Nov 1724 conveyed the lot to Alexander Moleston. The 1/2 lot is bounded by Market Street, by Second Street, by a lot of Richard Hinman, and by Moleston's lot. Alexr Moleston signs. Wits., William Moleston and Ephraim Darby. Ack. 12 Feb 1727.

Pages 252-253. Deed. 31 Jul 1727. From John Smith, sergin, of Sussex Co., DE., to Joseph Spencer,, of the same place. For 60 pounds 88 acres. Land is situated on the west side of Delaware Bay and on the south side of the Muspelion Creek and bounded by land of Mark Gendron, by a branch, and by land of Robert Hart. Land is part of a larger tract of 1000 acres granted by patent dated 20 Dec 1667 from Edmond Andrews, Governor of New York and Albany, to Richard Hill who on 11 Jul 1678 conveyed the tract to Benjamin Cowdry who on 26 Aug 1683 conveyed by deed of gift 500 acres to his daughter, Frances Spencer, wife of Major William Spencer. Joseph Booth, after marrying Frances Spencer following her husband's decease, sold 100 acres of the 500 acres to Mark Manlove. Mark Manlove sold the 100 acres to Henry Spencer who sold the 100 acres to John Smith except 12 acres which Henry Spencer had previously sold to Mark Gendron which William Spencer, son of Henry Spencer, conveyed to John Smith in Court in Aug 1721. John Smith signs. Wits., John May and Joseph Booth, Jr. Ack. 12 Aug 1727.

Pages 253-254. Deed. 12 Dec 1727. From Joseph Booth, Jr., yeoman, of Kent Co., DE., to Samuel Spencer, yeoman, of Sussex Co., DE. For 50 pounds 405 acres. Land is situated on the south side of Mispelion Creek, on the west side of Delaware Bay and part of a larger tract known as Hill's Content and is bounded by the first fast landing on the south side of Mispelion Creek and by a small hammock in the side of the marshes of the Mispelion. Land is part of a larger tract of 1000 acres formerly surveyed to Richard Hill who sold the tract to Benjamin Cowdry who by his deed of gift conveyed the land to Francis Spencer, mother of Joseph Booth, Jr., Henry Spencer, and Samuel Spencer. After a legal division of the land was made between Francis, Henry, and Samuel, Francis Spencer married Joseph Booth, father of Joseph Booth, Jr., who conveyed 150 acres of Francis's part to Samuel Spencer. Joseph Booth, as son and heir of Francis, now conveys all of Francis's part to Samuel Spencer including the 150 acres previously conveyed. Joseph Booth, Jr., signs. Wits., John Smith and Jonathan Ozbun. Ack. 14 Dec 1727.

Page 254. Deed of Gift. 17 Dec 1728. Decemr ye 17th 1728 then appeared in the office Willm Attkins who came by the order of his mother Ann Atkins widow & desired me to record one three year old bay horse (illegible) & one white (illegible) & branded on the near flank with IA wch horse she freely gives her daughter Tabitha Attkins & her heirs & assigns forever. pr Jacob Kollock D. Rolls

Pages 255-256. Deed. 15 Sep 1727. From Mary Cantwell, widow, of New Castle Co., DE., to Archibald Hopkins, yeoman, of Sussex Co., DE. For 30 pounds 300 acres. Land is situated in Sussex Co., DE., and known by the name of White Horse and is bounded by Luke Watson's land (Alexander Moleston's and Roger Gum's) and by Law's land. Land was granted by patent dated 27th da 12th mo 1684 by the Commissioners to John Oakey and John Oakey and Mary, his wife, conveyed on the 15th da 7th mo 1686 to Philip Russel. Philip Russel and Sarah, his wife, conveyed the land on 5 Jan 1686 to Elizabeth Frampton. Elizabeth Frampton, by Capt John Hill, her attorney, conveyed the land to William Dyre on the 8th da 12th mo 1686. Major William Dyre bequeathed the land to Mary Cantwell (by the name of Mary Dyre). Mary Cantwell appoints Henry Brook, Esqr., to be her lawful attorney. Mary Cantwell signs. Wits., Hen. Brook, W. Hammond and Sam'l Bullock. Samuel Bullock proves the deed on 12 Feb 1727. Ack. 12 Feb 1727.

Pages 256-257. Deed. 14 Dec 1727. From John Paynter, of Lewes, executor of Thomas Paynter, blacksmith, of the same place, to William Cornwallis and Rebecca, his wife, administrators of Elias Fisher, gentleman, of Sussex Co., DE. For (consideration not given) a lot with smith shop and stable and fencing. Lot is situated in Lewes adjoining the lot of Widow Clifton and Joseph Russel. Thomas Paynter conveyed the lot to John Fisher on 27 Oct 1708 and John Fisher died intestate before the deed was acknowledged in Court. John Fisher's estate descended to Elias Fisher as heir at law and Elias Fisher had administration of John Fisher's estate. Elias Fisher also died intestate and the administration of the estates of John and Elias Fisher became vested in their sister, Rebecca Cornwallis. John Paynter signs. Wits., John Paynter, Jr., and John Conwill. Ack. 14 Dec 1727.

Page 257. Deed. 15 Sep 1727. From William Cornwallis, gentleman, of Sussex Co., DE., to John Conwill, yeoman, of the same place. For 5 shillings and tender love and affection all the plantation on which Yeates Conwill lately dwelled and the marsh adjoining it and the 40,000 bricks standing in a pile on the plantation to build a house thereon. Land is situated between the Short Poynt, near the Salt Caody Marsh. Land to John Conwill and to his issue, if none, then to Elias Conwill and his issue, if none, then Hannah Conwill and her issue, if none, then to William Cornwallis's heirs. Wm Cornwallis signs. Wits., Wm Till and Jno Paynter, Jr. Ack. 15 Feb 1727.

Page 258. Deed. 14 Dec 1727. From William Cornwallis and Rebecca, his wife, administrators of the estate of Elias Fisher, yeoman, deceased, of Sussex Co., DE., to John Paynter, Jr., blacksmith, of the same place. For 5 pounds one lot. Lot is situated in Lewes on Mulberry Street and is bounded by the lots which were formerly Sarah Clifton's and Joseph Russel's. The lot was formerly sold by John Paynter, executor of Thomas Paynter, to William Cornwallis and Rebecca, his wife. Wm and Rebekah Cornwallis sign. Wits., Alexander Molleston and John Conwill. Ack. 15 Feb 1727.

Page 258. Deed of Gift. 1 Oct 1730. Then appeared in my office Willm Attkins who came by the order of his mother Ann Atkins and desired me to record for her daughter Tabitha Atkins one black year old horse with a white star in his forehead & branded with the letters IA on the near flank wch horse she freely gives to her afsd daughter Tabitha and her heirs & assigns forever. Recorded this 1th of Oct 1730. Test Jacob Kollock Dep Regr.

Page 259. Deed of Gift. 25 Nov 1727. From Richard Dobson, yeoman, of Sussex Co., DE., to Elenor Dobson, his wife. For love and affection 100 acres of land. Land is situated in Gitter's Neck. Richard Dobson appoints Joseph Pemberton to be his attorney. Richard Dobson signs. Wits., Robert Smith and Joseph Booth, Jr. Ack. 12 Dec 1727.

Pages 259-261. Deed. 12 Dec 1727. From Thomas Gray, yeoman, of Sussex Co., DE., and Temperance, his wife, to Philip Russel, of Lewes, DE. For 200 pounds 187 acres. Land is situated in a neck in the division of Pagan Creek and Cold Spring Branch and is bounded by a lane which divides this land from the land of John Prettyman which was formerly Daniel Brown's, by a Beaverdam Branch proceeding out of Cold Spring Branch, by the Sheep hole gut of the Beaverdam Branch, by two small hammocks, and surveyed by Robert Shankland. Lant is part of a larger tract called St(?) Piles patented to David Gray and Thomas Gray by warrant from the Commissioners to resurvey. Thomas Gray signs and Temperance Gray makes her mark. Wits., Woolsey Burton and R. Holt. Ack. 18 Dec 1727.

Pages 261-262. Deed of Release. 13 Dec 1727. From Richard Cooper, and Mary, his wife, of Sussex Co., DE., to James Claypoole, and Jean, his wife, of the same place, For 12 pounds 30 acres. Land is situated on the southwest side of Lewes and is bounded by Lewes Creek, by land that Nehemiah Field died possessed of, by land of Jonathan Bailey, Esqr., and by Pagan Creek. Land that James Claypoole died possessed of. Richard and Mary Cooper make their marks. Wits., John Dickson and John Welbore. Ack. 13 Dec (1727).

Pages 262-263. Deed. 15 Dec 1727. From Abraham Wiltbanck and Naomi, his wife, of Sussex Co., DE., to Jacob Philips, marriner, of the same place. For 23 pounds one lot 60 X 200 feet. Lot is situated in Lewes and is bounded on the northwest side with the lot in possession of Samuel Paynter, on the northeast side with Front Street, on the southeast side with a street running between this lot and the lot of Thomas Finwick now in the possession of Simon Kollock, and on the southwest side with Second Street. Abraham, Jr., and Naomy Wiltbank sign. Wits., Anderson Parker and Rob.

Smith. Naomi Wiltbank relinquishes her dower rights with Wm Till and Sam'l Davis in witness. Ack. 15 Dec 1727.

Pages 263-265. Deed. 6 May 1727. From Rives Holt, Esqr., Sheriff of Sussex Co., DE., to Richard Hinman, Esqr. For 92 pounds 1 shilling 200 acres. Land is situated in Rehoboth and is bounded on the east by land of Richard Hinman, on the west with land of Peter Marsh, and joining land formerly sold by Jno Morgan & Jemima, his wife, to Samuel Dickinson, and binding on a branch to Rehoboth Bay. Land is part of a larger tract of 800 acres called Avery's Rest. On 5 Nov 1726, Rives Holt, sheriff, was directed to choose good and lawful men of his baliwick to make known to John and Elizabeth Price, administrators of Jemima Green, that they should appear at a Court of Common Pleas on first Tuesday February next in regard to a tract of land which Nicholas and Jemima Green had mortgaged to William Till, trustee of the loan office, which mortgage had not been paid and the land was to be sold at public vendue and the money to be paid into Court on the 1st Tuesday of May next. Richard Hinman was the highest bidder. R. Holt vic.Comr. Comitatn. Readie., signs. Wits., Alexander Draper. Ack. 12 Dec 1727.

Pages 265-266. Deed. 15 Dec 1727. From Andrew Pennis and Mary, his wife, of Sussex Co., DE., to Andrew White, planter, of the same place. For 25 pounds 216 acres. Land is situated on the east side of Green Branch and on the south side of John Morris's land and is bounded by Green Branch, by John Morris's land, and on the south side of Summersett Road. Land was laid out by virtue of commissioners warrant from Jacob Taylor dated 11th da 4th mo 1717 to John Smith, dec'd, who bequeathed the land to his wife, Mary, who later married Andrew Pennis. Andrew Pennis signs and Mary Pennis makes her mark. Wits., Arch. Smith, Partick Allison, and E. Cummings. Ack. 15 Dec 1727.

Pages 267-268. Deed. 10 Dec 1727. From Philip Marsh, of Sussex Co., DE., to John Roads, Esqr., farmer, of the same place. For 39 pounds 140 acres. Land is situated in Sussex Co., DE., on the west side of Delaware Bay adjoining to the seashore and is bounded by John Roads' land, by the branch of a pond, by the seashore, and by land that did belong to the heirs of Peter Marsh, dec'd, and surveyed by Robert Shankland in 1727. Land is part of a larger tract of 227 acres which was part of a larger tract of 427 acres. The 427 acres was known by the name of Hatter's Land and contained in a patent now belonging to Jno Roads. The 227 acres was conveyed to John Marsh by Richard Hinman in 1726. Philip Marsh signs. Wits., Arch. Smith, John Walton, and Robert West. Ack. 12 Feb 1727.

Pages 268-269. Deed of Gift. 3 Aug 1727. From Comfort Burton to her son, Thomas Leatherberry, yeoman, of Sussex Co., DE. For goodwill and affection 315 acres. Land is situated between Indian River and Rehoboth Bay in a neck called Long Neck and is bounded by a corner post of 640 acres surveyed for Woolsey Burton, Esqr., and Francis Bagwell, dec'd, by the division line of the neck, by 25 acres of marsh of Woolsey Burton, and by the head of Ragged Hammock Creek or gut. Land that "I" purchased from John Adams and Agnes, his wife, on 3 May 1726 and the 315 acres includes part of the land that was allotted to Agnes Adams as her part of her father's, William Bagwell, estate as by the Orphans Court record of Sussex Co., DE., may appear. Comfort Burton makes her mark. Wits., Jos. Godwin and John Welbore. Ack. 2 Aug 1727.

Page 269. Earmark. 28 Mar 1728. William Reed his mark for cattle sheep & hogs &ct is a crop X slit in the right ear & a hole & over bitt in the left recorded this 28th day of March 1728. pr Jacob Kollock

Page 269. Earmark. 22 May 1728. William Woolf his marke for cattle sheep & hogs &ct is a swallow forke in the right ear & an over bitt in the left Recorded this 22th day of May 1728. pr Jacob Kollock

Page 269. Earmark. 18 Jul 1730. John Burton his ear mark for cattle sheep & hogs &ct is as follows A slit in the left ear a crop hole & under bitt in the right ear. Recorded this 18th day of July 1730. pr Jacob Kollock. Rgr.

Page 270. Deed of Release. 9 Feb 1727. From Richard Bracy and Annabella, his wife, to her children, Anne Stockly, Honor Tindal and Francis Stevens, daughters of John Crew, of Sussex Co., DE. For 5 shillings 900 acres. Land is situated on Delaware Bay and about 4 miles to the south of Rehoboth Bay and is called West Chester and is bounded by a creek that runs out of Rehoboth Bay. Land was granted by patent of Edmond Andross, Governor of New York, on 20 Aug 1679 to Robert Hignett and John Crew. Richard and Annabella Bracy make their marks. Wits., William Stevens and John Welbore. Ack. 6 Feb 1727.

Page 270. Earmark. 18 Jul 1730. Benjamin Burton his ear mark for cattle sheep & hogs &ct is a crop & hole in the left ear & a slit in the right. Recorded this 18th day of July 1730. pr Jacob Kollock Rgr. This mark recorded for Jno Burton son of sd Benjamin. pr Russel Recordr.

Pages 271-272. Deed. 7 Feb 1728. From Nicholas Williams, son and heir to Francis Williams, deceased, of Sussex Co., DE., to Abraham Inloes, of the same place. For 23 pounds 100 acres. Land is situated on the Indian

River and is bounded by the mouth of Swan Creek and running with it to the mouth of the Beaver Dam Branch, by land that Francis Williams, Jr., dec'd, bought from Francis Williams, Sr., and by Indian River. Land is part of a larger tract of 300 acres on the west side of Swan Creek which issues out of Indian River which Francis Williams, Sr., dec'd, bought of William Clark. Nicholas Williams makes his mark. Wits., Jno Prettyman and W. Russel. 6 Feb 1727.

Pages 272-273. Deed. 6 Feb 1727. From Thomas Walker, yeoman, of Sussex Co., DE., to Robert Lacey, yeoman, of the same place. For 30 pounds 187 acres. Land is situated in Sussex Co., DE., on the east side of Cowe Bridge Branch one of the branches which proceeds out of the Indian River and known by the name of Strife and is bounded another tract owned by Thomas Walker. Land was surveyed in Apr 1717 by Robert Shankland for John Cary, dec'd, who conveyed the land to Job Barker who sold to Thomas Walker. Thos Walker makes his mark. Wits., Francis Cornwell and John Welbore. Ack. 6 Feb 1727.

Pages 273-276. Deed. 13 Dec 1727. From Francis Cornwall, cordwainer, of Sussex Co., DE., to Thomas Walker, yeoman, of the same place. For 300 pounds 613 acres in one tract and two parcels. The tract is situated on the south east side of Cold Spring Branch and is bounded by Cold Spring Branch, by land of Michel Chambers, by land of Capt Henry Lingo, and by land of Samuel Gray. The 900-acre tract was granted by the Sussex Court on the 28th da 10th mo 1680 to William Trotter and surveyed on the 9th da 10th mo 1681 and William Trotter assigned the patent on 8 Sep 1685 to William Clark who assigned the patent on 8 Dec 1685 to Francis Cornwell, dec'd, father of the Francis Cornwell of this deed, on 8 Dec 1685 and is called Batchelor's Folly. One parcel is part of a larger tract situated on the west side of Delaware Bay and on the north side of Long Love Branch and known by the name of Gray's Inn and is bounded by land of Francis Cornwell. This tract of 632 acres was granted by the Sussex Court on 8 Dec 1681 to Samuel Gray, dec'd, and surveyed on 8 Dec 1682 and patented by William Penn on 26 Mar 1684. Samuel Gray conveyed 300 acres to John Roads, gentleman, who conveyed 100 acres to Robert Lodge, carpenter, on 5 Aug 1719 who on 8 Mar 1722 conveyed the 100 acres to Francis Cornwell. The last parcel is part of a larger tract called Watson's Purchase situated on the northwest side of a Beaverdam proceeding from the head of Love's Creek and is bounded by 50 acres of land of John Dyar. Land was granted by patent dated 30th da 1st mo 1684 from William Penn to Luke Watson, Sr., who conveyed on 30 Oct 1702 conveyed the tract to William White who on 8 Feb 1717 conveyed 115 acres of the tract to Francis Cornwell. Francis Cornwell conveys all this land except 300 acres (NOTE: or 15) already sold by Francis Cornwell to Mary Moore, widow, and 200 acres (NOTE: or 207) to John Atkins, carpenter, and 2 acres conveyed by deed of gift (NOTE: by Robert Lodge) to the congregation of the people called Quakers. Francis Cornwall makes his mark. Wits., Jno Russel and John Russell. Ack. 6 Feb 1727.

Pages 276-277. Deed. 5 Feb 1727. From Joseph Booth, gentleman, of Kent Co., DE., to William Samples, shipwright, of Sussex Co., DE. For 18 pounds 202 acres. Land is situated on the south side of the Mispelion and is bounded by the Herring Branch, by Manlove's clear ground, and by Robert Hill's land. Land is part of a larger tract of 600 acres known as Cedar Town granted by patent to William Carter on 29th da 8th mo 1686 who conveyed the tract to William Clark on 24th da 10th mo 1686 who conveyed 302 acres of the tract to James Brown on the 8th da 1st mo 1687 who bequeathed the 302 acres to Joseph Booth in 1703. Joseph Booth for 6 pounds conveyed 202 acres to Edward Burroughs, cordwainer, of Sussex, who, before a deed was made to him, for 18 pounds conveyed the 202 acres to William Samples. Joseph Booth appoints Rives Holt as his attorney. Joseph Booth signs. Wits., John May and Jno Edmunds. Ack. 6 Feb 1727.

Page 277. Earmark. 22 Dec 1731. John Bicknell His Ear Mark for Cattle, Sheap and hoggs &c is crop & under bitt in the right Ear & the Left Ear remaining hole as at first recorded the 22 day of Decemr 1731. Test Jacob Kollock D. R.

Page 277. Earmark. 29 Dec 1731. Hugh Vorgin his Ear Mark for Cattle, Sheap and hoggs &c is as follows (viz) Crop under bit over bit & slit in the left Ear and under bit the right Ear recorded the 29th day of Decemr 1731. Test Jacob Kollock Dep.

Page 278. Patent. 29 Sep 1677. From Edmund Andross, Esqr., Governor of New York and Albany, to Edward Cooke. A patent for 350 acres. Land is situated on the western side of Rebobah Bay and certified by the Court at the Whorekill and known by the name of Cooke's Rest. Examined by Matthias Nicolls, Jr.

Page 279. Deed. 6 May 1685. From Mary Southrin, administratrix of Edward Southrin, dec'd, of Sussex Co., DE., to Griffith Jones, merchant, of Philadelphia. For 4000 pounds of good sound merchantable tabacco 350 acres. Land is situated on the southwest side of Love Creek and is bounded by Love's Creek and by land of Jno Johnson. Land was granted by warrant from the Court of Sussex on 15th da 1st mo 1682 to Edward Southrin and surveyed on 17th da 8th mo 1683. Mary Southrin makes her mark. Wits.,

Wm Clark, Hercules Shepheard, and Wm Emmatt. Ack. 12th da 3rd mo 1685.

Page 279. Receipt. 29 Nov 1731. Rec'd 29 November 1731 of Mr. Robert Smith by the hand of Capt Edward Greenman the sum of forty pounds on account of the estate of Archibald Smith, deceased, for Mr. Willm Allen. pr Wm Coleman. The above sum was pd by ye sale of a negro man of Mr. Sam'l Davis. pr Jacob Kollock.

Page 280. Assignment of Patent. 12 May 1685. From Griffith Jones, merchant, of Philadelphia, to Thomas Loyd, president of the provinciall Councill of the province of pensilvania & Territories thereunto belonging. For 50 pounds the same land as on page 279 of this deed book. Griffith Jones signs. Wits., Wm Clark, Hercules Sheph'd and Wm Emmett. Ack. 12th da 3rd mo 1685.

Page 280. Assignment of Patent. 20 Aug 1690. From Thomas Loyd to Jno Vaughan, carpenter. For 50 pounds the same land as on page 279 of this deed book. Thomas Loyd appoints Morris Edwards as his attorney. Thos Loyd signs. Wits., Sam'l Richardson and Da. Loyd. Ack. 3rd da 10th mo 1690.

Page 281-282. Patent. 4 Jul(?) 1684. From William Penn, Governor of Pensilvania & the Territoryes thereunto belonging, to Griffith Jones. A patent for 350 acres. Land is situated on the southwest side of Love's Creek and is bounded by Love's Creek, by land Jno Johnson, and by a small branch. Land was granted by virtue of a patent dated 29th da 7th mo 1687 and by a warrant from the Court of Sussex dated 15th da 1st mo 1682 and surveyed on 17th da 8th mo 1682 (probably should be 1683) to Jno (probably should be Edward) Southrin who conveyed the land to Griffith Jones. Griffith Jones requested that the patent be confirmed to him. Wm Penn signs.

Pages 282-284. Deed. 1 Jul 1714. From Samuel Preston, merchant, of Philadelphia, and Henry Laurance, yeoman, of Haverford in Chester Co., PA., executors of the estate of John Vaughan, dec'd, carpenter, of Philadelphia, to William Shankland, yeoman, of Sussex Co., DE. For 9 pounds 17 shillings 2 pence 350 acres. Land is situated on the southwest side of a Creek formerly called Love's Creek and is bounded by Love's Creek and by land of John Johnson. Land was patented by William Penn to Griffith Jones who conveyed the land to Thomas Loyd who conveyed to John Vaughan. John Vaughan, by his last will and testament dated 23rd da 6th mo (August) 1712, devised that Samuel Preston and Henry Laurance should have authority to convey his lands. John Vaughan had previously sold the land to William Shankland but had not yet conveyed at the time of his death. Samuel Preston and Henry Laurance appoint Cornelius Wiltbank as their attorney. Sam'l Preston and Henry Laurance sign. Wits., Thos Wallace, Nath'l Starr, and Cha. Brockden. Ack. 7 Feb (1714?)

Pages 284-285. Deed. 4 Aug 1713. From Thomas Bedwell, Esqr., of Kent Co., DE., and Honor, his wife, to William Clark, merchant of Lewes. For 30 pounds 200 acres. Land is situated on the north west side of Cold Spring Branch and is bounded by the bridge of Cold Spring Branch and by a small branch that proceeds out of Cold Spring Branch. The land is part of a larger tract of 800 acres granted by patent by commissioners of William Penn, James Claypoole and Robert Turner, on the 2nd da 2nd mo 1686 to William Clark, dec'd, gentleman, of Sussex Co., DE., who on the 4th da 1st mo 1697 conveyed 200 acres to Mathew Osburn who conveyed the 200 acres to Thomas Bedwell on 1 Aug 1710. The 800 acres are bounded by Cold Spring Branch, by land called Abraham's Lot, the corner of land called Little Field, by Mill Creek and bridge and is called Mill Plantation. Thos. and Honor Bedwell sign. Wits., Cornelius Wiltbank and James Simson. No acknowledgement.

Pages 286-287. Deed. 3 May 1726. From John Adams, cordwainer of Sussex Co., DE., and Agnes, his wife, to Comfort Burton, widow of the same place. For 141 pounds 15 shillings 315 acres. Land is situated bewteen Indian River and Rehoboth Bay in Long Neck and is bounded by a corner post of 640 acres surveyed for Woolsey Burton and Frances Bagwell, by the division line of the neck, by the Neck Road, by 75 acres of marsh belonging to Woolsey Burton, and by the head of Ragged Hammock Creek or gut. Land is part of the land that was allotted to Agnes Adams as her part of the lands of her father, William Bagwell. John Adams makes his mark and Agnes Adams signs. Wits., John Welbore and Phil. Russel. Ack. May Court 1726.

Page 287. Deed of Gift. 12 Apr 172(5?). From Mary Hinman, widow of Jno Hinman of Sussex Co., DE., to her sons, Jacob and Edward Marshall. For natural love and affection 1/2 of all my goods, utensils, impelments, houshold stuff and wares, and 1/2 of the ready money and personal estate whereever it may be on the main of America. Mary Hinman makes her mark. Wits., Joseph Pemberton, Elizabeth Molleston, and Arch. Smith. Memorandum: The day of the Livery & Seisen was delivered by the within named Mary Hinman unto the sd Jacob & Edward Marshall one Take in the name of one half of the goods chattels & premises mentioned in the above written Deed to hold to the sd Jacob & Edward Marshall their Heirs &

assigns for ever according to the above written Deed in the presence of Arch. Smith and Jos. Pemberton.

Page 288. Deed of Release. 7 May 1728. From John Stevens and Frances, his wife, to John Harmonson. For 14 pounds 5 shillings their interest in 900 acres. Land is situated in Rehoboth Hundred and known as West Chester and is bounded by a Creek that runs out of Rehoboth Bay. The 900 acre tract was granted by patent on 20 Aug 1779 to Robert Hignot and John Crew. John and Frances Stevens make their marks. Wits., Arch. Smith, Phil. Russel, and John Welbore. Ack. 7 May 1728.

Page 289. Deed. 29 Apr 1718. From William Spencer, son of Henry Spencer, yeoman deceased of Sussex Co., DE., to Joseph Spencer, yeoman of the same place. For 5 shillings 52 acres. Land is situated in Cedar Creek Neck and is bounded by land Robert Hart, by Goites Branch, and surveyed by Robert Shankland on 7 Mar 1713. Land was formerly purchased by Henry Spencer from Robert Hart and subsequently sold by Henry Spencer to Mark Gendrone, dec'd, whose son, Gabriel Gendrone, for 13 pounds conveyed the land to Joseph Spencer but the conveyance was never executed. William Spencer signs. Wits., James Miers and Joshua Fisher. Ack. 7 May 1728.

Pages 289-290. Deed. 7 May 1728. From Anthony Johnson, yeoman of Sussex Co., DE., to James Holland, yeoman of the same place. For 70 pounds 100 acres. Land is situated on the north east side of Love's Creek and is bounded by Burton's(?) land, by Daniel Fling's Swamp, by Holland's land, Jonathan Baily's, Esqr., land, and Anthony Johnson's little field. Land is part of a larger tract of 311 acres, Anthony Johnson makes his mark. Wits., Sa. Richardson, Robt Cornwall, and Phil. Russel. Ack. 7 May 1728.

Pages 291-292. Deed. 13 Dec 1727. From Thomas Walker, yeoman of Sussex Co., DE., to Francis Cornwall, cordwainer of the same place. For 200 pounds 305 acres in 2 tracts. Land is situated on the east side of Cow Bridge Branch, one of the branches proceeding out of the Indian River and is bounded by John Cary's land, by Cow Bridge Branch, by a 100 acres of an ancient warrant surveyed dated 4 Jul 1709 to William Copes, and surveyed on 9 Jan 1717. This tract was granted by warrant from the commissioners dated 20th da 6th mo 1717 to Thomas Walker. The other tract is situated in Rosemary Neck on the west side of one of the branches of Indian River and is bounded by the branch, by the bottom of Rosemary Neck, and surveyed by Robert Shankland on 9 Jan 1717. The tract was granted by commissioners warrant to William Copes on 4 Jul 1709 who conveyed the warrant to James Pettyjohn who assigned the warrant to Thomas Walker.

Thomas Walker makes his mark. Wits., John Russel and John Russell. Ack. 7 May 1728.

Pages 292-293. Deed. 7 Nov 1727. From John Price, yeoman of Sussex Co., DE., to Woolsey Burton, Esqr., of the same place. For 16 pounds 10 shillings 210 acres. Land is situated on the south of Abraham's Branch in Indian River Hundred and is bounded by Abraham's Branch. Land was granted by warrant of the Commissioners dated 1st da of 7ber 1718 to Jenkin Price, brother of John Price, who happened to die before the warrant was actually laid out at whose death (to wit) the eighth day of December 1719, Jno Price as heir at law caused the warrant to be laid on the stated land which was surveyed by Robert Shankland. Jno Price makes his mark. Wits., Rives Holt and Phil. Russel. Ack. 7 May 1728.

Pages 293-294. Deed. 7 Mar 1727. From John Paynter, Jr., blacksmith of Lewes, to Roger Traine, blacksmith of Kent Co., DE. For 30 pounds 2 town lots 120 X 200. Land is situated in Lewes fronting Lewes Creek. John Paynter signs. Wits., James Simson and Patrick Allison. Ack. 7 May 1728.

Pages 294-295. Deed. 7 Mar 1727. Roger Train, blacksmith of Kent Co., DE., to John Paynter, Jr., blacksmith of Lewes. For 60 pounds 6 town lots. Land is situated near the town of Lewes. Lots are now in the possession of John Paynter; four of which were purchased by Roger Traine from James Finwick and other 2 lots from John Paynter, Sr. Roger Traine appoints Archibald Smith and Philip Russel of Lewes as his attorneys. Roger Train signs. Wits., James Simson and Patrick Allison. Ack. 7 May 1728.

Pages 295-296. Deed. 7 May 1728. From Alexander Molliston, yeoman of Lewes, DE., to John Shankland, blacksmith of the same place. For 24 pounds 5 acres. Land is situated near Lewes between two ponds and is bounded by land of Nathaniel Hall and Simon Kollock, Esqr. Alexander Molston signs. Wits., James Claypoole and Robt Shankland. Ack. 7 May 1728.

Pages 296. Manumission. 7 Sep 1728. Sussex SS. Discharge Joseph Ferdinando. To all to whom these presents may come I John Roades of the County of Sussex afsd Sends Greeting. Know ye that the bearer hereof Joseph Ferdinando a Spanish Negro, heretofore a slave to me hath lately purchased his Freedom therefore I hereby tolerate him the sd Joseph to Deal & traffick for him selfe as a freeman without being called to any acct hereafter by me Witness my hand at Lewes the Seventh day of Septembr Ano Dom. one thousand seven hundred & twenty eight. John Roades signs.

Wits., Henry Fisher and Phil Russel. Recorded the 9th day of Septemr 1728. pr Jac. Kollock. D. Roles.

Page 297. Bond of Assurance. 24 Oct 1721. From John Foster and Ann, his wife, executrix of Robert Clifton, yeoman deceased of Lewes, DE., to Patrick Delany, taylor of Lewes, DE. For 17 pounds bond a lot (60 X 200) and house. The condition of the bond is that John and Ann Foster will convey the lot upon reasonable request of Patrick Delany on the 1st day of November next. Lot is situated on Mulberry Street and is the same lot that Robert Clifton died possessed of. John and Ann Foster sign. Wits., Mary Russel and Phil. Russel.

Page 297. Assignment of Bond. 7 Mar 1721. From Patrick Delany to William Godwin, yeoman of of Sussex Co., DE. For 8 pounds a lot 60 X 200 as stated in bond above. Patrick Delany makes his mark. Wits., William Shankland and Phil. Russel.

Pages 297-299. Deed. 3 Aug 1728. From Andrew Magill, innholder of Sussex Co., DE., to Richerd Lonkomb, yeoman of the same place. For 20 pounds 63 acres. Land is situated on Delaware Bay in Cedar Creek Neck and is bounded by land of John Richards on the northeast side of a beaverdam, on the west of the other branch of the beaverdam and resurveyed on 7 Jan 1725 by Robert Shankland. Andrew Magill purchased the land from Henry Molleston of Kent Co., DE., on 9 May 1723. And. Magill signs. Wits., John May and Thomas Smith. Ack. 6 Aug 1728.

Page 299. Bond. 9 Jan 1723/4. From John Holland, carpenter of Sumer(set) Co., MD., to Nathaniel Ratcliffe, planter. Bond of 240 pounds. The condition of the bond is that John Holland will pay Nathaniel Ratcliffe 120 pounds - 40 pounds in silver or paper money between this day and 1 Jan next and 20 pounds 14 shillings in corn, wheat, pork or tabacco at market price and 41 pounds 6 shillings in corn, pork, wheat or tabacco at market price between this date and this time four years from now or in cows and calves at the current price or part in each commodities. Jno Holland signs. Wits., Jas Wyatt and Robt Stevenson.

Pages 299-300. Deed. 28 Mar 1728. From Daniel England, yeoman of Salem Co., West New Jersy, to Alexander Draper, merchant of Sussex Co., DE. For 40 pounds 400 acres. Land is situated in Sussex Co., DE., and known as (Twillings Neck?) and is bounded by Ceder Creek. Land was granted by the Court of Sussex to Robert Twilly and resurveyed for him on the 4th da 7th mo 1686 by John Barkstead, deputy surveyor to William Clark, who conveyed the tract to Daniel England on the 5th da 4th mo 1688.

Daniel England appoints Ryves Holt, Esqr., or Simon Kollock, or Jacob Kollock, Esqr., to be his attorney. Daniel England signs. Wits., John May, George Walton, and Jehu Spencer. Ack. 6 Aug 1728.

Pages 301-302. Deed. 5 Aug 1728. From Francis Cornwall, yeoman of Sussex Co., DE., to Thomas Walker, yeoman of the same place. For 30 pounds 50 acres of marsh. Marsh is situated on Pagan Creek and Cool Spring Creek which proceeds out of the Broadkill and is bounded by Paul Marsh's land now Anderson Parker's, on the south side of Cool Spring Creek, by David Gray's land in Gray's neck, on the south side of a gut that makes a beaverdam, by the mouth of a ditch that divides William Prittiman's marsh, the mouth of Honeycomb Gut, Robert Creig's marsh, and surveyed by Robert Shankland on 2 Aug 1728. Francis Cornwall makes his mark. Wits., John Jackson and Jno Welbore. Ack. 6 Aug 1728.

Pages 302-304. Deed. 9 Aug 1728. From Isaac Watson, administrator of William Townsend, yeoman deceased, to William Burton, gentleman of Sussex Co., DE. For 41 pounds 200 acres. Land is situated in Sussex Co., DE., and is bounded by land of John Lofley, by a beaverdam, and by the mouth of a small branch. William Townsend, at his death, was indebted 40 pounds to Elizabeth Watson, widow, who brought suit on the 1st Tuesday in Feb 1727. Isaac Watson requested to sell the lands of William Townsend since his personal estate was not sufficient to pay his debts. Isaac Wattson signs. Wits., Henry Draper and John Jackson. Ack. 9 Aug 1728.

Pages 304-305. Deed. 9 Aug 1728. From William Burton, yeoman of Sussex Co., DE., to Elizabeth Wattson, widow of the same place. For 41 pounds 200 acres. Land is situated in Sussex Co., and is bounded by land of John Lofley on the west side of a beaver dam, on the east side of a small branch, and by the mouth of a small branch. William Townsend died possessed of this land. William Burton signs. Wits., Henry Draper and Jno Jackson. Ack. 9 Aug 1728.

Pages 305-307. Deed of Mortgage. 10 Apr 1728. From William Orr, yeoman of Sussex Co., DE., to Mary Kollock, of Lewes. For 122 pounds 18 shillings 284 acres, houses, and water mill. Land is situated in Sussex Co., DE., and called Sun Dyall. Land is bounded by a beaver dam, and by Love's Creek. Land is part of a larger tract of 400 acres of which 116 acres was previously sold to James Holland and Patience Parker together with a parcel of land adjoining this land. William Orr is to pay 122 pounds 18 shillings by 10 Apr 1731 for reconveyance of this land to William Orr or his heirs/assigns. Mary Kollock is to keep the water mill, etc., in good repair.

William Orr signs. Wits., Woolsey Burton and Joseph Pemberton. Ack. 6 Aug 1728.

Pages 307-308. Deed of Release. 23 Sep 1728. From Thomas Clifton, marriner of Sussex Co., DE., to Elizabeth Godwin, widow of the same place. For 20 shillings one lot (60 X 200 feet) and house. Lot is situated in Lewes on Mulberry Street which the father of Thomas Clifton, Robert Clifton, died possessed of. Thomas Clifton appoints Ryves Holt as his attorney. Thomas Clifton signs. Wits., Cors. Edgell and Phil. Russel. Nov Court 1728, deed was proved by the oath of Philip Russel. Ack. 5 Nov 1728.

Pages 308-309. Deed of Release. 6 Nov 1728. From John Ryle and Elizabeth, his wife, daughter of Jno Dial, to John Atkins. For 10 pounds their interest in 50 acres. Land is situated in Sussex Co., DE., and is bounded by land of William White. Land was conveyed from William White to Elizabeth Dial and her sisters, Eleanor, Jean and Mary, on 4 Aug 1713. John Ryle signs and Elizabeth Ryle makes her mark. Wits., Isaac Atkins and Jos. Godin. Ack. 5 Nov 1728.

Pages 309-310. Deed. 4 Feb 1728. From Joseph Eldridge, carpenter of Sussex Co., DE., to John Clowes, merchant of the same place. For 6 pounds 10 shillings a lot of 12,000 square feet. Lot is situated in Lewes and is bounded by a lot of Joseph Eldridge, by the County Road, and by a street. Josep. Eldridge signs. Wits., Joseph Belcher and William Anderson Parker. Ack. Feb Court 1728.

Pages 311-312. Deed. 4 Feb 1728. From Ryves Holt, Esqr., sheriff of Sussex Co., DE., to Joseph Russel, yeoman, of the same place. For 10 pounds 10 shillings 44 acres. Land is situated on the south side of the Broad Kill and known by the name of Point and is bounded by the head of Peters' gut. Land belonged to Joseph Carpenter, weaver formerly of Sussex Co., DE., who absented himself from the government without paying his debts and at a Court of Common Pleas on 5 Aug 1728 Joseph Russel brought suit and the land was taken in execution and sold at public vendue on 8 Nov 1728. R. Holt signs. Wits., W. Rodeney and Phil. Russel. Ack. Feb Court 1728.

Pages 312-313. Deed. 20 May 1728. From Rebecca Clark, daughter of William Clark, Jr., late of Sussex Co., DE., merchant, deceased, to John Donalson, merchant of Sumerset Co., MD. For 60 pounds 50 acres. Land is situated by Lewes Creek and fronting Lewes Creek and is bounded by land of Abraham Wiltbanck and Nathaniel Hall and by Pagan Creek. Rebecca Clark signs. Wits., Za. Richardson, Jos. Hepburn, Lawrence Anderson.

Memorandum: On 30 Nov 1728 Joseph Hepburn proved the deed. Ack. Feb Court 1728.

Page 313. Receipt. 4 May 1725. Then rec'd of Thomas Gray the full payment or just ballance of all bills bonds depts dew and demands what ever. I say rec'd by me Christopher Topham. Rec'd of Thomas Gray the contents of note of twelve shillings one account of Willm Russel rec'd this 4th day of May 1725. by me Chris. Topham.

Page 314. Deed of Gift. 28 Jul 1729. Mary Bucher widow appeared in my office & desired me to record the following -------------- a black four year old heffor with a mottle face a crop & and underbitt in the rite ear and two howles in the left ear she freely gives unto her son Willm Bucher son of Robart Bucher to say the sd cow & her female future increase except the first calf wch ye cow shall have wch sd calf & the future female increase she gives to her son Robart Bucher & their increase. One thre year old Brindell mottle face heffor marked as above wch sd cow she freely gives unto her daughter Agnes Bucher (to say) the sd cow and her female future increase to her -------------- one black three year old heffor of the same marke as above she greely gives unto her daughter Rachell Bucher (to say) the sd cow and her female future increase to her and her heirs one black three year old heffor with a white streak in her face marked with a crop & under bitt in the right ear & crop & two holes in the left which she freely gives unto her daughter Mary Bucher (to say) the sd cow & her future female increase to her and her heirs. Test. Jacob Kollock Dp Rolls.

Pages 314-315. Deed. 7 May 1728. From John Allen, yeoman of Sussex Co., DE., to John Tomson, gentleman of the same place. For 12 pounds 12 shillings 100 acres. Land is situated on the south side of Long Love Branch adjoining land where John Tomson now lives and is bounded by Long Love Branch, intersecting with Indian River road that passes over the part of the Branch where Bundocks Bridge was, and by land of John Allen and John Tomson. Land is part of a larger tract purchased by John Allen from Jeremiah Claypoole, Esqr. John Allan signs. Wits., Francis Allen and John Welbore. Ack. Feb Court 1728.

Pages 315-316. Deed of Release. 6 Feb 1728/9. From William Stockly, yeoman of Sussex Co., DE., and Anne, his wife, to Cornelius Edgell, joyner of the same place. For 9 pounds 1/3 part of 8 acres. Land is situated in the town of Lewis and is bounded by land of Edward Naws. Land is one third part of the land of which Jno Crew died possessed. Willm Stockly signs and Anne Stockly makes her mark. No witnesses. Ack. Feb Court 1728.

Pages 316-317. Deed of Release. 25 Nov 1720. From Tabitha Attkins, dau of Willm Attkins, deceased of Sussex Co., DE., to her brother, William Attkins. For 30 pounds her part of her father's, William Attkins, plantation. Land is situated on Loves Creek in Angola Neck and adjoins land where Woodman Stockley now lives. Tabitha Attkins is coheiress with Mattilda, John, William, Isaac, and Elizabeth Attkins, children of William Atkins. At the end of the deed mention is made to Elizabeth Attkins as being the grantor which could be in error. Tabitha Atkins signs. Wits., Jacob Kollock and John Welbore. Ack. Feb Court 1728.

Pages 317-318. Deed. 5 Feb 1728. From William Stockly, yeoman of Sussex Co., DE., to Thomas Marriner, yeoman of the same place. For 25 pounds 100 acres. Land is situated on the south side of Ivy Branch and is bounded by Ivy Branch, and by land which formerly belonged to Gilbert Marriner. Land is part of a larger tract which formerly belonged to Amimadab Handzor. Willm Stockly signs. Wits., Samuel Dickeson and Oliver Stockly. Ack. Feb Court 1728.

Pages 319-321. Deed. 4 Feb 1728. From John Price, yeoman of Sussex Co., DE., to Henry Brereton, turner of of the same place. For 20 pounds 139 acres. Land is situated on the north side of Fishing Branch binding on Foxes land. Land is one half of a tract of 239 acres granted to Henry Touchbery, dec'd, by virtue of a commissioner's warrant dated 16th da 12th mo 1717 and surveyed by Robert Shankland, and situated in Indian River Hundred on the south side of Brace's Branch and bounded by Robert Richard's land, by land of Jacob Kollock, by Fishing Branch one of the branches of Middle Creek, and by Foxes land. John Price bought the land on 5 May 1721 from Elizabeth Touchberry, widow of Henry Touchberry. John Price makes his mark. Wits., Benjamin Stockly and Ann Barker. Ack. Feb Court 1728.

Pages 321-323. Deed. 7 Aug 1726. From John Price, yeoman of Sussex Co., DE., to Benjamin Stockly, yeoman of the same place. For (consideration not given) 93 acres. Land is situated in Indian River Hundred on the west side of Middle Creek and on the south side of Bracey's Branch that runs into Middle Creek and is bounded by land surveyed for John Hastings, by land of Henry Brereton, the headline of the tract, by land of Jacob Kollock and by Bracey's Branch. Land is 1/2 of a tract of land granted and surveyed to Henry Touchberry on 16th da 12th mo of 1717 and surveyed by Robert Shankland on 14 Apr 1726. John Price makes his mark. Wits., Robert West, John Russell, Jr., and Allexander Herrin. John Price appoints John Russell to be his lawful attorney to acknowledge the deed at the Court held in Lewes on the first Tuesday in Feb 1728/9. John Price makes his mark. Wits., Henry Brereton and Ann Barker. Feb. Term 1728. Power of attorney proven. Ack. Feb Court 1728.

Page 323. Bill of Sale. 8 Oct 1728. From William Till, Esqr., of Sussex Co., DE., to Mary Codd, gentlewoman of the same place. For 5 shillings 8 negro slaves. One negro woman named Hagor, four boys named Ishmall, Isaac, Harry and Cudgio, and three girls named Annis, Molly and Rose. Wm Till signs. Wits., Wm Becket and Mary Becket.

Page 324. Deed. 1 Nov 1728. From Philip Russel, yeoman of Lewes, to Benjamin Oram, sadler of the same place. For 18 pounds a 2-acre lot. Lot is situated on the south side of Lewes and is now in the possession of William Atchison and is bounded by the county Road, by land of Thomas Bell, by the lot of John Bywaters, and the southernmost street in Lewes. Phil. Russel signs. Wits., Arch. Smith and Robert Shankland. Ack. 4 Apr 1729.

Page 325. Deed. 6 Aug 1728. From John Chambers, wheelwright of Kent Co., DE., to Anthony Woodward, taylor of Lewes. For 5 pounds 74 square perches of land. Land is situated at the south end of Lewes and is bounded by the County Road, by land of Simon Kollock, by Kollock's road by the gate, and by lots of Anthony Woodward where he now lives. Lot is part of a larger tract and purchased by the grantor from James Finwick. John Chambers signs and Janet Chambers makes her mark. Wits., Anderson Parker and John Stewart. Ack. 6 May 1729.

Pages 326-327. Deed. 6 May 1729. From Ryves Holt, sheriff of Sussex Co., DE., to John Russel, Esqr of the same place. For 55 pounds 330 acres. Land is situated on the east side of Cow Bridge Branch one of the branches proceeding out of the Indian River and is bounded by land of John Carie (sic), and an ancient warrant surveyed bearing date 4 Jul 1709 to William Copes. Land was surveyed on 9 Jan 1717 and belongs to Francis Cornwell who was indebted to Thomas Walker, yeoman, for 93 pounds. On 6 Aug 1728, Thomas Walker obtained a judgment against Francis Cornwell for the recovery of the debt and the sheriff seized the land in execution and the land was sold at vendue. Ryves Holt signs. Wits., Woolsey Burton and Phill. Russel. Ack. 6 May 1729.

Pages 327-328. Deed. 6 Feb 1727. From John Chambers, yeoman late of Sussex Co., DE., and Janet, his wife, to Thomas Bell, taylor of Lewes. For 80 pounds 16 acres. Land is situated on the whorekill in Delaware Bay and is near Lewes between the County Road and the southernmost street and is bounded by the County Road, by the southernmost street, by land of

Alexander Molleston, and by Davis' plantation, and was surveyed by Robert Shankland on 2 Aug 1722 to contain 16 1/2 acres of which 1/2 acre was previously sold to Anthony Woodward. Land is part of 2 tracts. One tract was granted by warrant and laid out for John Kiphaven and was bounded by the whorekill, land of Allexander Molleston, by Pagan Creek, and contained 69 acres by return of a survey by Edmund Cantwell and patent dated in New York on 15 Jan 1675. John Kiphaven conveyed the land to William Clark who on 12 Apr 1681 conveyed to Capt Nathaniel Walker who bequeathed the land to Major William Dyer which land by warrant of resurvey belonging to William Carter was found to be surplusage 27 acres on 24 Dec 1686. William Carter conveyed the surplus to William Clark who conveyed on 4th da 3rd mo 1687 to Major William Dyer which made the tract now contain 96 acres. William Dyer and his mother, Mary Dyer, executors of Major William Dyer, conveyed the land to Thomas Finwick. The second tract of 440 acrew was sold by Alexander Molleston to Peter Lewes and is near Lewes and is called Middleborough. Peter Lewes sold the tract to Jacob Kollock, Sr., except 6 acres previously sold to Thomas Finwick of Lewes. James Finwick, son and heir of Thomas Finwick, sold to John Chambers a part of these 2 tracts containing 16 1/2 acres on 8 Aug 1722. John Chambers signs and Janet Chambers makes her mark. Wits., Anderson Parker and John Stewart. Ack. 6 May 1729.

Page 329. Deed of Release. 6 May 1729. From John Murrow and Elizabeth, his wife, Pashance Richerson, and Ellinor Richarson, daughters of Robart Richards, dec'd, to Mary Kollock, widow of Lewes. For 6 pounds their portion of the land their father died possessed of. John Morrow signs, Elliza Morrow makes her mark, Pahsunce Richorson and Ellinor Richorson make their marks. Wits., Anderson Parker and Jacob Kollock. Ack. 6 May 1729.

Page 330. Deed. 6 May 1729. From John Russel, yeoman of Sussex Co., DE., to David Hudson, yeoman of Somerset Co., MD. For 50 pounds 330 acres in 2 tracts. Land is situated in Rosemary Neck and is bounded by land of John Carey, by 100 acres granted to Wm Copes in 1709, and was surveyed 9 Jan 1717. Tract consists of one tract of 100 acres and one tract of 230 acres. Land was conveyed by Thomas Walker to Francis Cornwell. The land was extended by Rives Holt, Esqr., High Sheriff, and sold at vendue to John Russel on this same date. Jno Russel signs. Wits., John Shankland and Peter Robinson. Ack. 6 May 1729.

Pages 331-332. Deed of Release. 19 Feb 1728/9. From Robert Cade, cordwainer of Sussex Co., DE., and Matilda, his wife, John Russel, soriviner of the same place, and Elizabeth Stockly, his wife, to John Atkins, William

Atkins and Isaac Atkins, yeomen of the same place. For 30 pounds their portion of the land of their father, William Atkins, dec'd. Robert Cade signs, Matilda Cade makes her mark, Jhn Russell signs and Elisabeth Stockly Russell signs. Wits., Tabitha Atkins, Robert Shankland, and Ann Atkins. Robert and Matilda Cade and John and Elizabeth Stockly Russell appoint Philip Russel their attorney. Wits., Robert Shankland and Ann Atkins. 25 Feb 1729. Matilda and Elizabeth release their rights. Ack. 6 May 1729.

Pages 332-333. Deed. 25 Feb 1728. From John Atkins, William Atkins and Isaac Atkins, yeomen of Sussex Co., DE., to John Russel, scriviner of the same place. For 30 pounds 130 acres. Land is situated in Angola Neck and is part of a tract that belonged to William Atkins, dec'd, and is bounded by land of John Allen, land of John Atkins, land of William Atkins, land of Isaac Atkins, by Bundick's land, and by Love's Creek. John Atkins, Willm Atkins and Isaac Atkins sign. Wits., Tabitha Atkins and Robert Shankland. Ack. 6 May 1729.

Pages 334-335. Deed. May 1729. From Ryves Holt, Esqr., sheriff of Sussex Co., DE., to Martha Little, widow of the same place. For 37 pounds 232 acres. Land is situated in Sussex Co., DE., and is bounded by land formerly belonging to John Russel, by land of John Fox, and by a branch. At a Court of Common Pleas held on 15 Dec 1727, Ryves Holt was directed that he should cause Thomas McCosker, weaver late of Sussex Co., DE., to know that he is to appear in Court on the 1st Tuesday in Feb following to show cause why a tract of land which he had mortgaged to Wm Till, loan office trustee, should not be taken in execution. The land was sold at public vendue to Martha Little. R. Holt signs. Wits., Hen. Brook and Jonathan Baily. Ack. 6 Aug 1729.

Pages 335-336. Deed. 6 Aug 1728. From John Kain, planter of Kent Co., DE., to James White, yeoman of Sussex Co., DE. For 7 pounds 100 acres. Land is situated in Slaughter Neck and is bounded by land of Joseph Hickman and by land of James Carpenter and known by the name of Kain's Old Field. Land was purchased by Thomas Kain, dec'd, from Henry Bowman, the elder, dec'd. John Kain, son and heir of Thomas Kain, now sells the land. John Kain appoints Ryves Holt or Jeremiah Claypole as his attorneys. John Kain makes his mark. Wits., Samuel Berry and John May. Memorandum on 6 Aug 1729. John May proves the deed. Ack. 6 Aug 1729.

Pages 336-337. Deed. 11 Nov 1729. From John Stevens, planter of Sommerset Co., MD., and Francis, his wife, to John Adams, cordwainer of Sussex Co., DE. For 6 pounds 3 shillings and 9 pence 1/3 of 8 acres of land

(1/3 part of 2 four-acre lots). Lots are situated in Lewes on the NE side of the blockhouse pond and is bounded by Market Street the lowermost and the head of Mulberry Street. The lots formerly belonged to John Crew, dec'd. John and Francis Stevens make their marks. Wits., Tho. Cokayne and Eliz. Cokayne. Memorandum. On 11 Nov 1729, Francis Stevens releases her rights. Ack. 11 Nov 1729.

Page 337. Deed of Release. 1 Dec 1729. From John Harmonson to Ralph Tindall, yeoman of Sussex Co., DE., and Honor, his wife. For 15 pounds his interest in 900 acres. Land is situated in Rehoboth Hundred and known by the name West Chester and is bounded by a creek that runs out of Rehoboth Bay. Tract was originally granted by patent dated 20 Aug 1679 to Robert Hignet and John Crew. John Harmonson signs. Wits., Abner Hood and Phil. Russel. Ack. 4 Dec 1729.

Page 338. Deed of Release. 2 Dec 1729. From Mary Kollock, widow of Jacob Kollock, merchant of Sussex Co., DE., and Simon and Jacob Kollock, Jane Hirons, and Hesther Phillips, heirs of Jacob Kollock, dec'd, to John Prettyman, Sr., yeoman of the same place. For 41 pounds 13 shillings 128 acres in 2 tracts. Land is situated in Angola Neck and the first tract is bounded by Rehoboth Bay at the mouth of Love's Creek, land formerly laid out to John Johnson, negro, the mouth of a small gut which divides this land from Horse Island, by land that was formerly owned by John West and contains 80 acres. The second tract is surplusage land taken up by Jacob Kollock by virtue of a warrant containing 48 acres and adjoining the first tract. Mary Kollock makes her mark and Simon Kollock, Jacob Kollock, Jane Hirons, and Hesther Phillips sign. Wits., Joseph Pemberton and John Paynter. Ack. 4 Dec 1729.

Page 339. Deed. 5 Nov 1729. From Robert Lacey, yeoman of Sussex Co., DE., to William Prittyman, Jr., son of Robert Prittyman, yeoman dec'd, of the same place. For 5 pounds 50 acres. Land is situated on the north side of Indian River and on the east side of Swan Creek and is bounded by Swan Creek. The land is part of a larger tract of 200 acres. Robert Lacey signs. Wits., Thomas Stockly, Wm Field and Samuel Dickeson. Ack. 5 Dec 1729.

Pages 339-341. Deed. 5 Nov 1729. From Thomas Walker, yeoman of Sussex Co., DE., to John Prittyman, yeoman of the same place. For 12 pounds 5 shillings 20 acres. Land is situated on Pagan Creek and Cool Spring Creek which proceeds out of the Broadkill and is bounded by land of David Gray in Gray's Neck, a gut that makes a beaverdam, by the mouth of a ditch which divides this land from the marsh of Wm Prittyman, by Cool Spring Creek at the mouth of a gut, by the mouth of Honey Comb Gut, by

Sussex County, Delaware, Deed Book F-6

Beaverdam Gut proceeding out of Cool Spring Creek that divides Parker and Prittyman. Land is part of a larger tract originally granted by patent dated the 2nd da 2nd mo 1687 to Francis Cornwell and called Greenfield. Francis Cornwell, son of Francis Cornwell, obtained a warrant of resurvey dated the 13th da 11th mo 171(8?) and the tract was surveyed according to the ancient patent on 22 Aug 1718 by Robert Shankland. Francis Cornwell sold 50 acres, part of the tract, to Thomas Walker. Thomas Walker makes his mark. Wits., Robert West and Jacob Kollock. Ack. 4 Dec 1729.

Page 341. Deed of Release. 2 Dec 1729. From Abraham Wiltbank, yeoman of Sussex Co., DE., to John Harrison, of the same place. For 12 pounds 100 acres. Land is situated on the north side of Broad Creek and is bounded by land which was formerly John Donovan's but lately purchased by Edward Naws on the northeast, by land sold by Cornelius Wiltbank to John Jones on the southwest, and by Broad Creek on the southeast. Abraham Wiltbank makes his mark. Wits., Alexander Draper and Phil. Russel. Ack. 4 Dec 1729.

Pages 342-343. Deed. 3 Dec 1729. From John White, carpenter of Sussex Co., DE., and Esther, his wife, and William White, carpenter of the same place, to John Atkins, carpenter of the same place. For 30 pounds 150 acres. Land is situated on the west side of the Main Road as you go from Lewes Town to the Indian River Chapel and is bounded by land of Albert Jacobs on the southeast, and by land of the heirs of John Dyall and of Frances Cornwell now in the possession of John Atkins. Land formerly belonged to William White, dec'd, and by him bequeathed to his son, John White, party to this deed. John White, Esther White and Willm White sign. Wits., Fracs. Woolfe, John Ryle and John Russel. Ack. 4 Dec 1729.

Pages 344-345. Deed. 7 Nov 1729. From Ryves Holt, Esqr., sheriff of Sussex Co., DE., to William Atchison, gentleman of the same place. For 140 pounds a 2-acre lot. Lot is situated on the south side of Lewes. At the Court of Common Pleas on the 1st Tuesday in Nov 1728, William Atchison recovered against Benjamin Oram a debt of 171 pounds 12 shillings 3 pence and afterwards on 7 Feb 1728 the sheriff was directed to collect the debt from Benjamin Oram's goods and chattels and have the money in Court on the 1st Tuesday in May following. This land was taken in execution and sold at public vendue to William Atchison. Land purchased by Benjamin Oram from Phil Russel on 1 Nov 1728. Ryves Holt signs. Wits., Simon Kollock and Jonath. Beckett. Ack. 4 Dec 1729.

Pages 345-346. Deed. 9 Dec 1729. From Richard Hinman, yeoman of Sussex Co., DE., to Samuel Paynter, house carpenter of Lewes. For (no consideration given) a 60 X 200 foot lot. Lot is situated on Front Street in Lewes and is bounded on the front by the branch of Lewes Town Creek, on the SE by the lot of Jacob Phillips, on the SW by Second Street, and on the NW side by the lots of John and Albert Jacobs. Richard Hinman signs. Wits., Willm Molleston, Jos. Hepburn, and Phil. Russel. Ack. 9 Dec 1729.

Pages 346-347. Deed. 5 Nov 1712. From Anderson Parker, attourney of Robert Street, late of Sussex Co., DE., to David Hudson, of Summerset Co., MD. For 30 pounds 300 acres. Land is situated on the east side of Swan Creek and is bounded by 200 acres formerly owned by George Young, late of this County, on the south side, and by Swan Creek on the west side. Land was formerly sold by Wm Clark to John Street and Richard Ward. Anderson Parker signs. Wits., Staphan Woringtun and Wrixham White. Ack. 4 Aug 1715.

Pages 347-348. Deed. 26 Jul 1729. From Art Verkirk, Sr., and Art Verkirk, Jr., to Samuel Spencer, Jr. For 110 pounds 100 acres. Land is situated in Ceder Creek Neck and known as Bould Eagle Point or Art's Dairy and is bounded by land of John Walton and by land of George Walton. Land is part of a larger tract patented by Henry Bowman, dec'd. Art Verkirk, Sr., and Jr., first sold the land to Thomas Hemmons (presume he assigned the land to Samuel Spencer). Art Verkirk makes his mark and Art Verkirk, Jr., signs. Wits., John May and Isaac Warner. 5 Feb 1729. John May proves the deed. Ack. 3 Feb 1729.

Pages 348-349. Deed. 3 Feb 1729. From William Becket and Jacob Kollock, executors of Cornelius Wiltbank, yeoman dec'd of Sussex Co., DE., to Samuel Hopkins, yeoman of the same place. For 72 pounds 10 shillings for 185 acres. Land is situated on the NW side of Long Bridge Branch and is bounded by Long Bridge Branch and is on the north side of a larger tract. Land is part of a larger tract of 367 acres bounded by land of Thomas Davock, and by Long Bridge Branch. Tract previously belonged to Cornelius Wiltbank and Richard Paynter jointly and Cornelius Wiltbank authorized the executors of his will to make sale of his portion. On 3 Sep 1728, his executors requested the Orphans Court to divide the tract between the executors of Cornelius Wiltbank and the heirs of Richard Paynter. Wm Becket and Jacob Kollock sign. Wits., R. Holt and Phil. Russel. Ack. 3 Feb 1729/30.

Page 350-351. Deed. 4 Feb 1729. From James Claypoole, weaver of Sussex Co., DE., to Joseph Hazzard, yeoman of the same place. For 11 pounds 67 acres. Land is situated in Angola Neck near the southwest side of Love's Creek that runs out of Rehoboth Bay and is the third division of the tract and is bounded by Bracey's Branch. Land is part of a larger tract of 255 acres which is bounded by Robert Bracey's Branch one of the branches proceeding out of Middle Creek on the southwest. The land was granted to Richard Shoulster by warrant obtained from the Court of the Whorekill on 14 Feb 1681 and was surveyed by Cornelius Verhoofe on 1 Apr 1681. Land was afterwards conveyed to Thomas Smith, dec'd, on 5 Jun 1699 who bequeathed the land to his son and 4 daughters. The son afterward died and some of the daughters married Robert Clendening and William Conwill, yeomen. Robert Clendening in behalf of his wife, Alice (Smith), daughter of Thomas Smith, petitioned the Orphans Court on 5 Mar 1728 for a division of the lands of Thomas Smith, dec'd. James Claypool signs. Wits., Thomas Bagwell, Pettr Robinson and Tho. Cokayn. Ack. 4 Feb 1729/30 by James Claypoole, attorney of Robert Clendening and Alice, his wife.

Page 351. Power of Attorney. 11 May 1729. From Robert Clendening and Ealse, his wife, of Sussex Co., DE., to James Claypool, weaver of the same place. Authority to sell 67 acres in Angola Neck part of a larger tract called Shoulters Inheritance formerly belonging to the father of Ealse, Thomas Smith. Robert Clendenen signs. Ealse Clendenen makes her mark. Wits., Willm Donily and Robert Hill. 4 Feb 1729/30. Wm Donily proves the POA.

Page 352. Deed. 5 Feb 1729. From Baptist Newcomb, of Sussex Co., DE., to Edward Lay, of the same place. For 200 pounds 340 acres. Land is situated on the south side of the Broadkill and is bounded by land of Baptist Newcomb, by William Crage's point, by the head of Three Tree Hammock Gut, by Cold Spring Creek at the mouth of the gut, by the mouth of Link's Creek, by the mouth of Fork Gut, by the northwest fork of Fork Gut, by John Fisher's land and by the pasture Barrs on a point. Land was surveyed on 14 Mar 1728 by John Shankland. Baptist Newcomb signs. Wits., Sam'el Davis, Wm Russel, and Enoch Cummings. Ack. 5 Feb 1729/30.

Pages 352-354. Deed. 1 Nov 1729. From Zachariah Gofort, yeoman of Kent Co., DE., and Elizabeth, his wife, to Samuel Stewart, yeoman of Sussex Co., DE. For 55 pounds 224 acres. Land is situated on the northwest side of the Cypress Branch, one of the branches of the Broadkill and is bounded by the Cypress Branch above the bridge and County Road and by land (124 acres) which did belong to Thomas Carlile but now belongs to the heirs of Peter Marsh. Land where Capt Thomas Pemberton formerly lived who died possessed of this land and after his decease, it descended to his daughter, Elizabeth. Zachariah and Eliz. Goforth sign. Wits., Robert Craven and Ann Brown. Ack. 3 Feb 1729/30.

Pages 354-355. Deed 3 Feb 1729. From Samuel Stewart, yeoman of Sussex Co., DE., to Robert Cravens, yeoman of the same place. For 60 pounds 224 acres. Land is situated on the northwest side of Cypress Branch, one of the branches of the Broadkill, and is bounded by the Cypress Branch above the bridge and County Road and by 124 acres which was divided off for Thomas Carlile and Mary, his wife. Land which Capt Thomas Pemberton, dec'd, died possessed of and which descended to his heirs and by them conveyed to Samuel Stewart. Sam'el Stewart signs. Wits., Ryves Holt and Phil. Russel. Ack. 3 Feb 1729/30.

Pages 355-356. Deed. 10 Feb 1728/9. From George Clifton, house carpenter of Sumerset Co., MD., to William Samples, shipwright of Sussex Co., DE. For 24 pounds 112 acres. Land is situated on the north side of Ceder Creek and is bounded by land of John Richards and by the residue of the tract called Hart's Delight. Land is part of a larger tract of 412 acres called Hart's Delight which was conveyed to Henry Molleston who sold the tract to Thomas Clifton, dec'd, who bequeathed the 112 acres to his son, George Clifton. George Clifton appoints John May or Simon Kollock, to be his attorneys. George Clifton makes his mark. Wits., John Clifton and Elizabeth May, Jr. 4 Aug 1729. Elizabeth May proves the deed. Ack. 3 Feb 1729/30.

Pages 346-357. Deed. 4 Mar 1729. From Simon Kollock, Esqr., of Sussex Co., DE., to John Price, marriner of the same place. For 50 pounds 12 acres. Land is situated in the town of Lewes on the southeast side of Middle Street or Second Street and is bounded by a branch of Pagan Creek on the south, by Middle Street, by land of Cornelius Wiltbank, and by Third Street. Comfort Kollock relinquishes her dower rights. Simon and Comfort Kollock sign. Wits., R. Holt and Phil. Russel. Ack. 4 Mar 1729/30.

Pages 357-358. Patent. 25 Mar 1676. From Edmund Andross, Governor General under James Duke of York and Albany, etc., to Alexander Molestedy. Patent for (6?)11 acres. Land is situated on the Whorekill on Delaware Bay and is bounded by the Whorekill, by land of Abraham Clement, and a branch of Pagan Creek, and surveyed by Edmund Cantwell. E. Andros signs. Recorded by Matthias Nicolls, Sec.

Page 358. Confirmation of Patent. 19 Jun 1730. From Patrick Gordon, commissioner of Springett Penn grandson of Wm Penn and with advice and consent of Hannah Penn, widow of Wm Penn, to Henry Brook. Direction to honor letters of patent. Pa. Gordon signs. Recorded 7 Aug 1730. Jacob Kollock signs, Dep Reg.

Pages 359-360. Deed. 21 Apr 1730. From Rebecka Cornwalis, of Sussex Co., DE., sister of Elias Fisher, late of Sussex Co., DE., to Henry Fisher, chpurgain of Sussex Co., DE. For 60 pounds 30 acres. Land is situated in the town of Lewis fronting on Lewis Creek and is bounded by Lewis Creek and by Pagan Creek and a second parcel of land and marsh adjoining on Capt Baily and called The Point purchased by John Fisher, dec'd, from Nehemiah Field. Elias Fisher had given bond before his death to transfer the land to Henry Fisher. Rebekah Cornwalis signs. Wits., Simon Kollock, Anderson Parker and Josep Pemberton. Ack. 21 Apr 1730.

Pages 360-361. Deed. 2 Apr 1730. From Thomas Cade, house carpenter of Sussex Co., DE., to Abraham Potter, yeoman of the same place. For 50 pounds 169 acres. Land is situated on the northwest side of Cold Spring Branch and is bounded by land called Abraham's Lot, by Cold Spring Branch and by land of Joseph Russel. Land is part of a larger tract of 400 acres called Rotterdam which is bounded by the main branch of Marches Creek and on the mouth of a beaverdam dividing this land from the land of Henry Harmon. The 400-acres tract was granted by patent of Wm Penn on the 1st da 1st mo 1682 to Cornelius Johnson and since his death has been passed down from heir to heir and now Thomas Cade the only owner sells. Thos. Cade signs. Wits., Christop. Topham and Thomas Stockly. Ack. 4 Apr 1730.

Pages 362-363. Deed. 24 Apr 1730. From Christopher Topham, merchant late of Lewes, to Henry Breretton, yeoman of Sussex Co., DE. For 40 pounds 232 acres. Land is situated in Tuch Berries in Indian River Hundred and is bounded by Herring Branch one of the branches that proceeds out of Middle Creek on the south, by land of John Russel. Land was granted by virtue of a warrant dated 29 Sep 1718 and surveyed for Christopher Topham on 27 Apr 1719 By Robert Shankland. Christop. Topham signs. Wits., Abraham Potter and John Russel. Ack. 24 Apr 1730.

Pages 364-365. Deed of Release. 9 Dec 1729. From Nicholas Williams, yeoman of Sussex Co., DE., and Mary, his wife, to John Harmonson, yeoman of the same place. For 30 pounds 100 acres. Land is situated on the northeast side of Love's Creek in Rehobath Hundred and on the southeast side of 300 acres belonging to Harmon Harmonson which 300 acres is part of a larger tract called West Chester which did belong to John Crew and Robert Hignet and is bounded by the land called West Chester, by Love's Creek, by John Futcher's land, and by Harmon Harmonson's land. Nicholas and Mary Williams make their marks. Wits., William Orr and Jacob Kollock. Ack. 6 May 1730.

Pages 365-367. Deed. 3 May 1730. From William Woolfe, yeoman of Sussex Co., DE., to David Hazzard, yeoman of Somerset Co., MD. For 42 pounds 200 acres. Land is situated in Angola Neck at the head of Bracey's Branch and is bounded by the road(?) to St George's Chappel, by land of John Russel, by land of Woodman Stockly and by land formerly sold to Richard Holloway, dec'd. Land is part of a larger tract of 400 acres known by the name of Price which formerly belonged to Thomas Dennis and since to Robert Bracey, Sr., who conveyed to Robert Tomlinson who conveyed on 3 Mar 1696 to Mathew Stevens who conveyed on 3 Sep 1700 to Edmund Mcdaniel. Matthew Stevens obtained a judgment for debts due him from Mcdaniel on 5 obligations and the land was taken in execution by Luke Wattson, Esqr., Sheriff, who died before making the land over to Stevens. Afterward on 5 Feb 1705, Thomas Finwick, Esqr., sheriff, made the land over to Stevens, who bequeathed 200 acres of the land to Matthew and William Woolf and Matthew died before coming of age. William Woolf signs. Wits., Robert Shankland and Jacob Kollock. Ack. 6 May 1730.

Pages 367-368. Deed. 10 May 1720 (or 1730?). From Ryves Holt, attorney for John Kipshaven Johnson, Martha Johnson, and Peter Adams and Elizabeth, his wife, as by POA dated 24 Dec 1729, to Christopher Topham, merchant of Lewes. For 7 pounds 1/2 of 300 acres. Land is situated on the west side of Delaware Bay on the headline of a tract called Spooner's Hall and is bounded by the land called Spooner's Hall and by a branch. Land was granted by the Sussex Court to David Coursey whose attorney Richard Law assigned the land over to Adam Johnson on 12th da 1st mo 1687 and it was surveyed and laid out for Charles Spooner on 16th da 10th mo 1687. R. Holt signs. Wits., Peter Adams and John Russell. Ack. 10 May 1730.

Pages 368-369. Deed. 8 May 1730. From Ryves Holt, sheriff of Sussex Co., DE., to Daniel Harrison. For 20 pounds 75 acres. Land is situated at the lower side of Kings Road at the Round Pole Branch and is bounded by the Round Pole Branch, by a fork in the branch, and by Kings Road. Land belonged to Gideon Harrison who was indebted to Wm Till of the Loan Office who brought suit on 4 Nov 1729 and the land was taken in execution on 4 Dec 1729. The sheriff was directed to render the debt to Wm Till at the Court held on the 1st Tuesday in May next. The land was sold at public vendue to Daniel Harrison. R. Holt signs. Wits., Henry Fisher and Joseph Pemberton. Ack. 8 May 1730.

Pages 370-371. Deed. 3 Feb 1729. From Ryves Holt, sheriff of Sussex Co., DE., to Abraham Parsley, yeoman of the same place. For 18 pounds 85 acres. Land is situated in Sussex Co., DE., and is bounded by Long Bridge Branch, by land of the heirs of Cornelius Wiltbank, and by land of Dogood

Paynter. Land belong to Robert Cornwell and Margaret, his wife, who were indebted to Wm Till of the Loan Office. Robert and Margaret Cornwell were by order of the Court on 15 Dec 1727 to show cause on the 1st Tuesday of Feb next why the tract should not be sold for the money owed Wm Till. The land was thereafter taken in execution and sold and the sheriff was to have the money in Court on the 1st Tuesday in May next. The land was sold at public vendue to Abraham Parsley. R. Holt signs. Wm Rodeney and Wm White. 6 May 1730.

Pages 371-372. Deed. 18 Apr 1730. From Luke Davis, yeoman of Sussex Co., DE., to Henry Draper, yeoman of the same place. For 6 pounds 5 5/8 acres. Land is situated in Slaughter Neck and on the west side of 400 acres belonging to Alexander and Henry Draper and is bounded by Draper's land and surveyed on 4 Apr 1730 by Robert Shankland. Land is part of a larger tract of 255 acres belonging to Luke Davis. Luke Davis makes his mark. Wits., James Mires, Robert West and John Roades. Ack. 6 May 1730.

Pages 372-373. Deed. 18 Apr 1730. From Luke Davis, yeoman of Sussex Co., DE., to Henry Draper, yeoman of the same place. For 40 pounds 40 acres. Land is situated in Slaughter Neck and is bounded by Logghouse Branch, by Luke Davis' land, by Gabriel Henry's land, and surveyed on 4 Apr 1730. Land is part of a larger tract of 255 acres. Luke Davis makes his mark. Wits., John Roades, James Mires and Robert West. Ack. 6 May 1730.

Pages 347-375. Deed. 9 May 1730. From Jabez Maud Fisher, yeoman of Broadkill, and Sarah, his wife, to Abraham Wynkoop, gentleman of Sussex Co., DE. For 5 pounds 1/4 of 52 acres in 2 tracts. One tract of 32 acres is situated in Sussex Co., DE., and is bounded by a Kill. Land formerly belonged to Thomas Wynn who purchased 20 acres from Morrice Edward on 4 Jun(?) 1687 and 132 acres (of which the 32 acres is part) from Luke Watson on 4 Jun 1687. Thomas Wynn conveyed these 2 tracts to his wife, Elizabeth, and her 2 daughters by a former husband, Jane and Margery Maud, and his 2 daughters by a former wife, Sidney and Hannah Wynn, on 10 Aug 1687. Jabez Maud Fisher is son and heir of Margery Maud. Jabez Maud Fisher signs. Wits., Jno Clowes and S. Clowes. Ack. 9 May 1730.

Pages 375-376. Deed. 7 May 1730. From James Mires, yeoman of Sussex Co., DE., to David Smith, gentleman of the same place. For 11 pounds and 10 shillings 100 acres. Land is situated on the south side of Cedar Creek Branch and is bounded by Smith's land, by the marsh of Cedar Creek Branch, by Bellemies' land, by the head of Slaughter Branch. Land is part of a larger tract of 600 acres called Labanan granted to Luck Watson, Sr., dec'd, by patent dated 1 May 1685 by the commissioners of Wm Penn. Luck Watson, Sr., by deed dated 10th da 12th mo called Feb 1689 conveyed the land to Thomas Hazleam and John Monghan, sawyers, and Richard Rennall, planter, all of Sussex Co., DE., and Thomas Hazleum bequeathed his part to Mary Hazleum, his wife, who has since married John Mires, hatter, and John Monghan conveyed his part to John Mires on 8 Apr 1712 and sometime afterward John Mires also purchased the right of Richard Rennall. John Mires bequeathed the land to his wife, Mary, who bequeathed 100 acres of the tract to James Mires by her will dated 27th da 6th mo called Aug 1727. James Miers signs. Wits., Thomas Gorden and R. Shankland. Ack. 7 May 1730.

Pages 376-378. Deed. 6 May 1730. From George Chambers, yeoman of Sussex Co., DE., son and sole heir of Michel Chambers, dec'd, to Robert Crage, yeoman of the same place. For 2 pounds 3 shillings 246 acres. Land is situated about 2 miles to the westward of Lewes Town and is bounded by land now belonging to Abram Wiltbank, by a Beaver Dam Branch that runs into the Cold Spring Branch, by Crage's fence, by a small branch and resurveyed on 4 May 1730. Land is part of a larger tract of 500 acres called Orkney granted by patent dated 20 Mar 1684 by the commissioners of Wm Penn, Esqr., to Michel Chambers who conveyed 100 acres to Edward Crage, dec'd, on 30 Nov 1695 and also on 5 May 1702 Michel Chambers conveyed another 100 acres to Edward Crage, dec'd, and Edward Crage bequeathed the 200 acres to his son, Robert Crage, by his will dated 10 Sep 1717. Afterward Robert Crage had the 200 acres resurveyed and found the deeds of sale erroneous in the courses and distance and not containing the quantity of land therein mentioned. George Chambers makes his mark. Wits., Joseph Shankland and R. Shankland. Ack. 6 May 1730.

Pages 378-380. Deed. 9 May 1730. From John Gordon, yeoman of Sussex Co., DE., and Ruth, his wife, to Robert Smith of the Town of Lewis, gentleman. For 121 pounds 289 acres. Land is situated in Sussex Co., DE., and is bounded by a Creek on the west, by Mary Bell's land, by a line that divides this land from that of John Jacobs. Land was given by deed of release dated 1 May 1716 to Thomas Gordon by John Coe, of Kent Co., DE., and Thomas Gordon bequeathed by his will dated 10 Jan 1720 the land to his sons, Thomas and John Gordon, except 100 acres which he devised to his daughter, Mary. Land was known as Martin's Vineyard. John Gordon signs and Ruth Gordon makes her mark. Wits., David French and James Smith. Ack. 9 May 1730.

Pages 380-381. Deed. 21 Feb 1729. From Joshua Stockly, yeoman of Accomack Co., VA., to Oliver Stockly, yeoman of Sussex Co., For 37 pounds 10 shillings (not given) acres. Land is situated in Angola Neck on the north side of Braycey's Branch and is bounded by a beaverdam and by a branch. The land is part of a larger tract which formerly belonged to William Simons and John Hill and contained 600 acres as may appear by the several patents, deeds of sale, and articles of agreement between William Simons and John Hill dated 4 Apr 1716. William Simons' part was on the south side of the tract which he bequeathed to his wife, Jane Simons, who married Samuel Rowland after William Simons' decease. Samuel Rowland and Jane, his wife, gave the land by deed of gift dated 6 Aug 1725 to Joshua Stockly. Joshua Stockly signs. Wits., Thomas Gray and Willm Woodstock. Joshua Stockly appoints his brother, Benjamin Stockly, to be his lawful attorney. Joshua Stockly signs. Wits., Thomas Gray and Willm Woodstock. Ack. 6 May 1730.

Pages 381-384. Deed. 21 May 1730. From William Manlove, Esqr., of Kent Co., DE., and Daniel Clifton and Tabitha, his wife, of Dorchester Co., MD., to Abraham Wynkoop, merchant of Sussex Co., DE. For 78 pounds 365 acres. Land is situated in Cedar Creek Hundred on the south side of Mispilon Creek and is bounded by the marshes of Mispillion Creek, by land of James Brown, by land of John Rickards. Land is part of a larger tract known as Cedar Town which was formerly surveyed and laid out for William Carter who sold to William Clark who sold to James Brown who sold this part (365 acres) of the tract to Richard Manlove, dec'd. Richard Manlove at his death left one son and 2 daughters. The son died in his minority and without issue; therefore, the 2 daughters inherited the land. Elizabeth Manlove married Evan Morgan and they conveyed their rights to the land to William Manlove, Esqr.,; Tabitha Manlove married Daniel Clifton. William Manlove, Daniel Clifton and Tabitha Clifton appoint John May as their attorney. Willm Manlove signs, Daniel Clifton signs and Tabith. Clifton makes mark. Wits., Willm Selthridge and Josa. Fisher. P.S. Be it remembered that ye above sd Willm Manlove hath reserved one area of land as ye old burying place and only for the use and no other for himself and for his heirs forever. Joseph Booth, Esqr., of Kent Co., DE., deputed heir and executor of James Brown, for 10 shillings paid by Abraham Wynkoop quit claims his rights to this land and appoints John May his attorney. Joseph Booth signs. Wits., William Selthridge and Jean Pittettre. 28 May 1730. William Selthridge proves the deed. Ack. 2 Jun 1730.

Page 384. Deed of Gift. 7 Aug 1730. From William Atchison, of Lewis Town, to his kinswoman, Elizabeth Oram, of the same place. An inventory of goods and chattels of William Atchison which he has given and devised to Elizabeth Oram - some located at Mr. Hinman's and some in William Atchison's dwelling house. For love and affection these articles given to kinswoman, Elizabeth Oram. Wm Atchison signs. Wits., Jno Bywaters, Abram Hood. 22 Jan 1731.

Pages 385-386. Deed. 21 Apr 1730. From Henry Scidmore, of Sussex Co., DE., to John May, Esqr., of the same place. For 50 pounds 800 acres. Land is situated in Cedar Neck and is bounded by a corner tree standing below the bridge over Herring Branch where James Mires' mill dam now stands, by land of William Spencer that is partly now in possession of the heirs of old Henry Bowman, dec'd, called Timber Neck, by land formerly surveyed by Reed(?) Noble for Robart Hart now in the possession of Edward Stapelford, by land formerly in the possession of William Durvall. Land was taken up and patented to Henry Scidmore, dec'd, father of Henry Scidmore of this deed, and called Farmer's Delight. Henry Scidmore makes his mark. Wits., Willm Till and Henry Fisher. Henry Scidmore appoints Enoch Cummings as his attorney. Thomas Wilson's oath that he was personally acquainted with Henry Scidmore of this deed for about 40 years and that he was always the reputed son of Henry Scidmore, dec'd, who was an inhabitant of Cedar Creek Hundred for many years. Wm Till signs. Ack. 4 Aug 1730.

Pages 386-387. Deed 15 Jun 1730. From Richerd Loncome, planter, of Sussex Co., DE., to John May, Esqr., of the same place. For 30 pounds 159 acres in 2 tracts. Land is situated in Cedar Creek Neck and the 64 acres is bounded by land of Thomas Fleman and by a beaverdam and the 95 acres adjoins the 64 acres and was purchased from Art Verkirk by Richerd Loncome. Richerd Loncome appoints Simon Kollock, Esqr., or Abraham Parsley as his attorneys. Richard Loncome signs. Wits., John Callayhame and Mary Corwithen. Ack. 4 Aug 1730.

Pages 387-388. Deed 4 Nov 1730. From John Atkins, carpenter of Sussex Co., DE., to William Atkins, carpenter of the same place. For 12 pounds 60 acres. Land is situated in Angola Neck and is part of two tracts and is bounded by land of John Russell, by land of Woodman Stockly, by land of William Atkins. Land formerly belonged to William Atkins, dec'd, father of both parties. John Atkins signs. Wits., John Adams and John Russell. Ack. 10 Nov 1730.

Page 388. Earmark. 14 Oct 1731. Willm Woolf his ear mark for cattle sheep and hoggs &ct is a crop the right ear & hole in the left under bitt the left recorded this 14th day of Octobr 1731. Jacob Kollock signs.

Pages 389-390. Deed. 5 Nov 1730. From Mary McCullah, administratrix of John McCullah, yeoman dec'd of Sussex Co., DE., to Joseph Shankland, yeoman of the same place. For 50 pounds 10 shillings 130 acres. Land is situated in Angola Neck and is bounded by Love's Creek near the mouth of Woolfe Pitt Branch Gutt, by land of Joseph Cord. Land is part of a larger tract formerly owned by Alexander McCullah, father of John McCullah, and was called Woolfe Pitt Neck. Alexander McCullah died intestate leaving 2 sons and 2 daughters and the eldest son received 2 parts of his land, and the remainder was divided among the other 3 children. John McCullah, the eldest son, also died intestate leaving debts which could not be covered by his personal estate. The tract had not yet been divided amongst the children; therefore, upon petition in Court on 14 Jul 1730 an order was made that the land containing in the whole 316 acres should be divided amongst the heirs and John McCullah's part sold for the payment of his debts. Simon Kollock, Samuel Davis, John Jacobs, Esqr., Woodman Stockley and Joseph Hazzard and the sworn surveyor divided the land and the land being sold included the 4 1/2 acres John McCullah purchased from Richard Hinman. Joseph Shankland was the highest bidder. Mary McCullah makes her mark. Wits., R. Shankland and Sam'el Davis. Ack. 9 Dec 1730.

Pages 390-392. Deed. 20 Oct 1730. From William White, carpenter of Sussex Co., DE., to Frances Woolfe, carpenter of the same place. For 17 pounds 7 shillings 125 acres. Land is situated on the north side of Monties(?) Branch and another small branch both proceeding out of Long Love Branch and is bounded by land formerly owned by John Orr, dec'd, but now belongs to William Orr, by land of Richard Wesley/Westly, by the edge on the north side of a pond and valley that proceeds out of the Long Love Branch, by the fork of the Branch, by the other fork. Land was laid out and surveyed by Robert Shankland on 3 Jan 1718 and patented to William White, dec'd, father of William White of this deed, who bequeathed the land to his son, William White. Willm White signs. Wits., Tabitha Atkins and John Russell. William Atkins appoints John Atkins to be his attorney. Ack. 5 Feb 1730.

Pages 392-393. Deed. 10 Mar 1730. From Jeremiah Claypole, yeoman of Broadkill Hundred, and Sarah, his now wife, to Jacob Kollock, Esqr., of Lewis Town. For 100 pounds land that descended to Sarah from her grandfather, John Avery. Land is situated in Sussex Co., DE. Land was formerly owned by her grandfather, John Avery, dec'd, or Sarah's father, Hercules Shepherd, dec'd. Jeremiah Claypoole signs and Sarah Claypoole makes her mark. Wits., John Roades and Enoch Cummings. Ack. 10 Mar 1730.

Pages 393-394. Deed. 8 May 1730. From John Roades, Coroner, Esqr., of Sussex Co., DE., to Woodman Stockly, yeoman of the same place. For 8 pounds 110 acres. Land is situated at the head of Lawes' pond proceeding out of Bracey's Branch joining on the west side of Law's land and is bounded by land of Law and on the south side of a branch. Land previously owned by Thomas McCoske, weaver late of Sussex Co., DE., against whom Ryves Holt obtained a judgment in Court on 6 Feb 1727. Samuel Davis, then Coroner, by writ of execution, seized the land called The Glade and exposed it to sale after which for want of buyers at that time it was sold to Woodman Stockly. John Roades Coroner signs. Wits., David Smith and James Mires. Ack. 5 Feb 1730.

Pages 394-396. Deed. 20 Apr 1730. From Caleb Cirwithen and Rebecca, his wife, heirs of Preserved Coggeshall, and Rives Holt, Esqr., all of Sussex Co., DE., and administrators of Preserved Coggeshall, dec'd, to Joseph Pemberton. For 81 pounds 132 acres. Land is situated near Lewis and called the Two Little Necks and is bounded by land of John Hinman, by Alexander Molleston's land. Land is being sold to satisfy the debts of Preserved Coggeshall, dec'd, by his administrators. Caleb Cirwithen and Rebecca Cirwithin and Ryves Holt sign. Wits., Anderson Parker, Simon Kollock, Thoms. Gorden, Henry Fisher, and Wm Till. Ryves Holt one of the parties who executed the above deed signed and sealed & delivered the above deed in the presence of Henry Fisher & Wm Till. Ack. 23 Apr 1730.

Pages 396-397. Deed. 1 May 1731. From James Holland, yeoman of Sussex Co., DE., and Mary, his wife, to Robert Cale, planter of the same place. For 18 pounds and other consideration 220 acres. Land is situated in Sussex Co., DE. Land was granted by warrant to Thomas Carlile, miller, on 13 Feb 1717 and surveyed by John Shankland by order of Robert Shankland on 3 Feb 1720. Thomas and Mary Carlile by deed dated 12 Feb 1722 conveyed the land to Christopher Topham who on 3 Aug 1724 conveyed the land to William Cornwallis who on 1 Feb 1725 conveyed the land to James Holland. James and Mary Holland make their marks. Wits., John Clowes and John Bywaters. Ack. 4 May 1731.

Pages 397-398. Deed. 4 May 1731. From Charles Haynes, carpenter of Dorchester Co., MD., to Alexander Draper, merchant of Sussex Co., DE. For 45 pounds 250 acres. Land is situated in Sussex Co., DE., near a branch that proceeds from the north side of Cedar Creek and is bounded by land of William Stapleton being land on which he lives. Land formerly belonged to the estate of Henry Bowman, dec'd, and after his death, letters of administration were granted to William Clark, his principal creditor, dec'd, who sold the land on 25 Jul 1704 to Charles Haynes, physician and father to Charles Haynes of this deed. Charles Haynes appoints David Smith, Esqr., to be his attorney. Charles Haynes makes his mark. Wits., Elisabt. Conner,

James White, and Willm Carpenter. May Term 1731 the execucon of this deed was legally proved in open Court. Ack. 4 May 1731.

Pages 399-400. Deed. 5 May 1731. From Frances Woolfe, carpenter of Sussex Co., DE., to William Burton, gentleman of Somerset Co., Md. For 15 pounds 15 acres. Land is situated in White Oak Neck and is bounded by a gutt which proceeds out of Marshes Creek and by a large pond which heads up the gutt. Frances Wolf signs. Wits., Richard Burton and John Russell. Receipt for 15 pounds dated 5 May 1731. Francis Wolf signs. Wits., John Russell. Ack. 5 May 1731.

Page 400. Deed. 6 May 1731. From John Adams, cordwinder of Sussex Co., and Agnes, his wife, to John Simonton, cordwinder of the same place. For 10 pounds 1/3 of two 4-acres lots. The lots are situated in Lewis on the northeast side of the blockhouse pond and joining to and lying between Market Street (the lower part) and the head of Mulberry Street in Lewes. John Adams makes his mark and Agnes Adams signs. Wits., Jno Smith, Corn'l Edgell and Jonathan Jacobs. Ack. 6 May 1731.

Page 400. Earmark. 24 Mar 1731/2. Nick. Williams his ear mark for cattle sheep & hoggs &ct is as follows (vis) both ears swallow fork & under bitted. Recorded this 24th day of March 1731/2. per Jacob Kollock.

Page 401. Deed. 5 May 1730. From William Atchison, gentleman of Sussex Co., DE., to James Collet, saddler of the same place. For 10 pounds land 100 X 300 feet. Land is situated near Lewes and is bounded by land late belonging to Thomas Bell but now in the possession of James Collet. Land is part of a larger tract purchased by Benjamin Oram, saddler, late of Lewis town, from Philip Russel, gentleman of Lewes, and attached by William Atchison for a debt and afterwards sold at public vendue and was purchased by William Atchison. Willm Atchison signs. Wits., John Roades, R. Shankland and Rob. Smith. Ack. 5 May 1731.

Page 402. Deed of Release. 6 May 1731. From Mary Palmer, widow of Sussex Co., DE., to her brother, John Miers, mariner of Lewis Town. For 8 pounds her part of 100 acres. Land is situated on Cedar Creek Branch. Land is part of a larger tract called Lebanon bequeathed by her father, John Miers, dec'd of Lewis Town, to Mary Palmer. Mary Palmer signs. Wits., Woodman Stockley and Willm Shankland. Ack. 6 May 1731.

Pages 403-404. Deed. 25 Apr 1730. From Thomas Cade, carpenter of Sussex Co., DE., to Christopher Topham, merchant of the same place. For 20 pounds 130 acres. Land is situated on the northwest side of Coolspring

Branch and is bounded by Cool Spring Branch and by land of Arthur Johnson. Land is part of a larger tract of 300 acres called Abraham's Lott which is bounded by land of Cornalus Johnson which was granted by patent of James Claypole and Robert Turner, commissioners, to Abraham Potter in 1684 who conveyed the tract to Jacob Warrin who conveyed to John Hayns who on 2 Dec 1695 conveyed the land to Robert Cade, cordwinder dec'd, father of Thomas Cade. Robert Cade conveyed 130 acres to Thomas Cade in 1727. Thoms. Cade signs. Wits., John Russel and David Scudder. Ack. 4 May 1731.

Pages 404-405. Deed. 25 Apr 1730. From Robert Cade, cordwinder of Sussex Co., DE., to Christopher Topham, merchant of the same place. For 12 pounds 100 acres. Land is situated on the southeast side of a 300-acre tract which lies on the northwest side of Cold Spring Branch. Land is part of a larger tract of 300 acres which is bounded by land of Cornels. Johnson and called Abraham's Lott. Tract was granted by patent to Abraham Potter on 26th da 1st mo 1684 who conveyed the tract to Jacob Warrin who conveyed to John Hayns who on 2 Dec 1695 conveyed to Robert Cade, cordwinder dec'd, father of Robert Cade. Robert Cade signs. Wits., John Russel and David Scudder. Ack. 4 May 1731.

Page 406. Deed. 22 May 1731. From Christopher Topham, administrator of the estate of John Cooke, to Enoch Cummings. For 60 pounds 600 acres. Land is situated between the land formerly of Corn'l Johnson and the land where John Street formerly lived in Broadkill Hundred. John Cooke, dec'd, died possessed of this land and Christopher Topham, adm'r, sold the land because his personal estate was not sufficient to pay his debts. This was determined at a Court held on 10 May 1731 and sold at public vendue to Enoch Cummings. Christopher Topham signs. Wits., Rob. Smith and Anderson Parker. Ack. 25 May 1731.

Pages 407-408. Deed. 25 May 1731. From Enoch Cummings, Esqr., of Sussex Co., DE., to Christopher Topham, administrator of the estate of John Cook. For 100 pounds 600 acres. Land is situated between the land formerly the land of Cornelius Johnson and the land where John Street formerly lived in Broadkill Hundred. Land formerly belonged to John Cook and by order of Court held on 10 May 1731 was sold at public vendue to Enoch Cummings since John Cook's personal estate was insufficient to pay his debts. Memo: before ensealing & delivery of these presents this agreed by & between the parties within menconed that ye above named Enoch Cummings is not to be precluded any intrest in the above tract of land that he may have by haveing entered ye same in ye surveyors office as wheat land any thing in this deed anywise to ye contrary notwithstanding. Enoch

Cummings signs. Wits., Jacob Kollock and Andr. Parker. Ack. 25 May 1731.

Pages 408-409. Deed. 3 Aug 1731. From Phillip Russell, gentleman of Lewis Town, to James Collet, sadler of the same place. For 13 pounds 1 acres and 130 sq perches. Land is situated in Lewes Town and is bounded by land of Nathaniel Hall, by the road, a division line now or late of Benjamin Oram, by a public street of Lewes, and containing 6 2/3 lots. Phil. Russel signs. Wits., Thomas Gordon and Robert Turk. Ack. 3 Aug 1731.

Pages 409-410. Deed. 2 Aug 1731. From Woodman Stockly, yeoman of Sussex Co., DE., to Ann Sanders, widow of John Sanders, dec'd, of the same place. For 20 pounds 173 acres. Land is situated at the head of Long Love Branch and is bounded by land of Harrison, by land of James Fisher now William Pettijon, by land of Derval, on the north side of Bracy's Branch, by land of Ephram Darby and including the dwelling house formerly of Richard Law. Land is part of a larger tract of 550 acres which was granted by patent to Richard Law dated 24 Mar 1681 and is situated on the head of Bracey's Branch one of the branches of Middle Creek that runs into Rehobeth Bay and was surveyed by James Greenwood on 25 Nov 1708. Richard Law sold the tract to Jacob Kollock of Lewes, merchant, dec'd, who bequeathed by his will dated 13 Dec 1724 the land to his 7 children, Simon, Hannah, Jacob, Jane, Magdelon, Hester, and Cornelius. Mary Kollock, widow of Jacob, dec'd, Simon Kollock, Esqr., Hannah Wiltbank, widow, Jacob Kollock, Gent., and Jean Irons, and Jacob Phillips and his wife, Hester, heirs of Jacob Kollock, dec'd, sold the tract to Woodman Stockly on 30 Jan 1724. Woodman Stockley signs. Wits., Enoch Cummings and R. Shankland. Ack. 3 Aug 1731.

Pages 410.412. Deed. 2 Aug 1731. From Woodman Stockly, yeoman of Sussex Co., DE., to Ephraim Darby, carpenter of the same place. For 10 pounds 115 acres. Land is situated on the head of Bracey's Branch one of the branches of Middle Creek that runs into Rehobeth Bay and is bounded by land of Ann Sanders, by Bracey's Branch. Land is part of a larger tract of 550 acres which was granted by warrant dated 24th da 12th mo 1681 to Richard Law and was surveyed by Jonas Greenwood on 5 Nov 1708. Richard Law conveyed the tract to Jacob Kollock of Lewes who bequeathed the tract to his 7 children, Simon, Hanah, Jacob, Jane, Magdalin, Hesther and Cornelius, in his will dated 13 Dec 1720. Mary Kollock, widow of Jacob Kollock, dec'd, Simon Kollock, Esqr., Hanah Wiltbank, widow, Jacob Kollock, Gent., Jane Irons, and Jacob Phillips, Gent., and Hesther, his wife, heirs of Jacob Kollock, dec'd, on 13 Jan 1724 conveyed the tract to

Woodman Stockly. Woodman Stockly signs. Wits., Enoch Cummings and R. Shankland. Ack. 3 Aug 1731.

Pages 412-413. Deed. 3 Aug 1731. From Christopher Topham, merchant of Lewes, to John Lullham, yeoman of Broadkill Hundred. For 12 pounds 150 acres. Land is situated in Sussex Co., DE., and is bounded by Spooner's Hall. Land is part of a larger tract of 300 acres. Christr. Topham signs. Wits., John Shankland, Jas White and Richd Willson. Ack. 3 Aug 1731.

Pages 413-414. Deed. 4 Aug 1731. From Jacob Pride, Anne Middleton (alias Pride), and Esther Pride, heirs of Jacob Pride, yeoman of Sussex Co., DE., dec'd, to Francis Donovon, yeoman of the same place. For 50 pounds 200 acres. Land is situated on the northwest side of Mill Creek and is bounded by land of Richard Dobson, near Mill Creek. Land is part of a larger tract granted by patent to Christopher Sanders. Anne Middleton makes her mark; Esther Pride makes her mark; and Jacob Pride makes his mark. Wits., Enoch Cummings, John Russell, Jabes Maud Fisher and Thoms. Parker. Ack. 3 Aug 1731.

Pages 414-416. Deed. 2 Aug 1731. From Walter Reed, yeoman of Sussex Co., DE., to Richard Killum, yeoman of the same place. For 75 pounds 432 acres in 2 tracts. The first tract is situated on the northwest side of Long Bridge Branch is bounded by land of Davock, by Long Bridge Branch and contains 217 acres. This tract was granted by warrant dated 15th da 1st mo 1714 and surveyed to Walter Reed. The second tract adjoins the first tract and is bounded by Long Bridge Branch and contains 215 acres. This tract was granted by warrant to William Stewart on 15th da 4th mo 1718 who assigned the warrant to Walter Reed. Walter Reed makes his mark. Wits., Thos. Stockley and Phil. Russel. Cisely Reed, wife of Walter Reed, relinquishes her dower rights. Cisely Reed makes her mark. Ack. 3 Aug 1731.

Pages 416-417. Deed. 16 Aug 1731. From Nathaniel Hall, of Sussex Co., DE., to Hannah Addams, Mary Addams, John Addams, and Peter Addams, children of Jno Addams, cordwayner of the same place. For 24 pounds 90 1/3 sq perches. Land is situated near the town of Lewes and is bounded by land of Jno Addams, by land of Nathaniel Hall, by a small ditch. Nathaniel Hall signs. Wits., 17 Aug 1731.

Pages 417-418. Deed. 31 Oct 1731. From Robert Smith and Mary, his wife, of Kent Co., DE., to Sarah Clendenel, widow of Sussex Co., DE. For 25 pounds 100 acres. Land is situated in Ceder Creek Neck and is bounded by land of Robert Hart near the field of the plantation now in the possession of Mary Hall. Land is part of a larger tract which part Robert Hart bequeathed to his daughter, Margaret, and Margaret married Mark Manlove and they conveyed the 100 acres to Samuel Webster, who died intestate leaving one daughter, Mary, who married Robert Smith. Robert and Mary Smith appoint Simon Kollock to be their attorney. Robt Smith and Mary Smith make their marks. Wits., John May and Elizabeth May. John May proves the deed on 3 Nov 1731. Ack. 3 Nov 1731.

Page 419. Deed of Release. 14 Dec 1731. From Ralph Tindall, yeoman of Sussex Co., DE., and Honor, his wife, to John Harmonson and William Stockley, yeomen of the same place. For (consideration not given) 900 acres. Land is situated in Rehoboth Hundred and formerly granted by patent to John Crew and Robert Hignott. Ralph Tindall signs and Honor Tindall makes her mark. Wits., David Scudder and Phil. Russel. Ack. 14 Dec 1731.

Page 420. Deed of Gift. 16 Dec 1731. From Anderson Parker and Sarah, his wife, late wife of Robert Prittyman, cordwainer dec'd of Sussex Co., DE., to Sarah's son, Robert Prittyman. For love and affection 300 acres. Land is situated on the bay side of Ivey Branch one of the branches of Middle Creek that runs into Rehoboth Bay in Indian River Hundred and is bounded by Ivey Branch and surveyed and divided on 12 May 1730 by Robert Shankland. Land is part of a larger tract of 1117 acres belonging to Robert Burton, dec'd, father of Sarah, of whom Sarah was joint executrix. Anderson Parker signs and Sarah Parker makes her mark. Wits., Willm Burton and John Welbore. Ack. 16 Dec 1731.

Pages 421-422. Deed. 31 Jan 1731. From Cornelius Wiltbank, gentleman of Sussex Co., DE., to John Jones, of the same place. For 20 pounds 137 acres. Land is situated on the north side of Broad Kill Creek that runs into Delaware Bay and is bounded by the mouth of a small branch, by the north bank of Broad Kill Creek, by land that did belong to Bryent Roles, by land of John Harrison (his part of this tract). Land is part of a larger tract of 469 acres which was granted by warrant and surveyed on 3 Mar 1681 to Halmanus Wiltbank, dec'd, by Cornelius Verhoofe, surveyor. Later the land was confirmed by patent of Wm Penn to Halmanus Wiltbank for 469 acres called Hopewell on 1 Mar 1684. Halmanus Wiltbank died intestate leaving 3 sons, Cornelius, Abraham and Isaac, to whom the land descended. Cornelius Wiltbank received 2 shares as the eldest son, and the remainder divided between Abraham and Isaac. Isaac Wiltbank received 120 acres and died intestate leaving 3 sons, Samuell, Isaac and Cornelious, to whom the land descended and Isaac and Samuel died in their minority and without issue. Cornelius Wiltbank became the owner of the whole 120 acres and thereafter Cornelius Wiltbank along with other persons concerned that purchased part of the tract requested Robert Shankland to resurvey the tract according to the ancient boundary of the same adjoining upon the neighboring land on 23 Apr 1731 and by resurvey the tract contained 515 acres. Cornelius Wiltbank now owns 137 acres. Cornelius Wiltbank signs. Wits., Anderson Parker and R. Shankland. Ack. 2 Feb 1731.

Pages 422-423. Deed. 6 Aug 1731. From Thomas Gordon, yeoman of Sussex Co., DE., to William Cale, yeoman of the same place. For 14 pounds 17 shillings 35 acres. Land is situated in Rehobah Hundred and is bounded by land of Thomas Cale, the head of one of the forks of a branch, by both forks, by land called Martin's Vineyard. Land is part of a larger tract called South Hampton. Thomas Gordon signs. Wits., Simon Kollock and Richd Willson. Memorandum: Thomas Gordon agrees to pay all rents due on the land to 19 Aug 1724 according to a bond given to Thomas Cale on that date. Memorandum: On 2 Feb 1731 Catherine Gordon, wife of Thomas Gordon, relinquishes her dower rights. Catherine Gordon signs. Wits., Simon Kollock and Richd Wilson. Ack 1 Feb 1731.

Pages 424-425. Deed 2 Jan 1731. From Alexander Molleston, yeoman of Sussex Co., DE., to Capt Nathaniel Hall, marriner of the same place. For 100 pounds 100 acres. Land is situated on the southwest side of Lewis Creek and on the southeast of Lewes Town and is bounded by land of Turner, by land of John Shankland, by land of Archibald Smith, by land of Simon Kollock. Land was originally granted by patent of Edmund Andros on 25 Mar 1676 and was surveyed by Edmund Cantwill to Alexander Molleston, father of Alexander Molleston of this deed. Alexander Molleston, the elder, mortgaged the land to Jacob Kollock for a certain debt then afterward by deed of gift he gave the tract to his son, Alexander Molleston, on 8 Jan 1703 upon the condition that Alexander Molleston, the younger, redeem the tract by paying the mortgage. Alexander Molleston, Jr., has since paid the mortgage. Land is part of a larger tract which was divided and surveyed by Robert Shankland on 28 Mar 1730. Allexander Moleston signs. Wits., Josep. Shankland and Robt. Shankland. Ack. 4 Feb 1731.

Pages 425-427. Deed. 21 Feb 1731. From Roberson Lingoe, yeoman of Sussex Co., DE., and Anne, his wife, to Joseph Hazzard, yeoman of the same place. For 14 pounds 50 acres. Land is situated in Angola Neck near the southwest side of Loves Creek that runs into Rehoboth Bay and is bounded by land of Meggs called Rageltons, by a branch, and is the first division made on 15 Aug 1729 by Robert Shankland. Land is part of a larger tract which is bounded on the southwest side with Bracey's Branch and surveyed by Cornelious Verhoof in 1681 for 255 acres of land and was afterwards conveyed to Thomas Smith, dec'd, father of Anne, who bequeathed the land to his son, Thomas and 4 daughters. After the death of the son, Thomas, 2 of the daughters married to Robert Clandanel and William Conwell. Robert Clandanel in behalf of his wife, Alee Smith, petitioned the Court on 15 Mar 1728 for a division of the land among the 4 sisters. This division made to Anne, the younger daughter, wife of Roberson Lingoe. Robinson and Anne Lingoe make their marks. Wits., Woodman Stockley and John Russell. Memorandum: 22 Feb 1731 Woodman Stockley proves the deed. Ack. 22 Feb 1731.

Pages 427-428. Deed. 1 Feb 1731. From Abraham Wynkoop, Esqr., of Sussex Co., DE., and Hesther, his wife, to James Miers, yeoman of the same place. For 53 pounds 12 shillings 6 pence 19 1/2 acres. Land is situated in Lewes and is bounded by 13 acres which Jane Wiltbank bequeathed to Hesther, by Lewes Creek which divides this land from the 13 acres. Land is part of a larger tract belonging to Thomas Fisher, dec'd, which he bequeathed by his will dated 17 Nov 1713 to his daughter, Hesther. Abraham and Hesther Wynkoop appoint Simon Kollock to be their attorney. Abrahm. Wynkoop and Esther Wynkoop sign. Wits., John May and John Wynkoop. Esther Wynkoop relinquishes her dower rights. Ack. 1 Feb 1731.

Pages 428-429. Deed of Release. 4 Feb 1731. From Abraham Wynkoop, Esqr., of Sussex Co., DE., to James Miers, yeoman of the same place. For (no consideration given 13 acres. Land is situated in Lewes and is bounded by the Creek and is land which Abraham Wynkoop purchased from Jabez Fisher on 9 May 1730. Abrahm. Wynkoop signs. Wits., Thomas Gordon and Michael Gray. Ack. 4 Feb 1731.

Pages 429-430. Deed of Release. 3 Feb 1731/2. From Jabez Maud Fisher, yeoman, and Joshua Fisher, hatmaker, both of Sussex Co., DE., to James Miers, hatmaker, of the same place. For 40 pounds 350 acres. Land is situated on Herring Branch which proceeds out Mispillion Creek. Land is part of a larger tract of 2000 acres called Mill Range and was given by the last will and testament of Elizabeth Eyre, dec'd, to her brothers and sisters, Margret, Margery, Jabez, Joshua and James Fisher. Jabez Maud and Joshua Fisher sign. Wits., John Miers, Frances Cornwall, and Vertue Stauton. Ack. 3 Feb 1731.

Pages 430-432. Assignment of Patent. 26 Mar 1684. From Richard Patty to Baptis Nucomb. Land is situated on the west side of Delaware Bay between the Broad Creek and Marshes Creek near adjacent and is bounded by land formerly surveyed for Helmanious Wiltbanck, by land of Richard (surname not given), by Marshes Branch, by land of Henry Harmon. Land was granted by Sussex Court on the 19th da 1st mo called March 1685/6 to

Cornelious Johnson and since conveyed by the Court to Richard Peaty and surveyed on 7th da 7th mo 1682 to Richard Peaty who requested to confirm the land by patent. Wm Penn signs. Richard Patty did in a Court held on 8th, 9th, 10th, 11th days of the 12th month 1686 acknowledge the sale of the land to Baptist Newcome. Recorded on 24 Apr 1733. Jacob Kollock.

Pages 431-440. Appears to be audit records of the Loan Office (William Till) and receipts from the Committee, basically composed of Richard Hinman, Jacob Kollock, and John Roades. At the bottom of these pages if not completely full of audit records are other deed records, etc.

Page 435. Promissory Note. 17 Sep 1732. I promis to pay or cause to bee paid to Riece Merideth on order for vellew rec'd the sum of fifty nine pounds twelve shillings & tenn pence in manner following Twenty nine pounds sixteen shillings & fore pence in good and marchandable porke each barell fourty six shillings per bb: To hold thirty one gallons and to be delivered at Mrs. Ann Burtons on Indian river to be delivered by the tenth of Januy. The remainding sum being twenty nine pounds sixteen shillings & fore pence to be deliver'd in Long Black Tobacco suitable for Philadelphia marker at 14/ per hundred to be delivered on demand at the said above Mrs. Burton's. Riece Meridith pay half frait over the river as witness my hand. Aaron Lyen. Wits., Christopher Topham. Sep 17, 1732.

Page 441. Survey. 4 Mar 1685. By virtue of a warrant from the Court of Kent County bearing date ye (blank) day of ye (blank) month 168(blank) for marsh land to me directed by Willm Clarke chiefe survayor of Sussex & Kent. Land is situated on the west side of Delaware Bay in Sussex Co. and is bounded by a gut of a beaverdam, by Sedercreek, by land of Mager Spenser, by land of Robert Hart called Hart's Range. J. Barkstead deputy surveyor signs.

Page 441. Resurvey. 4 Mar 1685. Resurvey for Robert Harte for two tracts into one. One tract of 400 acres formerly laid out for Jeames Louton by Capt John Avery and left by will of Jeames Louton to Robert Hart, dec'd, father of Robert Hart. The other tract contains 500 acres and was laid out for Robert Hart for which Robert Hart holds the patent dated 29th da 10th mo 1677 from Edmund Andros and known by the name of Hart's Range. The tracts are situated on the north side of Sedercreek and are bounded by a branch of the beaverdam. The two tracts contained 900 acres. J. Barkstead dep surveyor signs.

Pages 441-442. Deed. 2 Aug 1715. From Francis Bagwell, yeoman of Sussex Co., DE., to Robert Burton, Sr., yeoman of the same place. For 60 pounds 340 acres. Land is situated on the north side of Indian River and is bounded by Rehoboth Bay, by land of William Bagwell, and surveyed by Jonas Greenwood. Francis Bagwell signs. Wits., Soloman West, Robt. West and Phil. Russel. Ack. 2 Aug (1715?).

Page 443. Deed. 18 Aug 1732. From Richard Poultney, of Sussex Co., DE., to Simon Edghill, merchant of Philadelphia. For 25 pounds 2 shillings sundry household item and other item as per a schedule. Schedule of items is included. Richard Poltny signs. Wits., Joseph Pemberton and Joseph Carter. Recorded 21 Aug 1732. Jacob Kollock signs.

Page 444. Bond. 7 May 1713. From John Coe, yeoman of Rehobah, to Thomas Gordon, yeoman of Sumerset Co., MD. John Coe is bound in the sum of 700 pounds to convey 700 acres. Land is situated in Rehobah and is part of 2 tracts, one named Martin's Vineyard and the other named South Hampton. John Coe is bound to convey the land after 10 Oct 1714 or at the reasonable request of Thomas Gordon. John Coe signs. Wits., Nehemiah Field, Phillip Russell, and Phillip Russel, Jr. Phillip Russell, the last named witness, proved the bond.

Page 445. Receipt &ct. 12 Feb 1728/9. My love I having this oppertunty I thought fitt to acquatt you that we goot safe of Elsonbory and rem'd my love to your son & my kind love to your self I desire you to deliver to ye berer Mr. Verkirt the goods that you goot in hour house of Capt Jacob Phillips leaft in your caire per James Forster. Mr. Verkirt he to pay you the chearges and storige sapauny Febr ye 13th 1728/9. Then recaved of Ranier Vankirt the sume of ten pounds currant money of America for goods left at James Forsters which ten pounds sd money is in full satisfaction as witness my hand. Henry Lueton. A list of household and other items is given. 24 Apr 1729. Then receved of Ranier Vankirt the sume of two pounds in full satisfaction for storeg'gdg for the goods left by Fillips orders per me Margret Foster. Personally apeared before me one of his majesties justices the within named Ranier Vankirt and being sollemenly sworn on the holy Evangilist of Almighty God saith that the within order hereunto annext given by James Foster to his wife was given by order of Henry Lueton and the severel charges & other things mentioned in the margent of the within recept for ten pounds were bought and ordered to be delivered to this deponont at the time of ye drawing the order & recept were the goods belonging to the within Henry Lueton which ware left in the hands of James Foster by order of Capt Jacob Phillips and after the sd Henry Lueton had sold the sd goods above mentioned he the sd Lueton told this deponent that he had Jacob Phillips recept for them and he would trobell him for them in the Island of Barbadus when he arrived there and further this deponent saith not. Octbr ye 6th 1731.

Ranier Verkirt signs. Sworn before me Jacob Kollock. Record: the 5th day of Feb 1731.

Page 445. Receipt. 4 Sep 1731. The division of monies received from the sale of a sloop apparently divided between Elizabeth Elisa Dyer and William Conwell and witnessed by Wm Wessell and Peter Egberts. Recorded 9 Mar 1731/2 by Jacob Kollock.

Page 446. Deed. 18 Dec 1731. From John Shankland, of Sussex Co., DE., to Mr. Brook, Esqr., of the same place. For the service of an indentured servant, John Welch. As per orders from Mr. George Brownell of New York but late of Philadelphia for John Shankland to hire John Welch, an indentured servant of Mr. Brownell's; however, Mr. John Shankland had not sufficient employment for him. Term of employment/indenture is three years. John Shankland signs. Wits., Henry Fisher and Rs. Holt. Recorded this 5th day of Januy 1731. Jacob Kollock. Nathaniel Hall of this County, marriner, having heard the contents of the letter in this book recorded in page 447 saith he knoweth ye same to be a true copy of one delivered to him at New York by Mr. Geo. Brownell dancing master there, directed to Mr. John Shankland of Lewis in the County above written. Nathaniel Hall signs. Sworn before me one of his majesties justices for the County afsd this 5th day of January 1731. Jacob Kollock.

Page 446. Receipt. 26 Feb 1731. Receipt Nick Loockerman to Cornwallas. Reseved of William Cornwallas the sum of nine pounds being in full of all accounts to this thirtenth day of August 1726. per me Nick. Loockerman. Recorded 26th of Februy 1731 per Jacob Kollock.

Page 447. Letter. No date. A letter from Mr. Brownell to Mr. Shankland concerning an indentured servant named John Welch which Mr. Brownell obtained from Mr. Allen. Letter makes reference to "your father Capt Hall".

INDEX OF NAMES

—A—

Abigail, 16, 44
Adams: Agnes, 39, 57, 69, 73, 97; Elizabeth, 90; John, 39, 57, 69, 73, 83, 94, 97; John J., 57; Peter, 90
Addams: Agnes, 57; Hannah, 100; Jno, 100; John, 100; Margret, 60; Mary, 100; Peter, 100
Allan: John, 79
Allen: Francis, 79; John, 28, 45, 53, 57, 79, 83; Mr., 106; Willm, 72
Allison: Patrick, 68, 75
Anderson: Lawrence, 78
Andrew, 44
Andrews: Edmond, 65
Andros: E., 88; Edmund, 102, 104
Andross: E., 42; Edmond, 5, 15, 18, 21, 23, 34, 50, 52, 63, 69; Edmund, 71, 88; Governor, 16
Annis, 81
Arey: William, 25, 26, 45, 46, 52
Askew: James, 42; Sarah, 42
Askie: Philip, 39; Phillip, 49
Atchison: William, 81, 85, 93, 97; Willm, 97; Wm, 94
Atkins: Ann, 65, 67, 83; Elizabeth, 15, 16, 18; Isaac, 1, 2, 78, 83; John, 1, 2, 18, 44, 71, 78, 82, 83, 85, 94, 95; Joseph, 15, 16, 18; Tabitha, 67, 80, 83, 95; William, 1, 2, 18, 80, 83, 94; Willm, 83, 95
Attkins: Elizabeth, 80; Isaac, 80; John, 11, 80; Mattilda, 80; Tabitha, 65, 80; William, 80; Willm, 65, 67, 80
Attkinson: Mary, 47
Avery: Elizabeth, 5; Jemima, 5; John, 5, 95; John, Capt, 104; John,Capt, 58; Mary, 5; Sarah, 5
Ayleff: Mr., 18
Aylif: Joseph, 50

—B—

Bagwell: Agnes, 57; Frances, 73; Francis, 33, 39, 49, 69, 104, 105; Mr., 39; Thomas, 33, 87; William, 33, 39, 57, 69, 73, 105
Bailey: Jonathan, 7, 67; Jonathan,Capt, 14
Bailly: Jonathan, 47
Baily: Capt, 89; James, 28; Jonathan, 45, 47, 57, 74, 83; Jonathan,Capt, 40; Jonathan,Capt,Esqr., 28; Nathaniel, 38, 39
Baly: Jonathan, 62
Barker: Ann, 80, 81; Job, 49, 58, 59, 70; John, 42, 50
Barkstead: J., 104; John, 76
Barnwill: Mr., 57
Barr: John, 9, 11
Barren: John, 49
Barsted: Joshua, 29
Bate: Thomas, 17
Bawler: Joshua, 54; Josuah, 51; Mary, 51
Becket: Mary, 81; William, 2, 24, 26, 27, 61, 86; William,Rev. Mr., 14; Willm, 81; Wm, 18, 27, 41, 44, 61, 86
Beckett: Jonath., 85
Bedwell: Honor, 7, 8, 9, 13, 37, 43, 63, 73; Thomas, 8, 12, 13,

32, 33, 37, 43, 63, 73; Thos., 73
Belcher: Joseph, 78
Bell: Mary, 92; Thomas, 81, 97
Bellamy: John, 3; William, 16
Bellemie: Mr., 91
Bendbrick: Edward, 18
Bennet: John, 39, 60
Bennett: John, 39; John,Jr., 39; John,Sr., 39
Berry: Samuel, 83
Besant: Thomas, 17
Bicknell: John, 71
Birch: Adam, 64
Blundall: Sarah, 8, 9
Bodall: Margt, 24
Booth: Francis, 65; Jos, 53; Joseph, 43, 52, 53, 54, 65, 71, 93; Joseph,Jr., 65, 67
Bowman: Elizabeth, 10; Henry, 10, 27, 42, 46, 57, 59, 83, 86, 94, 96; John, 10, 18, 50, 59; Mary, 10; Mr., 46; Patience, 18, 51
Bracey: Elizabeth, 19; Mary, 19; Richard, 25; Robert, 19, 22, 87; Robert, Sr., 90; Robert,Jr., 19; Robert,Sr., 19
Bracy: Annabella, 69; Richard, 3, 4, 50, 69; Robert,Jr., 50; Robert,Sr., 18
Branscomb: Thomas, 16
Brereton: Henry, 80, 81
Breretton: Henry, 89
Bright: Charles, 45, 46, 52
Brockden: Cha., 73
Brook: Hen., 66, 83; Henry, 66, 88; Mr., 106
Brooke: Hen., 2, 15, 16
Brooks: Henry, 62
Brown: Ann, 87; Daniel, 5, 9, 10, 36, 67; Elizabeth, 5, 6, 9, 10, 36; James, 62, 71, 93

Brownell: Geo., 106; George, 106; Mr., 106
Brush: Thomas, 14
Bryan: Denis, 31
Bucher: Agnes, 79; Mary, 79; Robart, 79; Willm, 79
Bullock: Sam'l, 66; Samuel, 66
Bundick: Mr., 83; Richard, 51, 52
Bundock: Richard, 2, 18, 31, 41
Burroughs: Edward, 71
Burton: Ann, Mrs., 104; Benjamin, 69; Comfort, 56, 69, 73; Jacob, 17, 47, 59; Jno, 69; John, 69; Joseph, 49; Mr., 74; Mrs., 104; Richard, 97; Robert, 3, 10, 11, 29, 56, 62, 101; Robert, Sr., 1, 2, 3, 104; Sarah, 101; William, 33, 48, 60, 77, 97; Willm, 101; Woolsey, 39, 47, 57, 67, 69, 73, 75, 78, 81
Bushop: George, 31
Butcher: Robert, 10
Bywater: John, 28
Bywaters: Jno, 94; John, 81, 96

—C—

Cade: Charles, 47, 63; Matilda, 82, 83; Robert, 44, 47, 51, 54, 62, 63, 82, 83, 98; Thomas, 19, 22, 61, 62, 89, 97, 98; Thoms., 98; Thos., 89
Cadwalader: Jno, 2; John, 2
Cale: Robert, 96; Thomas, 102; Thomas,Jr., 23; William, 102
Callayhame: John, 94
Camel: James, 63
Cantwell: Edmond, 40; Edmund, 88; Mary, 65, 66; Richard, 38
Cantwill: Edmund, 102
Carey: Edward, 58; John, 82
Carie: John, 81

Carlile: Mary, 5, 6, 9, 20, 62, 88, 96; Thomas, 5, 6, 9, 11, 20, 62, 87, 88, 96
Carlisle: Thomas, 20
Carpenter: James, 18, 27, 37, 83; Joseph, 9, 19, 78; Willm, 97
Carter: Joseph, 105; William, 40, 71, 82, 93
Cary: Bridget, 19; Jno, 59; John, 3, 18, 19, 37, 49, 70, 74
Chambers: George, 92; Janet, 81, 82; John, 4, 39, 40, 81, 82; Michel, 70, 92
Chancellor: William, 2
Chapman: John, 60
Chipman: Peris, 45
Cirwithen: Caleb, 96; Rebecca, 96
Cirwithin: Rebecca, 96
Clandanel: Robert, 103
Clandening: Mr., 29
Clark, 73; Honor, 12, 21; Mr., 25; Rebecca, 78; William, 2, 4, 6, 7, 8, 10, 11, 13, 15, 19, 21, 22, 24, 27, 29, 32, 33, 37, 40, 41, 43, 48, 49, 61, 62, 63, 70, 71, 73, 76, 82, 93, 96; William, Jr., 78; Wm, 72, 86
Clarke: Willm, 104
Classen: William, 33
Claypole: James, 98; Jeremiah, 83, 95; Sarah, 95
Claypool: James, 87
Claypoole: George, 31, 45; James, 1, 7, 8, 11, 31, 33, 43, 47, 62, 67, 73, 75, 86, 87; Jean, 67; Jeremiah, 31, 44, 45, 79, 95; Joseph, 31, 33, 45; Norton, 31, 33; Sarah, 95
Clement: Abraham, 88
Clendenel: Sarah, 100
Clendenen: Ealse, 87; Robert, 87
Clendening: Alice, 87; Ealse, 87; Robert, 87

Clifton: Daniel, 93; George, 88; John, 88; Robert, 16, 28, 76, 78; Sarah, 66; Tabitha, 93; Thomas, 78, 88; Thos, 78; Widow, 66
Clowes: Jno, 91; John, 78, 96; S., 91
Codd: Berckley, 3, 41, 51; Berkley, 15, 16; Mary, 15, 41, 81; St. Ledger,Mr., 41
Coe: John, 23, 40, 92, 105
Coggeshall: Preserved, 3, 8, 9, 15, 16, 17, 22, 24, 96
Cokayn: Tho., 87
Cokayne: Eliz., 84; Tho., 84
Coleman: Wm, 72
Colleman: John, 52
Collet: James, 97, 99; Symon, 45
Conner: Elizabt., 96
Conwell: Francis, 25; William, 103, 106
Conwill: Elias, 44, 66; Hannah, 44, 66; John, 44, 63, 64, 66; Rebecca, 41; William, 44, 87; Yeates, 41, 66
Cook: John, 98; Mary, 45
Cooke: Edward, 71; Francis, 31; John, 98; Mary, 31
Cooper: Mary, 67; Richard, 67
Copes: William, 74, 81; Wm, 82
Corbett: Roger, 6, 40
Cord: Anne, 29; Joseph, 3, 12, 29, 95
Cornwalis: Rebecka, 89; Rebekah, 89
Cornwall: Frances, 103; Francis, 11, 22, 29, 70, 71, 74, 77; Robt., 74
Cornwallas: Mr., 106; William, 106
Cornwallis: Rebecca, 63, 64, 66; Rebekah, 66; William, 20, 44, 45, 63, 64, 66, 96; Wm, 64, 66

Cornwell: Francis, 70, 71, 81, 82, 85; Margaret, 91; Robert, 49, 91
Corwithen: Mary, 94
Coulter: Charles, 59; Elener, 45; James, 59; John, 45, 46; William, 45, 59
Coursey: David, 5, 90
Cowdry: Benjamin, 52, 65; Joshua, 53; Josuah, 51
Cowthery: Joshua, 53; William, 53
Crage: Edward, 6, 37, 92; Robert, 92; William, 87
Crague: Edward, 4; Mr., 11
Craige: Robert, 52; William, 1
Crammer: Thomas, 24; William, 24
Craven: Robert, 87
Cravens: Robert, 88
Crawley: John, 38
Creig: Robert, 77
Crew: John, 15, 69, 74, 79, 84, 89, 101
Crige: Willm, 37
Crowell: Samuel, 32; Yelwerton, 32
Cudgio, 81
Cummings: E., 68; Enoch, 2, 22, 43, 44, 46, 58, 61, 62, 87, 94, 95, 98, 99, 100; Hannah, 2, 43

—D—

Darby: Ephraim, 64, 99; Ephram, 99
Darter: Margaret, 12; Mr., 12; William, 12, 20, 21, 45; Wm, 12, 21
Darval: Mr., 25, 57; William, 14
Darvall: Mr., 36; William, 23, 24, 46
Davis: Elizabeth, 57; Katherine, 6, 46; Luke, 91; Mr., 39, 82; Naomy, 8; Richard, 56, 58; Robert, 27, 28, 46; Sam, 38; Sam'el, 87, 95; Sam'l, 68, 72; Samuel, 2, 4, 14, 16, 34, 35, 39, 53, 95, 96; Samuel,Jr., 4; Samuel,Sr, 4; Thomas, 39, 46, 57, 58; Thomas,Jr., 46
Davock: Mr., 100; Thomas, 4, 21, 23, 86
Delany: Patrick, 32, 76
Dennis: Thomas, 90
Depree: Andrew, 15
Deprey: Andrew, 35; John, 35; John,Jr., 35; John,Sr., 35; Mary, 35
Derval: Mr., 99
Dewess: Lewes, 2
Dial: Eleanor, 78; Elizabeth, 78; Jean, 78; Jno, 78; Mary, 78
Dickason: Samuel, 30
Dickeson: Samuel, 80, 84
Dickinson: Samuel, 68
Dickson: John, 67
Dier: William, 63, 64
Dingee: Charles, 12
Dirnie: Philip, 60
Dixon: Henry, 41, 52; Ruth, 41, 53
Dobson: Elenor, 67; Richard, 28, 40, 44, 57, 67, 100
Dod: Joseph, 10, 25; Thomas, 10, 25, 26
Dodd: George, 52; Joseph, 56
Donalson: John, 78
Donily: Willm, 87; Wm, 87
Donley: William, 62
Donovan: John, 85
Donovon: Francis, 100
Dowling: Samuel, 51
Draper: Alexander, 7, 14, 15, 23, 24, 30, 46, 56, 58, 68, 76, 85, 91, 96; Ann, 47; Henry, 4, 5,

58, 77, 91; John, 57, 60; Sarah, 5
Duke of York and Albany: James, 88
Dunavan: Elizabeth, 38; Francis, 38, 58; Timothy, 12
Dunnavan: Elizabeth, 38; Francis, 38; Timothy, 13
Dupree: John, 5
Durvall: William, 94
Dyall: Eleanor, 44; Elizabeth, 44; Jean, 44; John, 44, 85; Mary, 44
Dyar: John, 70
Dyer: Elizabeth Elisa, 106; Mary, 82; William, 28, 64, 82; William, Major, 82
Dyre: James, 55; Mary, 40, 66; William, 4, 7, 40, 41, 49, 66; William,Major, 7, 40, 55, 66

—E—

Edgell: Corn'l, 97; Cornelius, 79; Cors., 78
Edghill: Simon, 105
Edmunds: Jno, 71
Edward: Morrice, 91
Edwards: Morris, 72
Egberts: Peter, 106
Eldridge: Josep, 78; Joseph, 28, 30, 78; Mary, 56
Emmat: William, 39
Emmatt: Wm, 72
Emmot: William, 23
Emmott: William, 50, 58
England: Daniel, 76, 77
Evans: David, 62
Everet: Thomas, 14
Everson: Gartharight, 61
Everston: Mathew, 46
Ewing: Jos, 64
Eyre: Elizabeth, 103

—F—

Farganson: Charles, 43
Fenwick: James, 3, 4, 7, 8; Sidney, 4, 7; Thomas, 4, 7
Ferdinando: Joseph, 75
Field: Nehemiah, 25, 31, 32, 53, 67, 89, 105; Rachel, 31; William, 25, 59; Wm, 84
Fillips: Mr., 105
Finch: John, 9
Finwick: Baltus(?), 40; James, 8, 19, 20, 28, 39, 40, 54, 59, 75, 81, 82; Sidney, 8, 9, 28; Thomas, 40, 54, 67, 82, 90; Thos, 8
Fisher: Elias, 8, 9, 25, 26, 33, 44, 47, 51, 57, 60, 66, 89; Elizabeth, 2, 13; Henry, 44, 76, 89, 90, 94, 96, 106; Henry,Dr., 44; Hesther, 103; Jabes Maud, 100; Jabez, 2, 5, 33, 35, 103; Jabez Maud, 9, 55, 91, 103; James, 14, 99, 103; John, 2, 13, 25, 26, 37, 43, 64, 66, 87, 89; Josa., 93; Joshua, 55, 58, 74, 103; Margery, 103; Margret, 103; Sarah, 26, 47, 91; Thomas, 9, 25, 33, 37, 41, 103; Thos, 51; Will, 47; William, 5, 7, 21, 39, 41, 53, 57, 60, 63, 64; Wm, 7, 64
Fleman: Thomas, 13, 94
Fling: Daniel, 50, 74
Forster: James, 105
Foster: Ann, 76; James, 105; John, 76; Margret, 105; Thomas, 48; Thos, 48
Fox: John, 17, 83; Mr., 80
Frame: Nathan, 47
Frampton: Elizabeth, 66
French: David, 92
Futcher: John, 89; Sarah, 42; William, 42

—G—

Garret: Barnes, 11, 62
Garrett: Barnes, 5, 51, 52
Gear: Mary, 17; Tho, 47; Thomas, 13, 17, 18, 20, 59; Thos, 17, 50
Gendron: Mark, 52, 64, 65
Gendrone: Gabriel, 74; Mark, 74
Gibb: John, 48
Gillesp: Robert, 64
Gillespe: Robert, 64
Ginkins: Thomas, 57
Glandon: Anne, 53; Robert, 53
Godin: Jos., 78
Godwin: Elizabeth, 14, 78; Jos, 61, 69; Joseph, 16, 40, 62; William, 2, 14, 16, 18, 26, 49, 76; Wm, 61
Gofort: Elizabeth, 87; Zachariah, 87
Goforth: Eliz., 87; Zachariah, 87
Goldsmith: Thomas, 52
Gorden: Thomas, 92, 96
Gordon: Catherine, 102; John, 92; Mary, 92; Pa., 88; Patrick, 62, 88; Robert, 62; Ruth, 92; Thomas, 3, 14, 38, 41, 92, 99, 102, 103, 105; Thos, 43
Goyt: Mary, 54; Peter, 54
Grafton: Richard, 62
Grainger: Nicholas, 2, 27
Gray, 4; David, 4, 10, 17, 22, 67, 77, 84; George, 60; Mary, 60; Michael, 103; Samuel, 10, 17, 22, 70; Temperance, 67; Thomas, 17, 18, 56, 67, 79, 93
Green: Jemima, 68; Margery, 9; Nicholas, 9, 47, 68
Greenman: Edward, Capt, 72
Greenwood: James, 99; Jonas, 33, 34, 35, 41, 99, 105
Greer: Thomas, 47
Groves: Thomas, 55, 57
Gum: Roger, 25, 65

—H—

Haggester: Jno, 38; John, 37
Hagor, 81
Halbert: Sam'l, 60
Hall: Capt, 106; John, 32, 33, 46, 61; John.Esqr., 32; Mary, 101; Nathaniel, 3, 8, 14, 17, 29, 33, 47, 59, 75, 78, 99, 100, 106; Nathaniel, Capt, 102; Nathaniel, Jr., 20
Hallands: Jehosaphat, 42, 62
Hammond: W., 66
Hand: Samuel, 19
Handzor: Amimadab, 80
Hanzer: Aminadab, 44, 47, 50, 58, 59; Elizabeth, 47; Rose, 58; William, 47, 59
Hanzor: Aminadab, 17; William, 17, 47, 48
Hardy: Frances, 48
Harford: Thomas, 8
Harmon: Henry, 19, 89, 103; Mr., 9
Harmonson: Harmon, 35, 89; Hendrick, 13; John, 13, 74, 84, 89, 101
Harrison: Charl., 32; Daniel, 32, 90; Gideon, 13, 90; Isaiah, 14; John, 85, 101; Mr., 99
Harry, 81
Hart: Margaret, 101; Robart, 94; Robert, 29, 30, 52, 65, 74, 100, 101, 104; Robert, Sr., 23
Harte: Robert, 104
Hassold: Thomas, 6
Hastings: John, 80
Haverloe: Andrew, 46; Anthony, 63, 64; William, 30
Haverly: Anthony, 41
Haynes: Charles, 54, 96; John, 47, 63

Hayns: John, 98
Hazard: Joseph, 59
Hazleam: John, 92
Hazleum: Mary, 92; Thomas, 92
Hazzard: Cord, 19; David, 19, 90; Joseph, 86, 95, 102
Heaton: Mary, 13, 22; Robert, 13, 22
Hemmons: Thomas, 86
Henry: Gabriel, 60, 91; Jonathan, 28, 37; Stephen, 18, 27
Hepburn: John, 4, 8, 21, 28, 47; Jos, 63; Jos., 40, 78, 86; Joseph, 11, 20, 21, 32, 48, 79
Herrin: Allexander, 80
Hickman: Joseph, 41, 42, 83; Joshua, 50, 51, 57, 60
Hide: Thomas, 47
Hignet: Robert, 84, 89
Hignett: Robert, 69
Hignot: Robert, 15, 35, 74
Hignott: Robert, 101
Hill: Capt, 21; Elizabeth, 5, 21, 64; John, 24, 38, 41, 45, 58, 64, 93; John,Capt, 5, 21, 64, 66; Mr., 57; Owen, 45; Richard, 10, 52, 65; Robert, 71, 87
Hines: John, 28
Hinman: Jno, 73; John, 13, 15, 53, 96; John,Jr., 21; Mary, 73; Mr., 93; Richard, 5, 10, 15, 22, 35, 36, 44, 48, 61, 63, 64, 68, 85, 86, 95, 104
Hirons: Jane, 36, 84
Hodgson: Robert, 22
Holland: Hester, 45; James, 45, 74, 77, 96; Jno, 76; John, 76; Mary, 96; Mr., 74; William, 45
Holloway: Richard, 90
Hollyman: Thomas, 54
Holt: Catherine, 19, 49; R., 67, 68, 78, 83, 86, 88, 90, 91;

Rives, 68, 71, 75, 82, 96; Rs., 106; Ryves, 14, 22, 24, 26, 36, 39, 54, 77, 78, 81, 83, 85, 88, 90, 96
Hood: Abner, 84; Abram, 94
Hopkins: Archibald, 65; Samuel, 86
Hoseman: Daniel, 1
How: John, 49
Howard: Knight, 64; Thomas, 5, 21
Hudson: David, 82, 86
Hueston: Anthony, 63
Huling: Martha, 11, 21; Walton, 7, 9, 12, 21
Hulling: Hester, 47; Martha, 47; Walton, 47
Hunter: John, 27
Huston: Willm, 31
Hyatt: Jno, 2

—I—

Inkins: Robert, 46
Inloes: Abraham, 69
Irons: Jane, 99; Jean, 99
Isaac, 81
Ishmall, 81

—J—

Jackson: Jno, 77; John, 44, 55, 77
Jacobs: Abigail, 28; Albert, 85, 86; Albertus, 28, 34, 38, 39; Hannah, 28; Jacobs, 22; Jno, 35; John, 8, 13, 17, 21, 22, 28, 32, 34, 35, 38, 86, 92, 95; Jonathan, 97; Thomas, 28
Jardyne: Jan, 33
Jenkins: Robert, 52; Thomas, 28
Johnson: Adam, 18, 34, 35, 38, 90; Anthony, 74; Art Vankirk, 51; Arthur, 27, 28, 47, 62, 63, 98; Corn'l, 98; Cornalus, 98;

Cornelious, 104; Cornelius, 19, 89, 98; Cornels., 98; Elizabeth, 34, 35; Isaac, 21, 34, 35; Jno, 71, 72; Jno Kiphaven, 31; Jno Kipshaven, 34, 35, 38, 39; John, 42, 72, 84; John Kiphaven, 21, 31, 34; John Kipshaven, 34, 35, 90; Martha, 18, 21, 34, 35, 38, 90; Marthew, 34
Jones: Griffith, 71, 72; James, 30; Jane, 41, 52, 53; John, 41, 52, 53, 85, 101; Ruth, 53; Thomas, 41, 52

—K—

Kain: John, 83; Thomas, 83
Keney: Steven, 47
Kening: Lazarus, 49; Martha, 49; Stephen, 49; William, 49
Kentwell: Richard, 38
Killingsworth: John, 1
Killum: Richard, 100
King: Hugh, 61; John, 5
Kiphaven: John, 4, 5, 7, 10, 25, 40, 82; Sarah, 5
Kipshaven: John, 16
Kirk: John, 1; John Sr., 1; John, Sr., 1
Kirwithen: Caleb, 16
Kollock: Comfort, 88; Cornelius, 35, 36, 99; Hanah, 99; Hannah, 36, 99; Hester, 99; Hesther, 36, 99; Jac., 76; Jacob, 7, 8, 10, 13, 19, 27, 31, 32, 35, 36, 43, 45, 46, 50, 58, 60, 61, 64, 65, 67, 69, 71, 72, 77, 79, 80, 82, 84, 85, 86, 88, 89, 90, 94, 95, 97, 99, 102, 104, 105, 106; Jacob, Sr., 82; Jacob,Jr., 41, 50; Jacob,Sr., 40, 41; Jane, 36, 99; Magdalen, 36; Magdalin, 99; Magdelon, 99; Mary, 36, 77, 82, 84, 99; Simon, 4, 5, 6, 8, 9, 13, 18, 32, 36, 67, 75, 77, 81, 84, 85, 88, 89, 94, 95, 96, 99, 101, 102, 103

—L—

Lacey: John, 48; Robert, 48, 70, 84
Laughland: John, 51, 53
Laurance: Henry, 72, 73
Law: Mr., 96; Richard, 36, 90, 99
Laws: Mr., 27
Lay: Edward, 87
Leatherberry: Thomas, 69
Leatherbury: Thomas, 56
Lemon: John, 16
Lewes: Peter, 4, 36, 40, 82
Lewis: Grace, 40; Peter, 4, 7, 40; Wrixham, 37, 40
Light: William, 38
Lingo: Henry,Capt, 70
Lingoe: Anne, 102, 103; Roberson, 102, 103; Robinson, 103
Little: Jean, 28; Martha, 83
Lodge: Robert, 8, 17, 22, 44, 55, 58, 70, 71; Robt, 44
Lofley: John, 77
Logan: James, 10, 12
Loncome: Richard, 94; Richerd, 94
Long: Jno, 44; John, 57, 58
Lonkomb: Richerd, 76
Loockerman: Nick, 106; Nick., 106
Loughland: John, 51
Louton: James, 30; Jeames, 104
Lovelace: Francis, 1, 3, 16, 32, 33
Loyd: Da., 72; H., 14; Henry, 14; Thomas, 7, 72; Thos, 72
Lucas: Peter, 23, 61; Sarah, 23, 61
Lueton: Henry, 105

Lullham: John, 100
Lyen: Aaron, 104

—M—

Maccarrel: Robert, 44
Mackbeth: Robert, 14
Mackelwan: James, 45
Magill: And., 76; Andrew, 76
Mahon: Aneas, 5; Offiah, 5
Manlove: Elizabeth, 93; George, 51, 54, 55; Geroge, 54; John, 7, 11, 12; Jonathan, 47; Margaret, 101; Mark, 52, 65, 101; Mr., 71; Richard, 48, 51, 62, 93; Sarah, 12; Tabitha, 93; William, 62, 93; Willm, 93
Margaret, 44
Mariner: Gilbert, 50; Thomas, 50
Marriner: Gilbert, 50, 80; Mary, 9, 10, 59; Thomas, 9, 10, 44, 59, 60, 80
Marsh: Elizabeth, 9, 10, 59; James, 6; John, 6, 9, 10, 48, 59, 60, 61, 68; Paul, 77; Peter, 3, 5, 6, 8, 48, 61, 68, 87; Philip, 6, 61, 68; Phillip, 6
Marshall: Edward, 73; Elizabeth, 60; Humphry, 57, 60; Jacob, 73; Tho, 52; Thomas, 28, 40, 52
Maud: Jane, 91; Margery, 91
May: Anne, 31; Elizabeth, 88, 101; Elizabeth, Jr., 88; Elizabeth,Jr., 54; John, 31, 43, 51, 52, 54, 60, 62, 64, 65, 71, 76, 77, 83, 86, 88, 93, 94, 101, 103; John,Esqr., 29; Thomas, 31, 53; Thomas,Jr., 31
McCoske: Thomas, 96
McCosker: Thomas, 83
McCullach: John, 23
McCullah: Alexander, 2, 95; John, 4, 29, 94, 95; Mary, 94, 95
Mcdaniel: Edmund, 90; Mr., 90
McDowell: John, 26
McGill: Andrew, 13, 14
McGraughan: William, 52
McSeachram: Daniel, 23
Meads: Francis, 38
Meggs: Mr., 102
Merideth: Riece, 104
Meridith: Riece, 104
Micky: Dan'l, 23; Wm, 23
Middleton: Anne, 100
Miers: James, 4, 7, 12, 30, 55, 58, 74, 92, 103; John, 1, 4, 30, 40, 97, 103; Margery, 55
Miller: Robert, 27
Milliner: William, 50, 51
Milner: William, 51
Milnor: Sarah, 12; William, 12; Willm, 12; Wm, 12
Mires: James, 91, 92, 94, 96; John, 92; Mary, 92
Molestedy: Alexander, 88
Moleston: Abraham, 50; Alexander, 3, 4, 6, 7, 10, 16, 18, 20, 22, 25, 30, 34, 35, 63, 64, 65; Alexander,Jr., 34, 35; Alexander,Sr., 40; Alexr, 64; Allexander, 102; Ann, 63; Elizabeth, 63; Hannah, 63; Hendrick, 13; Henry, 13, 43; Jhon, 63; Mr., 64; Naomi, 63; William, 7, 63, 64
Moliston: William, 20; Wm, 20
Molleston: Alexander, 66, 82, 96, 102; Alexander, Jr., 102; Allexander, 82; Elizabeth, 73; Hendrick, 13, 14; Henry, 14, 76, 88; Willm, 86
Molliston: Alexander, 75
Molly, 81

Molston: Alexander, 63, 75
Monghan: John, 92
Moore: Mary, 29, 71
Morgan: Elizabeth, 62; Evan, 62, 93; Evan Bradbury, 62; Jemima, 68; Jno, 68
Morris: Anthoney, 10; Edward, 16; Isaac, 10; John, 45, 52, 68; Phillip, 5; Sarah, 16
Morrow: Elliza, 82; John, 82
Moulson: Mr., 5
Mullinux: John, 48, 51; Mary, 48; Penellope, 51
Murphy: Thomas, 2
Murrow: Elizabeth, 82; John, 82

—N—

Naws: Edward, 3, 9, 58, 61, 63, 79, 85
Nelson: John, 14
Newcomb: Babtist, 37, 38; Baptis, 44; Baptist, 46, 58, 87; Daniel, 37, 38; Elizabeth, 38; Rd, 32; William, 38
Newcombe: Rd, 5, 8; Richard, 13
Newcome: Baptist, 104
Nicholas: Mr., 53
Nicholls: Matthias, 42
Nicolls: Matthias, 88; Matthias,Jr., 71
Noble: Reed(?), 94
Nucomb: Baptis, 103
Nutter: Christopher, 42, 56; John, 47, 56

—O—

Oakey: John, 65, 66; Mary, 66
Okey: Aminadab, 58
Ong: Isack, 54
Oram: Benjamin, 81, 85, 97, 99; Elizabeth, 93, 94
Orem: Benjamin, 64

Orion: William, 22
Orr: John, 64, 95; Patience, 6; William, 6, 64, 77, 78, 89, 95
Osborn: Mathew, 43; Thomas, 8
Osburn: Mathew, 9, 73
Owen: Griffeth, 12
Ozbun: Jonathan, 4, 65

—P—

Page: William, 6
Painter: Richard, 58; Richard,Sr., 58; Sarah, 58
Palmer: Daniel, 4, 5, 7, 11, 12, 17, 21, 36, 63; Mary, 4, 97; Mr., 11
Parker: Anderson, 3, 6, 7, 18, 23, 28, 38, 47, 50, 62, 64, 67, 77, 81, 82, 86, 89, 96, 98, 101, 102; Andr., 99; Edw, 63; Edward, 37; Patience, 6, 77; Sarah, 101; Thoms., 100; William Anderson, 78
Parsley: Abraham, 27, 54, 55, 59, 90, 91, 94; Frances, 55, 59
Parsly: Abraham, 50, 55
Parsons: John, 17, 19, 22, 47, 59
Pasley: Abraham, 54, 55; Frances, 54
Pattison: Tho., 41
Patty: Richard, 103, 104
Pawling: Simon, 63
Paynter: Dogood, 91; Doogood, 18; Jno, Jr., 8; Jno,Jr., 66; John, 8, 18, 66, 75, 84; John, Jr., 75; John, Sr., 75; John,Jr., 66; Margaret, 18; Margret, 18; Richard, 8, 86; Richard,Sr., 40; Samuel, 67, 85; Thomas, 66
Peaty: Richard, 104
Pecton: Samuel, 14
Pemberton: Capt, 5; Elizabeth, 87; Jos., 74; Josep, 89; Joseph, 67, 73, 78, 84, 90, 96, 105;

Mary, 11; Thomas, 9, 11, 16, 26, 44, 45, 60, 62; Thomas, Capt, 87, 88; Thomas,Capt, 5, 10, 11, 21
Penn: Hannah, 88; Springett, 88; William, 6, 10, 12, 19, 22, 50, 58, 64, 70, 72, 73; Wm, 1, 6, 7, 17, 62, 72, 88, 89, 92, 101, 104
Pennington: Henry, 31, 53
Pennis: Andrew, 68; Mary, 68
Pennoyre: Danet, 50
Peplo: Joseph, 3
Pepper: James, 32
Perrie: Robert, 20; Robt, 10, 11, 20, 28
Perrott: Richard, 3, 16
Peters: Mr., 78
Pettejohn: James, 60
Pettijohn: John, 53
Pettijon: William, 99
Pettyjhon: James, 60
Pettyjohn: Elizabeth, 25; Isabell, 25; Isabelle, 25; James, 10, 25, 74; John, 25, 26, 41; John,Jr., 25, 52, 53; John,Sr., 10, 25, 26, 31, 41; Richard, 26; Thomas, 25; William, 10, 25
Pettyjon: John, 41
Pevey: Jane, 45; Jean, 44; Joseph, 44, 45
Peyster: A. D., 27
Philips: Hester, 8; Jacob, 8, 36, 61, 67
Phillips: Hester, 99; Hesther, 36, 84, 99; Jacob, 36, 86, 99, 105; Jacob, Capt, 105
Phillipson: Christopher, 36
Pile: Wm, 2
Piles: John, 26; Joseph, 50
Pirrie: Robert, 32, 35, 37, 40, 46; Robt, 45, 46
Pirry: Robert, 49

Pittettre: Jean, 93
Poltny: Richard, 105
Ponder: John, 57; Mr., 57
Pope: Francis, 36; Margret, 36
Potter: Abraham, 11, 43, 44, 47, 62, 89, 98; Abrm, 23, 44
Poultney: Richard, 105
Preston: Sam'l, 73; Samuel, 72, 73
Prettiman: John, 63
Prettyman: Jno, 70; John, 28, 42, 67; John, Jr., 1; John, Sr., 84
Price: Elizabeth, 68; Jenkin, 75; Jno, 75; Jno., 75; John, 19, 20, 35, 68, 75, 80, 88; Thomas, 56
Pride: Abell, 9; Anne, 100; Esther, 100; Jacob, 100
Prise: John, 19
Pritteman: John, 14
Prittiman: John, Sr., 3; William, 77
Prittyman: John, 84; Robert, 84, 101; Sarah, 101; William, 59; William, Jr., 84; Wm, 84
Pyles: Capt, 16; Isaac, 1; John, 1, 26; Joseph, 1, 26; William, 1, 16, 26, 37; William,Capt, 16

—R—

Racklief: Nathaniel, 29
Ratcliffe: Nathaniel, 76
Reed: Cisely, 100; Walter, 100; William, 69
Rennall: Richard, 92
Reynolds: Richard, 12
Rhoads: John, 1
Richard: John, 62; Robert, 19, 50, 80
Richards: John, 24, 76, 88; Robart, 82
Richardson: Sa., 74; Sam'l, 72; Za., 78
Richarson: Ellinor, 82

Richerson: Pashance, 82
Richey: Alex'r, 43
Richorson: Ellinor, 82; Pahsunce, 82
Rickards: John, 93
Roades: John, 5, 17, 22, 23, 31, 36, 48, 57, 60, 61, 75, 91, 95, 96, 97, 104; Mr., 61
Roads: Jno, 68; John, 68, 70
Roberts: Edward, 2
Robeson: Andrew, 11; Patrick, 11
Robinson: Ebenezer, 2; Peter, 82; Pettr, 87; William, 55, 58
Rodeney: W., 78; William, 15, 32, 33, 54; Wm, 33, 91
Roe: Joseph, 11
Roles: Bryent, 101
Rolles: Bryant, 51
Rose, 81
Rowland: Jane, 55, 56, 93; Mary, 11, 62; Samuel, 11, 13, 20, 32, 33, 44, 46, 48, 49, 55, 56, 58, 62, 93; Thomas, 13; William, 13
Rowles: Bryan, 11, 60; Bryand, 62; Bryant, 5; Mr., 62
Royall: J., 36; Joseph, 6, 7, 8, 35, 36, 64; Magdelen, 8
Russel: Elizabeth Stockly, 82; Jno, 71; John, 39, 43, 75, 81, 82, 83, 85, 89, 90, 98; Joseph, 8, 9, 17, 40, 66, 78, 89; Mary, 7, 16, 26, 27, 29, 48, 76; Mr., 69; Phil, 1, 2, 4, 5, 6, 7, 8, 11, 12, 13, 15, 17, 18, 19, 20, 21, 22, 24, 25, 26, 27, 28, 29, 32, 33, 34, 35, 36, 37, 42, 44, 45, 46, 47, 48, 49, 56, 57, 59, 60, 63, 76, 78, 85, 86; Phil, Jr., 1; Phil,Jr., 3, 9, 23, 26, 37, 38, 49, 53; Phil., 73, 74, 75, 76, 78, 81, 84, 85, 86, 88, 99, 100, 101, 105; Philip, 2, 16, 24, 26, 28, 32, 33, 44, 54, 66, 67, 75, 78, 81, 83, 97; Philip,Esqr., 26; Phill, 81; Phill,Jr., 6; Phillip, 37; Phillip, Jr., 105; Ruth, 42, 43; W., 70; Willm, 79; Wm, 87
Russell: Elisabeth Stockly, 83; Elizabeth, 50, 83; Elizabeth Stockly, 83; Jhn, 83; Jno, 50, 57; John, 39, 50, 55, 71, 75, 80, 83, 90, 94, 95, 97, 100, 103; John, Jr., 80; Joseph, 8, 9; Mary, 8; Mr., 19; Philip, 26, 45, 51; Phillip, 99, 105; Sarah, 66
Ryle: Elizabeth, 78; John, 78, 85

—S—

Samples: William, 71, 88
Sanders: Ann, 99; Christopher, 100; John, 99
Sanderson: John, 37
Sangster: James, 34, 35, 49, 50
Savage: John, 53
Scidmore: Henry, 42, 94
Scott: Jeremiah, 16
Scudder: David, 98, 101
Seatown: Elizabeth, 55; James, 55
Seltheridge: William, 13
Selthridge: Lucilla, 31; William, 11, 31, 93; Willm, 93
Shankland: John, 3, 10, 20, 26, 28, 29, 34, 54, 75, 82, 87, 96, 100, 102, 106; Josep., 102; Joseph, 28, 92, 94, 95; Mary, 54; Mr., 106; R., 92, 95, 97, 99, 100, 102; Robert, 1, 4, 5, 9, 10, 11, 12, 13, 17, 18, 19, 23, 24, 25, 26, 27, 28, 29, 30, 31, 34, 35, 37, 39, 40, 45, 46, 48, 51, 53, 55, 57, 58, 60, 61, 64, 67, 68, 70, 74, 75, 76, 77, 80, 81, 82, 83, 85, 89, 90, 91, 95, 96, 101, 102; Robt, 17, 26,

27, 43; Robt., 75, 102;
William, 6, 13, 24, 29, 31, 41,
49, 72, 73, 76; Willm, 97;
Wm, 24
Sheltman: John, 6, 46, 52;
Tabitha, 6
Sheph'd: Hercules, 72
Shepheard: Hercules, 72
Shepherd: Hercules, 95; Sarah, 95
Shield: Luke, 18
Shiltman: John, 1
Shippen: Edward, 12
Shirley: James, 46
Shockley: Richard, 30
Shoulster: Richard, 87
Shurmer: Benjamin, 62
Simmonds: Williams, 56
Simmons: William, 50
Simons: Jane, 93; William, 93
Simonton: John, 97
Simson: James, 2, 6, 8, 9, 13, 15,
17, 22, 33, 35, 36, 57, 63, 73,
75; Margaret, 13, 22, 35;
Margret, 35; Margt, 35
Sipple: Lydia, 22
Skidmore: Henry, 56
Smith: Alee, 103; Alice, 87;
Anne, 102, 103; Arch, 26, 28,
31, 33, 36, 40, 57, 60, 68;
Arch., 73, 74, 81; Archibald,
11, 17, 18, 20, 21, 22, 27, 28,
34, 35, 59, 72, 75, 102; David,
26, 31, 35, 51, 91, 96;
David,Esqr., 26; Ealse, 87;
Henry, 3, 11, 62; Humphrey,
11; James, 92; Jno, 97; John,
30, 52, 64, 65, 68; Mary, 68,
100, 101; Mr., 91; Rebecca,
38; Rob, 28, 68; Rob., 97, 98;
Robert, 11, 13, 22, 43, 44, 67,
72, 92, 100, 101; Robt, 101;
Sarah, 26, 30; Smith, 59;

Thomas, 38, 76, 87, 102, 103;
William, 38
Solster: Richard, 38
Southrin: Edward, 71, 72; Jno,
72; Mary, 71
Spencer: Frances, 52, 65; Francis,
65; Henry, 52, 65, 74; Jehu, 2,
55, 77; Joseph, 64, 74; Samuel,
43, 65, 86; Samuel, Jr., 86;
Samuel,Jr., 55; Sarah, 25;
William, 25, 30, 52, 65, 74,
94; William,Major, 52, 65;
Wm, 27
Spenser: Mager, 104
Spicer: Matthew, 6
Spooner: Charles, 90
Stapelford: Edward, 94
Stapleford: Thomas, 14, 23, 24;
William, 24
Stapleton: William, 96
Starr: Nath'l, 37, 73; Nathaniel,
37, 43, 44
Stauton: Vertue, 103
Stevens: Frances, 74; Francis, 69,
83, 84; John, 74, 83, 84;
Mathew, 90; Matthew, 90; Mr.,
90; William, 69
Stevenson: John, 46; Robt, 76
Stewart: Jno, 54; John, 12, 23, 43,
54, 81, 82; Mary, 61; Sam'el,
88; Sam'l, 23, 61; Samuel, 87,
88; William, 23, 61, 100; Wm,
61
Stockley: Benjamin, 19, 41, 50,
56; Joshua, 55, 56; Oliver, 36,
56; Thomas, 28; Thos., 100;
William, 44, 101; Woodman,
1, 15, 36, 80, 95, 97, 99, 103
Stockly: Anne, 69, 79; Benjamin,
80, 93; Joshua, 92, 93; Oliver,
59, 80, 92; Thomas, 84, 89;
William, 79, 80; Willm, 79,

80; Woodman, 90, 94, 95, 96, 99, 100
Street: John, 86, 98; Robert, 86
Stretcher: Edward, 20; Henry, 15, 54
Stringer: Hillary, 53
Stutchbury: Elizabeth, 19; John, 34
Sumerford: Anne, 52; Jefray, 52
Summerford: Anne, 51, 52; Jeffrey, 51, 52

—T—

Taylor: Jacob, 14, 19, 20, 28, 49, 57, 60, 68
Thomas: Gabriel, 63
Thomson: Anne, 40; Georg, 40; George, 40; John, 5, 41; William, 14
Till: William, 44, 68, 81, 104; Willm, 94; Wm, 15, 27, 41, 44, 66, 68, 81, 83, 90, 91, 94, 96
Tillton: Thomas, 46
Tindal: Honor, 69
Tindall: Honor, 84, 101; Ralph, 84, 101; Robert, 101
Tomlinson: Robert, 90
Tomson: John, 79
Toole: Tho., 39; Thos. 49
Topham: Chris, 44; Chris., 79; Christop., 89; Christopher, 5, 20, 21, 31, 44, 45, 79, 89, 90, 96, 97, 98, 100, 104; Christr., 100
Touchberry: Elizabeth, 19, 20, 80; Henry, 19, 80
Touchbery: Henry, 80
Townsend: Costin, 56, 58; John, 49; William, 31, 77
Train: Roger, 4, 8, 10, 21, 31, 36, 51, 75
Traine: Roger, 40, 75

Trippit: William, 45
Trotter: William, 70
Turk: Robert, 26, 99
Turner: Mr., 102; Robert, 1, 7, 8, 11, 43, 47, 62, 73, 98
Twilley: Robert, 6
Twilly: Robert, 76

—V—

Vankirk: Art, 27, 43, 55; Art Johnson, 29, 48, 53; Arthur Johnson, 51
Vankirt: Ranier, 105
Vaughan: Jno, 72; John, 72, 73
Venus, 44
Verhoof: Cornelious, 102
Verhoofe: Cornelius, 16, 61, 87, 101
Verkirk: Art, 86, 94; Art, Jr., 86; Art, Sr., 86
Verkirt: Mr., 105; Ranier, 106
Vines: Jno, 11; John, 23
Vorgin: Hugh, 71

—W—

Walker: Alee, 47; Capt, 7; James, 18, 19, 22, 39, 42, 46, 47, 49, 56; Nathaniel, Capt, 82; Nathaniel,Capt, 4, 7, 40, 63; Thomas, 49, 59, 70, 74, 75, 77, 81, 82, 84, 85; Thos, 70
Wallace: Jane, 16; Tho., 30; Thomas, 9; Thos, 73
Walton: Esther, 47; George, 7, 12, 27, 29, 43, 47, 54, 55, 77, 86; John, 23, 24, 27, 30, 43, 68, 86; Mary, 47; Mr., 53; Patience, 27; William, 27, 30
Waples: Peter, 49
Ward: Richard, 48, 86; Thos, 32
Warner: Isaac, 86

Warren: Jacob, 47; John, 18; William, 18
Warrin: Jacob, 63, 98
Watson: Elizabeth, 77; Isaac, 30, 56, 77; John, 30; Luke, 10, 14, 25, 30, 65, 91; Luke, Sr., 91, 92; Luke,Jr., 5, 21, 42; Luke,Sr., 70; Samuel, 30; Sarah, 30
Wattson: Elizabeth, 77; Isaac, 30, 57, 77; John, 16; Luke, 46, 57, 90; Luke,Jr., 16; Samuel, 3, 14, 16, 18; Samuell, 51; Sarah, 3
Webster: Mary, 101; Samuel, 101
Welbore: Jno, 77; John, 42, 45, 48, 58, 60, 61, 62, 63, 67, 69, 70, 73, 74, 79, 80, 101
Welch: John, 106
Wells: John, 55
Wesley: Richard, 95
Wessell: Wm, 106
West: John, 53, 84; Robert, 68, 80, 85, 91; Robt., 105; Soloman, 105
Westly: Richard, 95
Wheeler: John, 42, 43
White: Andrew, 68; Esther, 85; Hannah, 8; James, 2, 3, 14, 15, 16, 18, 24, 25, 30, 31, 42, 44, 50, 51, 83, 97; Jas, 28, 46, 56, 57, 58, 60, 62; Jas., 100; John, 85; W., 17, 18; William, 11, 44, 70, 78, 85, 95; Willm, 85, 95; Wm, 91; Wrixham, 86
Whitehead: Mary, 22; Nathan, 22
Whiteman: Stephen, 16
Whitman: Stephen, 16
Wickes: John, 14
Wilbore: John, 47
Williams: Francis, 37, 50, 69; Francis,Jr., 70; Francis,Sr., 70; John, 15, 36, 37; Mary, 54, 89; Nicholas, 69, 70, 89; Nick, 97;
Patrick, 21; Peter, 54; Rebeckah, 15; Rebeckah,Jr., 15; Richard, 1; Ruth, 54; Thomas, 53
Willson: Mercy, 42; Rebecca, 42; Richd, 100, 102; Thomas, 41, 42, 56, 58
Wilson: Richd, 102; Thomas, 14, 94
Wiltbanck: Abraham, 24, 67, 78; Cornelius, 1, 21, 24, 27, 33, 43, 47, 61; Halmanius, 24; Hanah, 36; Hannah, 36; Harmanus, 33; Harmanus Fredrick, 32, 33; Helmanious, 103; Hermanus Fredrick, 1; Isaac, 24; Naomi, 67
Wiltbank: Abraham, 85, 101; Abraham,Jr., 67; Abram, 92; Cornelious, 101; Cornelius, 4, 8, 9, 11, 15, 17, 73, 85, 86, 88, 90, 101, 102; Halmanus, 101; Hanah, 99; Hannah, 99; Isaac, 101; Jane, 103; Naomi, 68; Naomy, 67; Samuel, 101; Samuell, 101
Wolf: Frances, 97; Francis, 13, 97
Woodstock: Willm, 93
Woodward: Anthony, 3, 20, 29, 81, 82; Mary, 57
Woolf: Matthew, 90; William, 69, 90; Willm, 94
Woolfe: Fracs., 85; Frances, 95, 97; Francis, 29; Mary, 29; Rice, 29; William, 90
Woolgast: Otto, 26, 28
Woringtun: Staphan, 86
Wyatt: Jas, 76
Wynkoop: Abraham, 91, 93, 103; Abrahm., 103; Esther, 103; Hesther, 103; John, 103
Wynn: Elizabeth, 91; Hannah, 91; Sidney, 91; Thomas, 91

Wynne: Jonathan, 53

—Y—

Young: George, 86

Sussex County, Delaware, Deed Book F-6

INDEX OF LAND NAMES

—A—

Abraham's Lott, 98
Abraham's Lot, 73, 89
Abraham's Lott, 11, 19, 43, 47, 62, 98
Art's Dairy, 86
Avery's Rest, 5, 68

—B—

Batcheller's Folley, 11
Bottle & Cake, 59
Bottle and Cake, 17, 47, 48
Bould Eagle Point, 86
Bowman's Farm, 46
Bowman's Farms, 42, 46
Bury, 11

—C—

Callis, 53
Cedar Town, 71, 93
Cooke's Rest, 71

—D—

Dods Farm, 10
Dyer's Choice, 28

—E—

Ebenezer, 58

—F—

Fairfield, 30
Farmer's Delight, 94
Finch Hall, 10

—G—

Good Hope, 6
Granger's Field, 55

Gray's Inn, 17, 22, 70
Green Meadows, 21
Greenfield, 85

—H—

Harlem, 46
Hart's Delight, 88
Hart's Range, 30, 104
Hatter's Land, 61, 68
Hill's Content, 51, 54, 65
Horse Island, 84
Howard's Choice, 5, 21

—J—

Johnson's Purchase, 42, 56

—K—

Kain's Old Field, 83
Knight Howard's Land, 64

—L—

Labanan, 91
Lebanon, 97
Little Field, 11, 43, 73
Love's Choice, 15, 16
Luck by Chance, 27, 59

—M—

Maiden Plantation, 14
Martin's Vineyard, 92, 102, 105
Middleborough, 4, 7, 40, 82
Mill Plantation, 2, 43, 73
Mill Range, 103
Millborrow, 46
Millford, 13, 49
Mulberry, 11

—N—

New Hall, 63
New Heveloe, 62
Nutter's Farm, 56

—O—

Orkney, 92
Orphans Choice, 46, 62

—P—

Pennington, 31
Persimon Island, 57, 60
Point, 78
Price, 90

—R—

Rageltons, 102
Richland, 55
Rotterdam, 19

—S—

Schoolfield, 56
Scidmore's Choice, 42
Shoulters Inheritance, 87
Soulsters Inheritance, 38
South Hampton, 23, 102, 105
Spooner's Hall, 90
Spooner's Hall, 90, 100
St(?) Piles, 67
Strife, 49, 59, 70
Sun Dyall, 77
Susan's Pallas, 46

Swan Point, 11, 62

—T—

Tanner's Hall, 50
The Cold Spring, 8
The Glade, 96
The Glades, 27
The Point, 7, 89
Timber Hill, 11
Timber Neck, 94
Trotters Point, 38
Twillings Neck?, 76
Two Little Necks, 96

—V—

Virgin's Choice, 58

—W—

Walton's Choice, 23
Warren's Choice, 18
Watson's Choice, 10, 25
Watson's Marsh, 30
Watson's Purchase, 70
Webley, 19, 22
West Chester, 69, 74, 84, 89
West India Fort, 33
White Horse, 65
Woolfe Pitt Neck, 95

www.ingramcontent.com/pod-product-compliance
Lightning Source LLC
Chambersburg PA
CBHW070502100426
42743CB00010B/1731